ADMINISTRATIVE ORGANISATIONS

ADMINISTRATIVE ORGANISATIONS

Compiled & Edited
by
Dr. R.K. Pruthi

D P H

DISCOVERY PUBLISHING HOUSE
NEW DELHI-110002

First Published-2005

ISBN 81-8356-005-9

Published by

DISCOVERY PUBLISHING HOUSE
4831/24, Ansari Road, Prahlad Street,
Darya Ganj, New Delhi-110002 (India)
Phone: 23279245 • Fax: 91-11-23253475
E-mail:dphtemp@indiatimes.com

Printed at
Arora Offset Press
Laxmi Nagar, Delhi–92

Preface

Organisation is a framework. When certain goals have to be achieved and when individuals have to come together and share the work and act with understanding over a period of time a framework is organised. It facilitates proper utilisation of men, material and money for achievement of the goals.

Aim of the book is to make available to our readers material on some important aspects of administrative organisation. The selection of the essays have been made in order to cater to the students and teachers requirements.

In preparing this work we have incurred indebtedness of the authorities on the subject. We record our acknowledgements to them.

We have received every possible help from the librarians and their staff members. We thank them all.

My publisher and his staff members have worked hard. Our readers satisfaction will be our best reward.

R.K. Pruthi

Contents

1

Introduction

Before we Study the Administrative Organisations Let us Examine Elements of Development Administration

Edward Weidner, way back in 1962, defined Development Administration as a "goal-oriented" and "change-oriented" administration.

To Weidner Development Administration is concerned with maximising innovation for development.

According to Riggs Development Administration refers to organised efforts to carry out programmes or projects initiated by those involved in serving developmental objectives.

To Martin Landau Development Administration has come to mean the engineering of social change. He sees it is a directional process which is intended to make things happen in a certain way over intervals of time.

A number of other scholars also defined and refined the concept. Over the years, its meaning has expanded in accordance with the added implications attached to it. As a result, one would find it, difficult to precisely define the concept of development administration. At best one can attempt to explain what it implies and includes as per the current usage of the term. In the following section, we would outline a few of the most important elements of Development Administration existing in the literature of Public Administration.

Change-Orientation

Development Administration is change-oriented administration. Change involves the movement of a system or a structure from one point to another. The reverse of 'change' could be status-quo or inertia.

Thus, a development administrative system would be dynamic and not 'Static'. There is an in-built philosophy of Development Administration that values change. This change is a strategy for increasing the coping ability of an Administrative system in relation to its external environment as well as a mechanism to activate its internal structures.

Goal-Orientation

As we have pointed out above, Development Administration, as defined by Weidner, is a 'goal-oriented' administration. One might ask a simple question: Is an administrative system not necessarily goal-oriented? Do we not define administration as a collective human activity that is designed to achieve certain specific goals? Yes, it is true that all administrative systems as such are goal-oriented. Yet what distinguishes the general Public Administration from Development Administration is the dominant focus on goal-achievement in a more systematic manner. In other words, Development Administration is that aspect of Public Administration which is dominantly goal-oriented. And these goals, as Weidner points out are progressive in nature.

Thus Development Administration is concerned with the achievement of progressive political, economic, social and cultural goals.

Progressivism

The element of 'progressiveness' of goals is an accepted feature of Development Administration. What is progressive for one society may not be so for another society. Nevertheless, there appears to be a broad consensus on the nature of progressiveness of these goals in most of the countries, particularly those which are 'developing' societies.

'In political systems, progressivism would imply greater participation of the people in governmental affairs. In a democratic system, participation could imply strengthening of the pressure groups, political parties, free voting in elections and greater respect for public opinion in governmental affairs. On the other hand, as in totalitarian country, participation would be more of a symbolic character. But in both types of systems, increasing participation would involve greater share of the common man in the formulation and implementation of government policies, plans, programmes and projects. It is a very difficult goal to achieve, particularly by an administrative system. Nevertheless, it is expected of a development administrative system to create and promote such conditions that will facilitate greater participation of the people in the process of development.

In the economic sphere, a progressive approach would involve faster pace of economic development and a more equitable distribution of income and wealth. It would involve an approach of economic justice where opportunities to develop economically are equitably distributed to all sections of society.

In the socio-cultural sphere, a progressive approach would involve universalisation of education, promotion of health facilities for all section of society, social justice based on equity, secularism and adequate opportunities to all social groups to promote their respective cultural distinctiveness.

Development Administration, thus, is an administration designed to achieve progressive political, economic and socio-cultural goals. You can observe this from Figure 1.1.

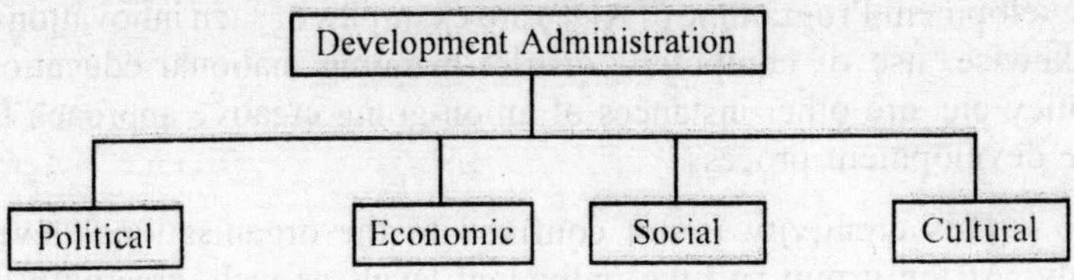

Figure 1.1: Progressive Goals

Planning

Planning is not a prerequisite to Development Administration. but it is the most helpful aid to the whole process of goal-oriented change. An Indian scholar, Pai Panandiker looks at Development Administration as administration of "planned change". Weidner, however opines that planning may or may not be a necessary condition for Development Administration. Nevertheless, it is true that planning is a strategy that facilitates maximum possible utilisation of human and material resource. And in poor countries, where such resources are scarce, planning gains a central importance. As a programme of action to achieve certain specified goals in a given period, planning helps in the maximum possible utilisation of time and other resources that make the whole process of development effective. Little wonder, almost all developing counties have adopted socio-economic planning as a strategy of development, and even the developed socialist countries continue to place great reliance on the mechanism of planned development. Further, capitalistic developed nations such as Great Britain and France have some form of 'indicative' planning.

Innovativeness

Development administration is not dogmatic and traditional in its approach to problem-solving. Instead, it stresses upon identification and adoption of new structures, method procedures, policies, plans, programmes and projects which would help achieve the developmental objectives with the greatest possible facilitation. Experimentation and adaptation are the hallmarks of Developmental Administration. In India, for instance, organisations such as District Rural Development Agency (DRDA) and Command Area Development Administration (CADA) and programmes such as Integrated Rural Development Programme (IRDP) and Tribal Area Development Programme (TADP) are examples of such innovations. Likewise, use of computers, district planning, national education policy etc. are other instances of an on-going creative approach to the development process.

This creativity is not confined to the organisational level only. At the group and the individual levels as well, creativity in administration is feasible and its overall contribution to effectiveness of goal-oriented change can be immense. A development administrative system has the responsibility to create an organisational environment which would be congenial to creativity and innovations.

Flexibility in Organisational Procedures

Generally, a bureaucratic administration is considered as a synonym of rule-oriented administration. While it is true that no bureaucracy or administration can function without an adequate set of rules, it is also true that a totally "rule-oriented" administration can fall in the trap of treating rules as ends rather than as means. Such a dogmatic approach can make an administrative system straight-jacketed and inflexible and thus make it unfit for promoting development as a faster pace. Development oriented administration requires an optimum flexibility of operations which would allow an administrator the required autonomy to apply rules with discretion to certain unique and significantly distinctive administrative situations. Though accountability for any decision made shall remain with the administrator, yet he will be granted adequate leeway in using the set of rules of the advantage of the organisation and to the best of his ability and judgement. Yes, the risk is likely to remain of misuse of any discretionary powers. yet this little inevitable risk should not become an obstruction in the process of making a Development Administration optimally flexible in its functioning. Otherwise, the ideal notions of creatively and innovation will remain only myths.

High Degree of Motivation

Motivated personnel are the backbone of any organisation designed to achieve certain progressive goals. A development administrative system needs a set of highly motivated personnel at top, middle and lower levels. Such personnel should be committed to the progressive goals designed to be the achieved and should have a high degree of enthusiasm to accomplish those goals. Their narrow vested interests or comforts should not deter them from acting in the highest interest of the organisation and the society.

What factors can motivate the personnel functioning in development administrative organisation? Essentially, the maxim of need-fulfilment will apply to any group of individuals entrusted with the responsibilities of achieving certain goals. For the developmental administrative personnel too, the bases of motivation will remain the same. Notwithstanding this commonality, it may be stressed that in a development administrative system, the personnel need to possess and demonstrate extra zeal, extra dedication and even perseverance to achieve lofty progressive goals of change. In case it is not possible to create such a cadre of motivated people, there is a likelihood of routinisation of administration resulting in only modest performance.

How to get a group of highly motivated people to guide and man development administrative organisations is a difficult question. Yet, a rigorous exercise in building individuals and groups in a planned manner through proper training can be attempted. Behavioural training for attitudinal change can be effectively employed for creating a new class of motivated individuals.

Client-Orientation

A development administrative system is a client-oriented or a beneficiary-oriented administration. It aims at providing maximum benefits of its services and products to the very people for whom the organisation is designed. In other words, Development Administration is "people-centred" administration which accords primacy to the needs of its beneficiaries and tries to tune its programmes, policies and actions to these needs.

Here it may be appropriate to refer to a very important aspect of motivation that is pre-eminent in any service-oriented or beneficiary-oriented administration. It is called "extension" motivation, which means motivation to "help" people. Western motivation theorists such as Maslow, Herzberg and McClelland have not highlighted this particular type of motivation, but Indian social psychologists have been successful in identifying and highlighting this notable phenomenon.

The assumption of extension motivation is that there is a desire in every man to be of use to others. There are varying intensities of extension motivation among people, depending on their socialisation and orientations. It can be suggested without much risk of contradiction that in a beneficiary-oriented administration, existence of functionaries with a high degree of extension motivation will be a great asset in moving that organisation towards its goal of responsiveness. No doubt, a development administrative organisation is a "responsive" organisation. It is responsive to the needs, wishes and aspirations of the people that it purports to serve. Responsiveness is a trait that would do good to any administrative system, but for a development administrative organisation, it is a fundamental prerequisite to its successful existence.

Participation

We have discussed earlier that progressive political goals in a society will involve greater participation of the people in governmental affairs. The notion of participation gains added importance in the actual functioning of a development administrative system.

Development Administration involves the participation of the people or the beneficiaries in the formulation and implementation of development programmes. In identifying goals, prescribing objectives formulating plans, designing action strategies, implementing projects and evaluating performance, the role of the beneficiaries is of utmost importance. That is why the block level and district planning are gaining increasing importance in Development Administration in India. Not only participation helps in making policies and plans more realistic and down-to-earth, it also mobilises people's cooperation and support in implementing development programmes with minimum cost in terms of manpower, time and money.

Participation of the people in development programmes depends on three factors. These are:

(i) Ability to participate which in turn depends on their level of formal and informal education;

(ii) Willingness to participate which in turn depends on the socio-psychological framework of society, groups and individuals, and

(iii) Opportunity provided to the people by the governmental organisation to participate. Their absence may cause low participation.

Participation has an important concomitant in decentralisation. A development administrative system effectively utilises the strategies of delegation and consultation and thus makes the administration "gross-root" oriented. People's willing cooperation is sought and mobilised by the governmental authorities and this cooperation and collaboration becomes a potent instrument for making the process of Development Administration successful.

Effective Integration

Bringing together a host of groups and authorities for the achievement of common developmental goals would require a high degree of integrative capacity in an administrative organisation. Verily, Development Administration is characterised by a high degree of coordination or integration. And in case the level of integration is low, the developmental results are likely to be adversely affected.

In a development administrative situation, coordination is required to be affected at various levels, among different organisations and units, among various positions and functionaries and among the resources available for the achievement of goals. Lack of coordination is bound to result into wastage of resources and mitigation of effectiveness.

As is well known, any developing society experiences a proliferation of structures to equip itself to undertake specialised tasks. But what generally happens is that the level of specialisation of functions and structures increases. But this is not accompanied by a required level of coordination. This gap between specialisation and coordination is termed as "integration lag". Fred Riggs calls that society "Prismatic" where the level of integration (coordination) is less than that of differentiation (specialisation). In a Prismatic Society,

I<D (I stands for "integration lag", D stands for Development)

Coping Ability

A development administrative system is an "open" system. It receives inputs regularly from the environment and attempts to respond through its outputs, viz., decisions and actions. No doubt there is a continuing interaction between a system and its environment and this reciprocity of relationship is an important trait of Development Administration.

Every development administrative system functions in an environment which has its set of sub-structures. For instance, there are the political, economic, social and cultural (including technological) environments in which the Development Administration has to function. Obviously, the influences of these environments affect the nature of functioning and effectiveness of Development Administration. The political environment places demands for a change and provides direction of movement, the economic environment outlines the agenda of action of the administrative system and puts constraints of resources administrative system has to operate. This is clear in Figure 1.2.

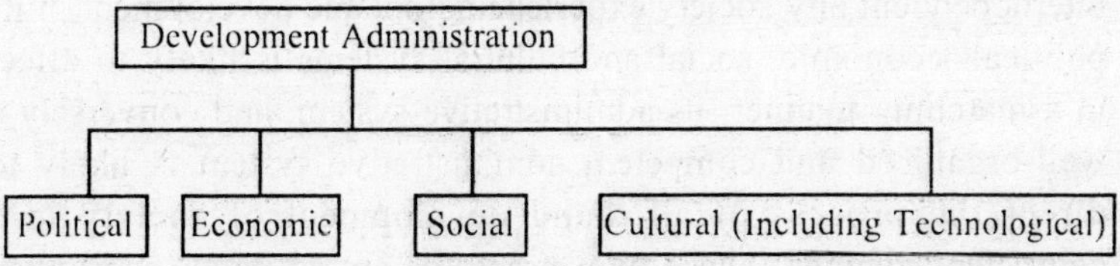

Figure 1.2: Environment of Development Administration

It does not imply that Development Administration is only a dependent variable and lacks its own mechanism to influence the environment. Essentially, the process of Development Administration is international and therefore it would be a mistake on the part of theorists to present it only as an uni-directional process.

One thing is clear in this context: Development Administration has to respond to the demands and challenges arising from its environment. Sometimes these challenges are moderate and modest and thus do not strain the development administrative system. However, on occasion, the challenges are serious and test the coping ability of the administrative system. A development administrative system, therefore continuously tries to enhance its coping capacity. This is done through a process of greater sensitivity and responsiveness to the environment and the capacity to strengthen its administrative structures, behaviour and processes. This is what is known as "Administrative Development" about which we would discuss in the next section. At this stage it should be adequate to mention that Development Administration is goal-oriented, change-oriented, progressive, planned, innovative, flexible, motivational, client-oriented, participative, it is a highly integrated administrative system with substantial coping ability.

Development Administration and Administrative Development

In the literature on Development Administration, two notions have been interwoven: *first* the "administration development" and *second,* the "development of administrative capacity". The former is termed as "Development Administration", and the latter "Administrative Development". Both the phenomena are interdependent any society experiencing notable development in its political, economic, social and cultural systems is likely to affect in a matching manner, its administrative system, and conversely a well-organised and competent administrative system is likely to direct the process of all-round development of society in a competent manner. These twin processes are so much interlinked that it is difficult to assert as to which would be more prominent and which would precede the other. Little wonder that Fred Riggs has found in "Development Administration" and "Administrative Development" a "chicken and egg" relationship.

Whatever be the sequence, it is undeniable that administrative development is an essential corollary to Development Administration. Administrative Development implies the enhancement of the capacity and capability of an administrative system to achieve the prescribed progressive goals. The process depends on modernisation of administrative structures and processes, induction of a spirit of innovation, cultivating a highly motivating climate, increasing differentiation, effective integration, and positive attitudinal and behavioural changes among the administrators. The strategies of administrative reform are a part of the process of Administrative Development.

Development Administration and Traditional Administration

With the emergence of development administration, some scholars have attempted a distinction between development and traditional administrations. The term traditional administration is used as a synonym for 'general' administration and even revenue and law and order administration. The distinctions are generally made on the following lines:

(i) The objectives of traditional administration are simple while those of Development Administration are multiple and variegated.

(ii) Traditional administration has a limited scope of operations, while Development. Administration has a much vaster scope of functioning.

(iii) Development Administration is more complex in its parts and procedures than traditional administration.

(iv) Development Administration is larger in size than traditional administration.

(v) Development Administration is much more innovative and creative than traditional administration.

(vi) Development Administration is dynamic in its functioning, while traditional administration stresses upon stability.

(vii) Rule-orientation is valued in traditional administration, while flexibility is considered a virtue in Development administration.

(viii) Participatory style of administration is a characteristic of Development Administration while traditional administration is bureaucratic and authority-oriented.

(ix) Development Administration is administration of planned change, while traditional administration does not rely as much on planning.

(x) Colonial bureaucracy is engaged dominantly in the performance of general administrative functions, while the administrative system of an independent country is primarily developmental in character.

(xi) The administrative systems in developing countries are basically developmental in orientation, while those in developed countries focus on general administration.

It has become clear over the years that to attempt a neat distinction between development and traditional administration is, at best, being over-simplistic. The nature of operations in revenue, finance, police and para-military administrations has become so complex, consequently in these sectors of administration, not only the complexity has increased manifold and their objectives multiplied and intertwined but also the structures and processes in these organisations have undergone notable changes. The techniques and technologies in general administration have become modernised and sophisticated; planning has become an integral part of their functioning: innovativeness and creativity in their operations are being valued immensely; people's cooperation in taxation and law and order administration is being sought and mobilised; and flexibility is being introduced in their procedures. No more, the 'general' administration is 'traditional': it has already adopted the maxims of modernisation with vigour. Thus, to attempt an absolute distinction between general administration and Development Administration would be untenable and unrealistic.

Further, to assert that the colonial administration is engaged mostly in performing traditional administrative functions of law and order and revenue administration would be an over-simplification. It is well known that even the colonial bureaucracies, such as the Indian, were engaged in promoting so-called 'developmental' activities (railways, roads, tele-communication, education, health etc.). Even a Planning and Development Department was set up in the Government of India before Independence. Conversely, in the independent countries, the focus is not on Development Administration alone. The crises of stability, nation building, internal security and national integrity have forced the governments in developing countries to strengthen their law and order maintenance systems. In a country beset with problems of internal disharmony, communal riots and violence, it is difficult to promote socio-economic development in a whole-hearted manner. Time, energy and resources are distributed between the developmental and the non-developmental activities. In fact, both are interdependent and changes in one lead to changes in the other. Both prosperity and poverty can lead to discontentment and even violence. It may be pointed out that even the developed countries face problems of change, and challenges from their dynamic environment. In order to meet the progressive goals of development, their administrative system have also to be goal-oriented, change-oriented, innovative, responsive, motivational and integrated. That is why the New Public Administration, a movement started twenty years ago, stressed on almost the same premises that characterise Development Administration. Thus to say that development administration is a dominant feature only of developing countries would be an over-generation. And when we look at the developed 'socialist' countries (such as the U.S.S.R.), the distinction further loses its validity.

The characteristics of Development Administration enumerated are also associated with general administration, but their intensity is greater in the case of the former.

There are scholars (including William Wood) who say that to distinguish between development and traditional administrations would involve an undue undermining of the latter and thus belittling the importance of the fundamental bases of a nation's existence, security and financial resources. How can, it is argued, a process of development take place without adequate resource base? The argument has validity.

Instruments of Development Administration

The problems of development are many and complexity of developmental tasks are varied. It is very difficult to depend only on administrative system tó realise the developmental goals. There is need to employ other instruments also. We would examine the four important instruments that can be employed to realise the goals of development. They are:

- administrative system
- political organisation
- voluntary associations, and
- people's organisations.

Administrative System

Public Administration of any country is an indispensable instrument to implement development policies and programmes. Administrative system performs specialised services and undertake vast range of developmental and non-developmental activities. As administrative systems have specialised skills and have rich experience there is a heavy dependence on this instrument to realise development goals. But, because of the number of the goals there is need to enlist other instruments also.

Political Organisation

Political parties mobilise people in support of developmental programmes. They resolve social conflicts and pave the way for development. Therefore it is considered an important instrument of Development Administration.

Voluntary Associations

In transitional societies there will always be gap between the people and the governmental system. This should be filled to expedite the process of development. It is here that the voluntary organisations can play a very crucial and significant role. Higher level of motivation, flexibility in the organisation and approach, apolitical nature, commitment to the cause make them fit instruments to undertake developmental tasks.

Peoples Organisations

We have discussed earlier that development requires greater participation of people. Participation can be at the level of decision-making, or implementation or in sharing benefits or in evaluation. This requires skills as well as devoted work and calls for mass movement. Peoples organisations contribute to quicken the process of development and social transformation.

We have to bear in mind that development strategy cannot depend only on one strategy for national building and socio-economic progress. We have to use all the instruments or a combination or different instruments.

Further, there are several administrative positions, such as those of District Collectors and Chief Secretaries in India, which are intricately involved in performing developmental as well as traditional functions. To separate their functions would at best have only academic relevance.

Therefore, the most acceptable approach would be to look at Development Administration as a type of administration which has its distinctive characteristics, but in an inseparable form from general administration.

2

Organisation

General Aspects

The term, organisation, is used in two senses—to connote a status and a process. If used in the former sense, it describes the existing arrangement of the parts of a whole; for example, the organisation of a plant or an animal. If used in the latter sense, then it means a process of establishing or reshaping relationships between the parts. For example, we in India often talk of the need of organisation of a sound system of administration, or organising a Students' Union.

In the former sense, the term is used substantively, to describe an institution. While in the latter sense it is the activity of organising—that is, the dynamic aspect—which is emphasised. Used in the sense of an institution, the term imports a static sense of completeness into the idea. This is a somewhat misleading use of the term, because organisation in the active sense is essentially dynamic.

In Public Administration, however, the term is used in both the sense. It means a status as well as a process and may be described as "an arrangement of the working relationships of individuals." Prof. J.M. Pfiffner defines it thus:

"Organisation is the structuring of individuals and functions into productive relationship."

Prof. John M. Gaus defines it thus:

"Organisation is the arrangement of personnel for facilitating the accomplishment of some agreed purpose through the allocation of functions and responsibilities."

Mr. J.R. Simpson, Director of Organisation and Methods Division of H.M. Treasury defines organisation as a "harmonious inter-relation of functions and staff". According to Dr. E.N. Gladden "Organisation is concerned with the pattern of relationships between persons in an enterprise, so construed as to fulfil the enterprise's function."

A sound system of organisation, that is, grouping of positions and definition of functions and responsibilities, is very essential for the proper performance of the duties of the public officials. The effectiveness of an administration depends not only upon the efficiency of its personnel but also upon its organisation. A poor organisation may lead to lack of clear responsibility, duplicity of work, lack of co-ordination, loose supervision, ineffective delegation, and lack of balance and may thus lead to loss of human effort, confusion of purpose and conflict of wills. But a good organisation will not only avoid these defects but would act positively by creating unity of purpose and command and proper machinery of co-ordination and co-operation. Prof. Gaus has rightly said that organisation is "the relating of efforts and capacities of individuals and groups engaged upon a common task in such a way as to secure the desired objective with the least friction and the most satisfaction to those for whom the task is done and those engaged in the enterprise."

Therefore, the need of a sound system of organisation was felt quite early in human history. The need, however, became more urgent with the growth of large scale organisations since the advent of the Industrial Revolution. The dual principle of Division of Labour and Specialisation resulted in the breaking down of work into small pieces. But instantaneously the problem arose of integrating, or reintegrating, these functional units into a composite whole, so that the whole machinery may function harmoniously for a single purpose. Therefore, there arose, in the last quarter of the 19th century, a movement for Scientific Management of business. This movement began with Frederick N. Taylor and is known after him, as the 'Taylor System' or 'Scientific Management' system. This movement was carried on, after the death of Taylor, by two disciples, Gautt, and Galbreth.

Scientific Management System

Scientific Management System is one in which the character of activity engaged in, rather than the end sought, is made the basis of determining the jurisdiction of the units of organisation. In other words, under this system, organisation of administration is based upon the nature of activity. For example, census work may be divided into units of computation and compilation of data, despatch and receipt of schedules, editing of returns etc. Under this system, manpower is taken as an expendable commodity which could be purchased in the open market and could be controlled through money incentive. Therefore, in dividing up work, these pioneers did not take the human factor into consideration. Organisation was based upon paternalistic and authoritarian considerations.

During the present century, however, there has begun a reaction against the Scientific Management Movement. Elton Mayo, President of the Harward Business School has called it a system based upon the "robble hypothesis". Studies of Social Psychologists like William McDaugall, Jung, Eugene Bleular and Alfred Adler have further strengthened the view point of the Harvard Business School. According to their view point, man is a social animal and hence his behaviour is determined primarily by his relationship with his immediate associates. Therefore, instead of money the determinant factors, which go to make up the efficiency of the employees, are social sentiments, group feeling, sympathy, and similarity of cultural backgrounds. Therefore, instead of basing organisation on authoritarian grounds, they base it on democratic leadership which recognises human dignity, fosters satisfying social environment, cultivates a feeling of belonging and a two-way communication. Whitley Committee system is a manifestation of the same trend in public management.

Which is the better of the two systems?—that is the question which naturally arises at the end of the above survey. The former emphasises the importance of form, structure, methods and procedure, while the latter emphasises the importance of human factor. Perhaps, a blending of the two systems will go a long way in building up an effective organisation. While we must have a well-defined system of positions, functions and relationships, we should not make it too rigid. While we should have unity of command in administration, we should not deny to the employees a voice in its management.

General Aspects of Organisation

What are the main features of the arrangement of parts of a large scale organisation? They are:

1. Position and its Incumbent—The Unit Cell of Organisation.
2. The Formation of Administrative Units.
3. The Form of Organisation—Hierarchical.
4. The Location and Delegation of Authority, and
5. The Co-ordination of Parts into an Effective Whole.

1. *The Unit Cell of Organisation.* Organisation is a method of dividing up work. It presupposes two things, viz., one, that there is a job to be done and two, that a number of individuals are involved in accomplishing that job. In a relatively simple situation, organisation is informal and even implicit. But as the job becomes larger and purpose more complex and the number of persons for performing that job increases, organisation tends to be formal and well-defined.

Hence job or position and its incumbent are the unit cell of organisation. These two terms, however, are not identical. All large-scale organisation is built up on positions rather than on incumbents. And although a position cannot be of any utility without an incumbent, yet it is quite possible to conceive of position without an incumbent. The U.S. Personnel Classification Board in its closing Report of Wage and Personnel Survey of 1931 defined position thus:

"A position is a specific civilian office, employment or job, whether occupied or vacant, calling for the performance of certain duties and the carrying of certain responsibilities by one individual either on a full-time or a part-time basis..."

So the concept of position is different from that of its incumbent. It is characterised by the duties and responsibilities attached to it rather than with the character of the person occupying it. In fact, the position may be either occupied or vacant. An employee or incumbent is a person who occupies a position. A sound system of organisation is one which brings about the effective relationship between positions and employees. But this relationship is to be brought about, not by changing the character of the position to suit the qualities of its incumbent but *vice versa*. A position is first created according to the principle of Specialisation and Division of Labour and then an incumbent is selected to suit the job.

2. *The Formation of Administration Units*. The Doctrine of Division of Labour in modern organisation reflects a double influence of specialisation and combination. Specialisation operates constantly to divide and subdivide work into units and thus to segregate workers, while combination operates to re-integrate these working units into a composite whole for the accomplishment of the desired purpose. For example, in the preparation of a suit of clothes, the suit cutter, as expert cutter, cuts the cloth according to a suit pattern, the tailor, as expert sewer, stitches the parts, and only then is the suit ready. Some of the tailors may sew shirts, while some others, trousers. The work of each must be systematically allotted in order to achieve the desired purpose. This systematic allocation of work is called organisation.

   (i) *The Line*. In government, major administrative units are called "agencies" or "departments". These agencies are organised on the basis of major substantive purpose. Thus we have an Education Department, Health Department and so on. But as these functions are quite large and varied, they are split up into a umber of divisions and sub-divisions and for the sake of effective action all are put in a 'chain of command'. So they are also called as "Line agencies". Line is a term borrowed from military usage which means "the subordinate division of operating responsibility" in

which there runs a single line of command. In military organisation, the line runs from the Head of the State to the soldier through the Army Commander, Corps Commander, Division Commander, Battalion Commander, Company Commander and the Platoon Leader. In civil administration it runs from the Head of the State to the lower employee (clerk) through the Secretary Deputy Secretary, Assistant Secretary, Superintendent, Deputy Superintendent and Assistant.

Now, the operating services may be organised in either of the two ways. They may be divided into functional stages i.e. horizontal levels, or into a vertical order. In the first system the whole task of the service is broken into pieces and each piece is assigned to an expert or body of experts. In the latter system, the whole work is broken into units and each unit has to deal with all the processes needed to complete the task. But, whatsoever may be the system of breaking the work, each department is divided into Branches or Bureaus on the basis of the relative distinctness and specialisation of function. The basis of their organisation also is purpose, but it is more specific, narrow and unitary. For example, the Education Department of the Government of Punjab has a Directorate of Public Instructions, an Archeological Branch and so on.

The sub-divisions of Branch or Bureau are called "Divisions". They are based on subject-matter specialities, specific projects or special kinds of work. For example, the Directorate of Public Instructions has Divisions of Elementary, Secondary and Higher education.

The sub-divisions of Divisions are called "Sections". They too are based on subject-matter specialities. For example, the Division of Elementary Education may have a section for Basic Education, another for Social Studies and so on.

Besides, there may be field stations in Departments whose operations are carried on not only in the Headquarters but also outside the H.Q. For example, the Police Department has police stations and sub-stations scattered all round the country.

(ii) *Auxiliary Agency.* Till recently each purpose Department used to be a self-contained unit. For carrying its purpose, it had to perform a number of subsidiary activities which, though not essential in themselves, had to be carried on for the performance of main functions of the Department. For example, personnel has to be recruited, training has to be imparted to them, and certain types of material have to be purchased. Now, due to the impact of the principle of specialisation, the major purpose Departments are losing control over these secondary activities which are now being separately organised partly outside and partly inside the departments. The work specialised outside is usually organised directly under the Chief Executive but is sometimes attached to the Central Financial Department as well.

These services are called by different names. Willoughly calls them "House-keeping" or "Institutional" activities; Gaus names them "Auxiliary Technical Staff Services" and Dr. L.D. White suggests the name of "Auxiliary Services" for them. These services usually comprise of Purchasing agency. Personnel agency, and Account offices. The topic will be discussed fully in the next chapter.

(iii) *Staff Agency.* In larger organisations, another type of specialisation is developing. We saw earlier that the functions of the administrator are many. They have been described by the word posdcorb which stands for planning, organising, staffing, directing, co-ordinating, reporting and budgeting. Now, all these functions cannot be adequately performed by any one man single-handedly. Nor can responsibility be divided at the top of the administration. So in order to increase the resourcefulness of the administrator, without breaking the line of responsibility, an expert or body of experts is attached to his office who or which advises him in matters of policy. This is a recent development and is called "Staff Organisation". Again, the term is borrowed from military usage. There the 'Line' commands, while the 'staff' plan and advise. Similarly, in the civil administration, the operating services act while the Staff agencies prepare matters for their action. They plan, advise, suggest and assist but do not operate.

3. *The Hierarchical form of Organisation.* Large-scale organisation always runs in quest of organisational unity. This unity is brought about through what is called as the "Hierarchical system". This system of organisation is also called "Scalar". As already indicated, organisation begins with some major substantive purpose and proceeds by dividing the job into various functional units. These units are further divided into sub-units and the sub-units in their turn, get further multiplied until we reach the workers who make the base of the cone. All authority proceeds from the top-management in this descending order. This is called the hierarchical or scalar principle of organisation.

Hierarchy may be defined as "the grouping of units into a larger unit for direction and control of activities." In the words of John D. Millett "it is the method whereby the efforts of many different individuals are geared together". It is through it that a unified direction can be achieved from one central point and broad purpose be translated into action. Every position, the unit cell of organisation, finds its appropriate place in the hierarchy, designated by a distinctive title, the incumbent possessing authority to give orders to sub-ordinates and bearing responsibility to receive and obey orders from superiors. Under this system, the Chief Executive is united to each individual worker through link after link.

The main advantages of the Hierarchical system may be summed up as follows:

(i) It serves as a channel of communication, downward and upward.

(ii) It is a means of preventing congestion in the flow of business by establishing subordinate centres for taking decisions on specified matters.

(iii) It helps to make clear relative responsibilities.

(iv) It is the normal means of contact between the central office and the remote parts of a dispersed department like the Police Department.

4. *The Location and Delegation of Authority.* The next problem in large scale organisation is that of location and delegation of authority, that is, whether administrative authority, like political authority should be centralised or decentralised? In other words, should it be concentrated in one hand or dispersed into various hands? If administrative authority is concentrated by law into the hands of the Chief Executive, then it is called an "Integrated system" or Departmental system and if the authority is vested in a number of independent offices and commissions, then it is called "Independent" or Disintegrated system of organisation.

In the Integrated system, responsibility runs upward in a scalar order and thus the whole department is brought under the supervision, direction and control of the Legislature through the Chief Executive. But in the Independent system, the operating Commission or Board is directly responsible to the Legislature without the intervention of the Chief Executive. There are some such offices in U.S.A. For example, Civil Aeronautic Board, Federal Communications Commission, Federal Power Commission, General Services Administration etc. We in India do not follow this system either at the Centre or in the States. As a matter of fact, it does not suit our political theory of Parliamentary Government.

Coming to the Integrated or Centralised system, here all administrative power is vested in the Chief Executive. This, however, does not mean that all these powers are actually exercised by the Executive. Powers have necessarily to be delegated to the subordinate officials. But what powers the officials enjoy are only delegated powers. The Executive delegates certain powers to the officials but she cannot delegate responsibility to them. Hence the main difference between the Integrated and the Independent systems is not in the devolution of powers but in the devolution of responsibility. In the former system, responsibility always remains concentrated at one point, while in the latter it is dispersed among various Boards and Commissions. So far as the delegation of powers is concerned, there are wide degrees of integration even in the Integration system. Either powers may be concentrated in the hands of top management as in the Prussian Administration during the 18th and 19th centuries, or they may be diffused amongst the top, middle and lower management as in the Education Departmental in India.

5. *The Co-ordination of Parts into an Effective Whole.* In any large-scale organisation proper co-ordination of parts is very essential for the sake of effective management. Lack of co-ordination may lead to duplicity of work, waste of money, friction and departmental jealousies and rivalries. On the other hand, a sound system of co-ordination leads to efficiency and economy, healthy competition. Co-ordination is primarily a duty of the Executive. But the Executive cannot provide means of co-ordination at lower levels, while co-ordination at lower levels is as essential as at the centre. Hence a complete machinery of co-ordination has been evolved. The best means of co-ordination so far discovered are:

   (i) *Conferences of High Executives under the Chairmanship of the Chief Executive:* For example, in India Finance and other Minister's Conferences are held periodically under the Chairmanship of Union Ministers. Similarly, there may be conferences of Deputy Secretaries and Under Secretaries under the chairmanship of the Secretary of a Department. These Conferences lay down broad policies regarding their departments and also lay down procedure of establishing inter-departmental contact.

   (ii) *Interdepartmental Committees:* are committees composed of equal number of representatives of two or more related departments. For example, the Economic Welfare Departments may have an Interdepartmental Committee for co-ordinating the policies and activities of their respective departments.

Such committees are very useful as they bring co-operation and harmony in the related activities of different departments.

(iii) *Specialised Co-ordinating Agencies* Sometimes permanent bodies of experts are appointed for the purpose of bringing about co-operation, and avoiding frictions, between related Departments. The Staff agencies are example in question. They can serve this purpose very nicely because their studies of the internal working of the department make them more familiar with the consequences of poor co-ordination. They can suggest means of co-ordination to the executive. The Cabinet Secretariat in India functions as a permanent co-ordination body.

In conclusion, it may be said that a sound organisation itself is conductive to easy co-ordination. Co-ordination of jobs must precede co-ordination of men, as Money, a great industrialist, has said. Not only arrangement of jobs is essential for easy co-ordination but also the arrangement of secretariat offices. Secretarial architecture plays an important role in developing a sound organisation.

All these aspects of administrative organisation will be discussed in some detail in the ensuing chapters of this Part.

3

Principles of Organisation

The functions or duties of Government determine the number and character of the parts of branches of administration. These parts or branches are called Departments. According to a great authority the departments of administration are to be determined and allocated only according to two alternative principles.

These principles are:

1. Distribution according to the persons or classes to be dealt with.
2. Distribution according to the services to be performed. According to the former principle each Minister and head of a department would be responsible for the activities of the Government which affect the sectional interests of particular classes of persons. Thus there may be a department for the depressed or a department for children, a department for farmers, a department for strangers and aliens and so on. This principle has only to be illustrated in order to be proved to be out of the question. A tendency to Lilliputian administration, we are assured, is the inevitable outcome of this method of organisation. As the authority we have referred to says, it is impossible that the specialised service which each department has to render to the community can be of a high standard when its work is at the same time limited to a particular class of persons and extended to every variety of service for them. For instance, the department for children would have to provide medical and educational and other welfare services for children and a department for farmers

would have to provide them in addition to the facilities of the department of agriculture. The duplication of services and institutions and the consequently enormous cost would lead to an early breakdown of administration.

The other method is the time-honoured method of defining the field of activity for each department according to the particular service it renders to the community. Thus a department of education would be occupied with the supply of the service of education of all kinds and grades wherever and by whomsoever needed. It is not possible to avoid some overlapping even if this principle of division of departments were adopted. The sanitary arrangements of a school or the health of the pupils may be the primary concern of the Department of Health and the latter may have to enter into the jurisdiction of the Department of Education in regard to these services. But such small and incidental mixing up of the work of departments is inevitable. And any difficulties to which such overlapping gives rise can be easily solved by arrangements for the collaboration of departments. But on the whole and as a rule, the division of departments according to the nature of the service to be rendered to the community is likely to lead to the minimum of confusion and the maximum of efficiency. For, if specialisation is necessary in the performance of any service this division according to services provides for that specialisation in study, thought and action. It is only in rare cases when the State feels called upon to undertake the promotion of the rapid progress of a section of the people long neglected and oppressed or depressed that it might create a special department to secure their progress. Thus in some States in India a department for Harijans has been created. But time only can show whether this is the best method of achieving the end in view and whether it would not have been better to entrust each of the Departments of Education, Health, Land Revenue with special directions to see to the special provision for the supply of their respective services to this special class of people for the Department for Harijans will still have to depend on them for any service it may render them. And that will to serve of the other departments may have weakened by the establishment of this special department.

That the division between the departments according to services cannot be rigid and exclusive is also proved by the experience that within each of some of these departments it may be necessary to provide for other services normally provided by other departments of a specialised character. Thus the Defence Service may have to provide not only specialised education required in the army, the navy, the air force but general education of the not-so-well educated members of this service. Thus there are army schools provided by the Army for the general education of soldiers. The Defence Service has also its own medical department. This difficulty in classification and division of departments is got over by the differentiation between the primary and the secondary services of departments. The main principle of classification is that the main services rendered by departments should be different and distinct and each department should have a main service of its own. The practical principle also should not be lost sight of that the grouping of Governmental business into departments must observe the principle that each department be each under a responsible head and that the grouping should be based on the correlation of services and limited by the amount of work which one man can efficiently supervise.

The work of modern Governments may be distributed among the following chief departments classified as basic, Social Welfare, Economic Protection, and Business Departments.

1.	National Defence	Basic
2.	Finance	
3.	External Affairs	
4.	Home Affairs	
5.	Education	Social Welfare
6.	Medical	
7.	Public Health	
8.	Labour, Poor and Backward Classes	Economic Protection or Welfare
9.	Agriculture, Industry, Commerce, Forests, Fisheries and Supplies	

10. Railways, Transport and Post-Office Irrigation, Hydro-electric works etc. } Business

Of these the first 4 are concerned with indispensable duties and functions of the State without the performance of which no State can exist. Education and Health, Medical, Public Health, Labour Departments have been added as State services as soon as it was realised that modern conditions of life required that the State should organise them if the conditions of the people were to be improved. Still later, the State, again to accelerate the rate of progress and prosperity and welfare of the peoples in the complex and complicated conditions of national and international life in modern times has had to do something to promote the prosperity of agriculture, industry, trade and commerce. And if the State goes still farther and decides to become a producer and distributor of wealth, so far left to individual initiative and activity, new departments will have to be added. Each nationalised industry will have to be looked after by separate department or a separate section in a general Production Department. There would have to be a Coal Board, a Steel Board, a Transport Board. The Business State of Socialist and Communist conception and contrivance has still further added to the number of departments of administration.

As the multiplication of departments is a tendency to which modern administration is addicted, its appetite growing by eating, it is as well to lay it down as a sound principle that new departments should be established only when and where the powers and duties it has to exercise or perform are of so special or so separate a nature they cannot be placed in the hands of an existing department or official. The cost of administration is a limitation on the number of departments in a State. A poor State cannot endow itself with departments that adorn the administrative life of an industrially advanced State. Administration is only part of a system of government and some systems of government can be very costly. A government that attempts to follow the latest fashion in welfare work, and to be the fairy godmother of its people would have to create a large number of expensive departments. But unless it wishes to founder and be wrecked it will have to resist the temptation. As Burke said "an economical constitution is a necessary basis of an economical administration."

THE FINANCE DEPARTMENT

"Finances are the nerves of the State" said Richelieu; he called it the lever of Archimedes which being firmly established give one the means to move the world. First and foremost therefore among the departments of administration stands the Department of Finance. Money is necessary not only for meeting the cost of maintenance of the several departments but it is necessary to enable them to perform the several services required of modern departments, like education, public health, promotion of agriculture, industry, trade and commerce. Money has to be taken from the people in the way of taxes and loans and spent on them in the form of services like defence, internal security, schools, hospitals, irrigation works, roads. The Budget as it is called, i.e. the statement of the revenue and expenditure of a modern State runs into millions of pounds sterling or billions of dollars, or crores of rupees. The modern State also borrows money from its own people or from foreigners and the National or Public Debt which a century ago counted only a few millions now runs into hundreds of millions. Some States have entered into business and have begun producing and distributing wealth and the Capital Budget of such a Business States also is to be counted in millions. All these millions and billions of modern currency have to be either managed directly or controlled indirectly by the Finance Department. It has to supervise the banking and currency of the State. It has not only to see to the collection of the revenue or income of the State and to distribute to the spending departments the monies sanctioned for them but to see that the money is properly spent on the objects specially sanctioned and only to the extent of the amount sanctioned for each. And as Burke pointed out in constitutional systems of government, "in every question of expense there is a mixture of constitutional considerations". For the Finance Department has to see to it that income and expenditure of or on behalf of the Government are according to the provisions made by the authority competent to do it according to the law and custom of the constitution of the State.

It is the special duty of the Finance Department to keep constant watch on the cost of government in general and the cost of administration in particular. Although it is true that the cost of the government and the administration may depend on decisions made elsewhere, in the Legislature and the Cabinet, yet it is the duty of the Finance Department to watch and report and advise the Government on the course of the financial administration of the State committed to its charge. It is the duty of the Finance Department and its head that the "means of order and foresight it keeps all the objects of this office, their state, conditions and regulations constantly before them".

To sum up the duties of the Finance department, they are:

1. Imposition and regulation of taxation according to law and the collection of the revenue from taxes and other sources.

2. Control of public expenditure through the preparation and supervision of estimates and through a proper system of account and audit.

3. Provision of funds required from day to day to meet the necessities of the public services for which purpose it is invested with extensive borrowing powers.

4. Management of the property of the State.

5. Management of the public debt.

6. Supervision of the currency and banking system of the country.

7. Supervision and control of the business enterprises of the State if there should be any.

From the enumeration of the powers of the Finance Department it follows that it is largely a department of control and supervision, apart from its main business which is the management of the finance of the State.

But it is its main business which is the control and supervision over the finance of the state that the Finance Department exercises that gives it its importance. If only because its approval is necessary for any expenditure of public money and it is charged with the duty of the accounting and auditing of the finances of the State it exercises a dominant voice in the management of the affairs of the State. Colbert in monarchical times and Gladstone under parliamentary government have proved the pre-eminence of the Finance Department. From a consideration of the powers and duties of the Finance Department it will be realised that it is the most important department of Government. There was one political system in the world that recognised the supreme importance of the Finance Department and its head. And that was the often and much decried ancient regime of France. The head was the Controller General who attracted to himself gradually all the business of the State that had to do with money that is to say the whole of the public administration of France. He was the Finance Minister, the Minister of the Interior, Minister of Public Works. He was in fact Prime Minister of France. (Nor must it be forgotten that the official title of the Prime Minister of England is, First Lord of the Treasury).

Revenue and Expenditure

Its main business consists of:

1. The collection of the revenue or income of the State.
2. The issue or distribution of parts or portions of this income to the several departments or on behalf of the several services offered by the State to the people. Each of these duties or functions of the Finance Department has its appropriate office and sets of officials.

Should Revenue and Expenditure be under the same head?

It has been the practice in well-governed countries, especially with à constitutional system of government to combine under the Finance Minister and his administrative chief the offices of revenue and expenditure. It has been proved by experience for instance in England that it is essential to a sound system of finance that the Minister and department responsible for raising the revenues should also have a predominant voice in deciding on the amount and in some degree on the character of the expenditure. For only in this way can the Finance Department exercise the necessary check and control on the demands made by the spending departments of Government. It is only thus that the Finance Department which is responsible for the management of the finances of the country can have a proper appreciation of the liabilities to which it is being committed by the policy of the other departments.

As Burke recommended, "all obstacles ought to be abolished that obscure the prospect of the general superintendent of finance, which destroy his super tendency, which disable him from foreseeing and providing for charges as they may occur for presenting expense in its origin, checking it in its progress, securing its application to the proper purpose." It is only he that can judge any proposal of any other Minister or Department, as the result as Burke called it, of "the total collected exigencies of the State". If as has been well put the Finance Department is to be held responsible for filling the reservoir and maintaining a certain depth of water in it, it must also be in a position to regulate the outflow. While each department looks upon its demands as if it stands alone and standing alone as being not formidable, it is the Finance Department that keeps account of each item of expenditure and knows how many a mickle of the several departments makes the mickle of the governmental expenditure on the whole. While not interfering with the details of the administration of the other departments, the Finance Department has to see to it that expenditure by each department takes account of the financial burden of the country and once sanctioned according to law if it exceeds the amount sanctioned.

Napoleon's device of separating the Ministry of Finance which was responsible for revenue from the Ministry of the Treasury which dealt with public expenditure was justified by his theory of dividing and ruling departments of Government. It will be remembered that he also thus divided and hamstrung the Legislature and his device was perhaps justified by the chaotic condition of administration in which the Directory had left it.

Revenue Offices

All revenue is collected by ubiquitous revenue officials and sent to local treasuries or banks to be settled in due time to the account of the Finance Department or a Central Bank or Treasury

The number and character of these offices depends on the number and character of the chief items or sources of revenue or income of the State. Thus we have in most countries:

1. An Inland Revenue Office, charged with the duty of collecting taxes and other revenues like rents from land or other property of the State, excise duties, death duties, judicial stamp, duties, etc., within the country mainly from the citizens or subjects of the state. An important section of this office is the Income-tax section which collects income-tax, profits tax, excess profits tax which fill a large and growing place in the tax system of modern States.
2. A Customs Office that has to collect customs and other duties (tariffs) levied on commodities imported into the country from abroad and those exported from the country abroad. As these duties are collected at the points where these goods come into the country or go out of the country, these customs offices are located mainly at the ports of the country especially when the country has a large sea-board like India, England and U.S.A. But countries with a land border also have Inland Customs Offices placed along the frontier of the country. As collection of customs has to combat against smugglers and smuggling on an organised basis the customs office has to organize a protective armed force to enable it officials to perform their duties. In such countries like U.S.A. the Coast Guard which has to prevent smuggling by sea is under the Customs Office.
3. Other important sources of revenue are the contribution made by certain modern businesses undertaken by the State like Posts and Telegraphs, Telephones, Broadcasting and Railways and Irrigation and Hydro-Electric systems. The amounts contributed by these businesses are so large that separate departments have been established to deal with the collection of the monies they gather, but the amounts go into the Treasury.

Expenditure Offices

As the most important business of the Finance Department is to superintend, check, and control the expenditure of the State revenue or income by the several departments and on behalf of the several services the offices and sections of the Department are concerned with this business.

ESTIMATES SECTION

The estimate of revenue and expenditure is the most important act of this the main section of the Finance Department. Estimates said Burke is the foundation ann corner-stone of all regular provident economy.

ESTIMATES OF REVENUE

Sometimes, say not more than 6 months before the Budget that is the annual statement of revenue and expenditure is submitted to the country or the Parliament, the Finance Department in the Estimates section proceeds to collect information from the revenue and other departments of the amount that would accrue during the financial year on the basis of the existing provisions, according to law of permanent and annual revenues. A statement of the actual receipts during the current financial year is also called for, provision is also made for supplementary estimates of unforeseen items and also uncalculated surpluses die to god-sends.

As these estimates are of tariffs, customs duties and other duties, the greatest secrecy is necessary. If it were known before the end of the financial year that customs duties were to be increased or reduced there would be much manipulation of customs and excessive clearances of the goods effected by merchant shippers and producers. If an increase were expected there would be what are called forestallment making the receipts abnormally high in the expiring year and during the early part of the new, and vice versa, from an anticipated reduction. To say the least there would be much derangement of the revenues calculation and a net loss to the State, gain to the tax or duty-payer with gains also to the merchant or trader.

Most revenues of the State are permanent, and this estimate of the amount contributed by them in any year is easily calculate any increase being mainly due to greater efficiency of collect. obi A common fault prevalent in estimates of revenue presented not an elected Parliament is to underestimate the revenues as a corresponding fault is to overestimate expenditure. This fault only makes the Budget look pretty but nobody is taken in by this dodge.

Estimate of Expenditure

About six months before the Budget is presented to the Parliament the Finance Department calls upon the other departments to send estimates of their expenditure with a warning or advice that in view of the state of the country's finance—s state which is more or less permanent—the departments should exercise the greatest restraint in proposing items of expenditure. But with a popular Minister dependent on a popular Assembly which again is dependent on the votes of the people, it is the Finance Department that has to play the restraining hand. A good estimate of expenditure should secure only what is necessary for the department during the year. It will avoid resorting to supplementary estimates and demands. The Finance Department in regard to expenditure has to see that the appropriations which are the allotment of supply to service made by the Legislature are properly spent by the several departments. The Finance Department is the watch-dog of the Government and the State.

Relation between Revenue and Expenditure

The relation between revenue and expenditure is best understood by the simile of a reservoir. All tax and other monies that form the revenues of the State collected by the officers of Revenue must be poured into a reservoir kept in a Bank or in its own Treasury, the tap of the reservoir cannot be opened except by authority with which the Finance Department is satisfied—generally in Parliament-governed countries by what is known as an Appropriative Act, and the people that collect the water are the spending departments of government.

Control of Expenditure—Account and Audit

Account—It is by the tried instruments of accounting and audit that the control of expenditure by the Finance Department is exercised. First, account must be kept of every payment made and it must come before payment. The capital use of an account, said Burke is that the reality of the charge, the reason of incurring it and the justice and sincerity of discharging it should all appear antecedent to the payment for no man ever pays first and calls his account afterwards because he would thereby let out of his hands the principal and indeed the only effective means of compelling a full and fair use, and in national business there is an additional reason for a previous production of every account, it is a check and perhaps the only one upon a corrupt and prodigal use of public money and an account after payment is to no purpose a rational account." And a modern authority modernizes this old injunction when he says there is no machinery for the control of expenditure except accounting.

In addition to the Accounts section of each department which must keep the tale of the receipt and expenditure made each day by or on behalf of each department, there must be a general Accounts section of the Finance Department which consolidates all these several accounts received from time to time and present a picture of the accounts of the State at the end of the financial year.

The Accounts section of each department and the General Accounts section of the Finance Department are charged with the following duties.

1. Watching expenditure before, during and after it is incurred.
2. Planning and accounts to the satisfaction of the head of the department and of the Finance Department.
3. Arranging and maintaining a system of internal audit of the accounts and money in the custody of the department and its officials—day to day check is thus kept on the expenditure of the department.
4. Examining and certifying the appropriate account.
5. Preparing accounts and relative books and documents for audit by the auditing department.
6. Preparing the annual accounts for the Public Accounts Committee of the Legislature.

As the easy and decisive fixation of responsibility is necessary of this section is to secure any useful purpose the head of this section of the Finance Department cannot delegate his responsibility to subordinates. In England he is the person whom the Parliament and the Treasury regard as primarily responsible for the balance in the custody of the department, although he may not keep a farthing of it. Responsibility for the proper conduct of financial business cannot be delegated to subordinate officers who may be placed in charge of the departmental accounts; otherwise the signature appended to the appropriate account would be otherwise an ideal form calculated only to mislead Parliament. A further device to fix the responsibility of the Head of the section is to make him personally and directly responsible to the Minister and to insist on every objection of the Accounts officers to what he considered to be improper expenditure to be in writing and on the overriding official also recording him instruction in writing. A further safeguard is required that all Accounts offices should submit their accounts to the Public Accounts Committee of the Legislature which is thus given an opportunity and power to exercise additional check and control over all the finance of the country.

In parliamentarily governed countries the Public Accounts Committee of the Legislature examines accounts of all departments and passes its observations and criticisms of the financial behaviour of departments to the finance department who passes them on to the departments concerned for future guidance. According to English practice the leader of the Opposition is chairman of the committee and an officer of the Treasury is in attendance at meetings of the committee.

The relationship between the Public Accounts Committee and the accounts officer is that of a judicial tribunal and a respondent. It does not give orders to him and has no responsibility for what he does. If it approves of his account it discharges him of his liabilities to Parliament, if it does not approve it reports him to the house to that effect; in the latter event the Legislature calls the attention of the Minister who is then expected to take suitable action.

In order to ensure the accuracy and control of finance by means of accounts, the system of book-keeping with double entry should be maintained in each accounts section. It is a tried means of strict control of financial administration which nothing can escape, as well for check as for defence. The system of book-keeping by double entry follows every financial operation from start to finish, it gives guarantee of exactitude of date and ever by insisting on putting down everything as soon as it happens, not only does it group related facts in their chronological order but it maintains the accounts thus composed in such wise that they can at any time be compared, balanced, closed and every account could be judged as a whole and in each one of its items. This was the system introduced into French State finances when Napoleon with the aid of men like Mollien attempted to evolve order out of the chaos into which the finances like other parts of the administration had been thrown in the last phase of the ancient regime and the early days of the Revolution.

From business must be copied the practice of cost accounting the great detector of waste and inefficiency.

Not the least, though it is the last of the principles of good public accounting is that all sorts of accounts should be closed sometime or other—by payment by composition or by oblivion.

Audit

One of the greatest administrative inventions of modern times was the Audit invented early in the 19th century, although an office corresponding to it is said to have existed in the later days of the Chinese Empire. When the Chinese Censor or Auditor thought it essential to criticise the financial acts of His Celestial majesty but was weighed down by the seriousness of his act he promptly committed suicide. Audit has served to put down the waste of public money and corruption that had been rampant in most countries.

Auditing although allied to is different from accounting. Accounting only sees to it that the amount of money provided for in the Budget and only that amount is used by the department, that spending by the department as a whole and by each section is according to law or the orders of the head of the Department. Auditing goes one step further and sees to it that each department spends the amount allotted to it only for the specific purpose for which it is allotted and in such a way that the purpose is served by the specific expenditure. The Audit Department checks all accounts of tall departments and has access to all ledgers, store accounts, trading accounts, etc. The audit known in England as the Appropriation Audit is called upon or on behalf of the Legislature and the people to see that the money expended has been applied to the purpose or purposes for which the grants made by the Legislature were intended to provide, and that the expenditure conforms to the authority which governs it. The Audit Department has to satisfy itself that every item of expenditure falls within range of the heads of expenditure voted and has been classified and charged to the specific sub-head of the vote. It must see that laws passed are duly observed, that the specific sanction of the Finance Department has been obtained, that the amounts are correct and all payments are supported by documents and vouchers. For convenience and increased efficiency of all concerned the auditing should be done continuously or periodically throughout the year; irregularities should thus have a better chance of being detected immediately. A large office like the British Admiralty, for instance, has members of the Audit Department permanently housed within its own building and this periodical and continuous audit is good for the Admiralty as well as convenient for the Audit Department. This interim audit of the Audit Department must not be confused with the internal audit of each department which is a domestic convenience and does not exempt it from the external audit of the Audit Department.

Such a system helps the Audit Department to serve the two main purpose of an audit, the check, the prevention and the detection of errors and frauds. It has to prevent not only misappropriation but mismanagement. Periodical and continuous auditing furnishes us with the preventive mechanism to be applied at the danger points, to stop abuses from going to excess so that we may not be faced with monstrous scandals or loss at the end of the year. Even if as in the judgment in the Kingston Cottom *Mills* case audit is shown to be a watchdog rater than a blood-hound, a policeman rather than a detective, it would still render a great service to the State.

Audit is of two kinds—Pre-audit and Post-audit. Generally it is Post-audit that is used—that is to say auditing is mostly postmortem checking of accounts of the expenditure incurred by departments. The Auditor-General's functions are largely of reporting on the operations authorised of the departments of Government. They have been humorously described as follows. The Auditor-General starts the hare, the public accounts committee runs it down, the treasury breaks it up. But is has also been said that if an Auditor-General is popular with departments he is not doing his work properly.

Separation of Audit from Accounts

The separation of Audit from Accounts is necessary for the efficiency of either. It is especially necessary if audit is to enable the departments or officer charged with to perform the important duty of controlling the expenditure of public money by Government Departments. The independence of audit of all departments of Government of even the Finance Departments, has been called for by the democratic form of government where the pressure of the electorate and of the Minister dependent on the votes of the electorate has become more or less irresistible. So much has the need for the independence of audit been felt in modern democratic times that the Head of the Audit Department has been given the status of a judge and made independent of the Finance Department and even the Government, although he may owe his appointment to the Government to the Treasury in England and to the Head of the State in U.S.A.; and India, being made irremovable except by formal and special vote of the Legislature.

As against the British system of accounts and audit is the continental system which consists in a Court of Accounts which tries the accounts and grants final certificates of discharge and then reports results to the Legislature. While the British system is primarily a post-audit system after payment, the Belgian and Italian systems, involve and pre-audit before payment. In some countries e.g., Japan before the war there was also what is known as efficiency audit which is not satisfied that public expenditure is correct and authorised but finds whether the State has received value for its money by its expenditure. For this the Japanese Auditor-General was helped by a committee or technical men attached to his office.

To conclude, the object of all Accounts and Audit system is the practice of economy, not, as President Coolidge of the U.S.A. said, in order to save money but to save the people from burdens they need not bear.

Other Sections of the Finance Department

1. The Banking and Currency Section:

The Banking work of a Government may be done by a private Bank as was done by the Bank of England ever since it was started and where the monies collected by the State were deposited, or by a State Bank. Some States have a Central Bank under Government auspices. While it may be agreed that, as Lord Keynes argues, the functions of a Central Bank are a collective activity and one in which private profit should not play a part and the business of a Central bank is to pursue a defined technical purpose, the important question is whether this particular collective activity is of a kind that should be subject to Ministers who are subject to the Cabinet who in their turn are subject to daily criticism in Parliament. Thus, even when the Central Bank is a Government or a Government controlled institution it should be a semi-autonomous body not subject to political interference it its daily work. But to the ultimate control of the Ministry and Parliament such a Central Bank should be subject. Large matters of currency policy should be determined by the Ministry and parliament, whether for instance, it is to be parity with gold, or whether it has to have regard to the state of internal prices, or the state of employment. In the decision of such questions the advice of and recommendations of the Finance Department would be decisive. Even when the Central Bank is a private bank as was the Bank of England till recently Government have powers of control over it as illustrated in the power given the Chancellor of the Exchequer to suspend the fiduciary limit on note issue.

Currency administration has become an important business of modern Governments. The problem of inflation alone throws this business on Governments and their Finance Departments.

The revenue of the State that comes from permanent income or annual taxation or loans is enormously large. The money collected is not spent at once; it has therefore to keep a central treasury or Bank; a modern Government has to do a lot of banking work. It has to issue Bills for temporary accommodation when it may not have the money to make certain payments as its income takes time to collect. In some countries a Reserve Bank is set up which does banking work for the Government, it keeps the money of the State and issues money as and when Government or departments of Government need it. The Governing Board or Board of Directors is nominated by the Government and elected by the shareholders in due proportion.

The right to issue public money is one of the rights of a sovereign State. The right to issue paper money now a popular substitute for it is a corollary. Manufacture of metal coins is done in one or several State mints which may have the machinery for making paper money.

All work connected with currency is entrusted to a section of the Finance Department. The decision to add to the coinage or paper money of the country rests with the Government

The Public Debit Section

It is a long time since Government have lived on their revenue. We have travelled far from the times of Colbert who warned the French Finance Department of his days against beginning to borrow for the State or they had in their King Louis XIV's penchant for grand schemes of war and peace a powerful temptation to extravagance, once this comparatively easy method of getting money was made known to him. Our times must be pleasing to Alexander Hamilton who thought and argued that "a national debt is a national blessing". Governments have had to borrow not only in times of need like individuals. Welfare and business schemes make Governments borrow and the ease with which Governments can float loans on account of the security they offer which is the security of the State, its wealth, its production, its income encourage them to borrow. The Public or National Debt of modern States soars into hundreds of millions. The management of this debt and its account is given to a section of the Finance Department. Although the decision to raise a loan is the decision of the Finance Minister and of the Ministry, the details of the loans are suggested by this section. All the preparation for the floating of the loans is made here. The administration of such a loan is in its hands, the payment of the interest, the repayment of the loan. The sinking fund and fund from which the debt is to be repaid is also in the hands of this section. Government securities, annuities, etc., have to be administered by it.

THE DEPARTMENT OF DEFENCE

The defence of the life and liberty of a State against attack from outside and internal disorder within is one of the most important duties of a Government. The Department of Defence is charged with the duty of organizing the defence of the freedom sovereignty and independence of the State against all those that challenge them from without or within. The instruments of that defence are the Army, the Navy, the air Force and other services and the Department of Defence is concerned with the organisation of these services and with making them carry out their several duties to the highest point of efficiency. The nature of the work of these services calls for a division into two sections, concerned with.

1. The personnel and material required.
2. Strategy and tactics.

On account of the tremendously important character of the latter class of concerns they have been put under a special organisation known in England as the Committee of Defence under the direct supervision and control for the Head of the Executive. This organisation provides for the frequent meeting of the heads of the chief services, the Army, the Navy and the Air Force for consultation and decision in regard to important question.

With regard to the Departments of Defence itself the question has been raised whether the Army, the Navy and the Air Force should have separate departments or should be united under a single Minister. Separate departments like the Admiralty, the War Office in England are accounted for by history. But where history has not operated it is best to have the defence under a single political and administrative Head, with different sections under their own sectional chiefs.

The peculiar importance of Defence Department charged as it is with looking after the safety of the State and where safety must come before parsimony, its finances and its financial administration are committed to a special section in the Ministry of Defence as in England and not to the Finance Department as are the finances of other departments.

The Defence Department is only the administrative head of the defence services, the army, the navy, the air force. As these are professional and technical services their organisation is governed by the laws and principles appropriate to each of them although the general principles and methods of administration are found operating in each of them *mutatis mutandis*. But like any other service they work and operate under the ultimate authority of the Government which is represented for them by the Defence Department or departments, with one Minister or more at the head.

The Department of Foreign or External Affairs

A great French Minister of Foreign Affairs D'Argenson spoke of the super-eminence of his office over other departments of the Government because the army, the navy and the finances of the State depend largely on its management of its business and the decisions it takes on the relations between the State and other States. Some of the greatest statesmen of France have been ministers of foreign affairs, Richelieu, Mazarin, Talleyrand. Statesmen of other countries also like Castlereagh and Palmerston of England Machiavelli and Cavour of Italy, Gorstschakoff of Russia, Bismarck of Germany owe a large part of their fame to their work as Ministers in charge of the foreign affairs of their respective countries. The Secretary of State in the U.S.A. is the minister in charge of foreign affairs. The Department of Foreign or External affairs as it is now called in some countries is one of the most important departments of the State. It strikes the imagination of the people and almost has a glamour about it. For, on account of the nature of its work, representatives of foreign States—ministers envoys, plenipotentiaries, consuls, hover about it.

Alone among the departments of the State it holds receptions and organizes entertainments at which duty and beauty and pleasure, native and foreign, meet in social conviviality. Its officials and servants and other representatives are spread all over the world. It is one of the most costly departments of State next only perhaps to that of defence and even the cost of the Defence Department, of the defence services depends on the work and decisions of the Department of Foreign Affairs. For whether the country is to continue to enjoy peace or be thrown into the cauldron of war depends on the work of this Department.

For it has to do with:

1. Formulation and conduct of the foreign policy of the State, i.e., the conduct of its relations with other states.
2. Help in building up the foreign trade and commerce of the State.
3. Protection of the rights of the citizens of the State and other property in the territory of other States.

In doing this work it has to perform the following duties:

1. It supervises and controls the work of the official representatives of the State to other States—the ambassadors, the ministers, envoys, plenipotentiaries delegates, consular and other trade officers through whom the department maintains contacts and relations with foreign Governments and protects its citizens and their rights abroad.
2. Aids in the making and enforcing of treaties and other agreements with other States.
3. Arranges for the reception by the Head of the State of foreign ambassadors and ministers accredited to it.
4. Gathers information about the political and social and economic conditions (these latter have become very important on account of the predominance of economics in modern political problems) of other countries.
5. Arranges for trade agreements with the Governments of other States.

6. Issues passports to citizens who wish to travel abroad and visas to travellers from abroad.

7. Controls the immigration of foreign people to the territory of the State.

8. Administers the nationality and nationalisation laws of the State.

The work of the Head of the Foreign Affairs department has been summarised thus by a great Secretary of State of the U.S.A. It is:

1. To aid the head of the Government in every possible way in the formulation and conduct of foreign policy.

2. To make use of his department's life-long experts on each important question of foreign policy concerning every country in the world and to keep in touch with the best informed experts in every department from top to bottom.

3. To foresee and appraise to the fullest possible extent questions and problems arising or about to arise.

4. To formulate his own ideas of foreign policy in conference with the associates in his department and then recommend such policy to the Government for their approval or disapproval and recommend the necessary action.

5. If the Head of the Government or the Government should themselves suggest a policy he should furnish them with all information relating to it and then carry it out through his department.

On account of the nature of the work of the Department of Foreign or External Affairs, having to do not only with different countries but with different kinds or work in one and the same country the question arises of the principle on which its several sections should be divided. Should these be divided according to the groups of regions with which this Department is concerned or according to the groups of subjects that have to be dealt with by this department in relation to foreign countries. For instance, should the English Foreign office be divided into a West European Section and an East European section and an Asiatic section, or the U.S.A. Secretary of State's Department be divided into a European section, a South American section and a pacific Ocean section or the Indian Department of External Affairs be divided into a European section, an Asian section and an American section? Or, on the other hand should this department be divided into a political section, an Economic section, a Military section, a Naval section, and a Trade and Commerce section each dealing with their particular subject in all countries. The choice of the principle to be followed has been determined by the character of the work of the department which is to organize relations with other States. It is the sum of the interests political, military, economic represented by each State that has to be taken into account to determine their relations. And so a department of Foreign Affairs is divided according to groups or regions of States, for obviously it would not be possible to have one section for each foreign country.

Thus the English Foreign Office since its reorganisation in 1918, has been divided into the Eastern section (dealing with the affairs of Eastern Europe, Turkey, Persia, Central Asia, Egypt) the Western section taking Western Europe, the American section taking North, Central and South America, the Far Eastern section taking China, Japan, Siam. But there are still subjects that are of such important and specific character that they have a section to themselves. Thus there is the Consular section dealing with British Consuls, throughout the world, (as Consuls are concerned with the promotion or trade in the countries to which they are) sent. There is a Treaty section which does the important and specialised work on Treaties, preparing drafts for them and dealing with other technical questions, as extradition, nationality, copyright, the Foreign Enlistment Act.

It is only when foreign affairs occupy a large part of the attention of the Government that the division into regional sections is called for. Great Britain and the U.S.A. and Russia whose contacts with foreign States are world-wide would have such section. But States like India with few interests in other countries and States to be in touch with should be satisfied with sections divided according to subjects.

The Department of Foreign Affairs cannot work in isolation although its subject may make it look like a thing apart and in some States like England of the 19th century it did look and act thus. In any time it has to work in conformity with the Defence Department, otherwise its policy may be in the air and of no force or effect. It has to work also in touch with the Department of Home Affairs as in the matter of extradition and the treatment of aliens. And modern economic problems call for work in harmony with the Departments of economic affairs. The evil consequence of the Department of Foreign Affairs working in isolation is illustrated for instance in the consequences to Russia on the eve of the war of 1914-18 when Russian foreign policy was divorced from the home policy of the Tsars and remained solely the province of the Foreign office which became more and more cut off from the rest of the Government resulting in weakness and even danger. The Russo-Japanese war might not have been undertaken if the internal state of Russia had been known. Similarly the Kaiser entered into the war of 1914—18 on the advice of the war ministry without any reference to the foreign office and Hitler worked the war machine of Germany in the II World War without any reference to foreign affairs or to his foreign office under Ribbentrop which had no mind of its own.

Diplomats

As the Department of Foreign or External Affairs has to deal with other States and the questions that have to be settled with them cannot in the nature of these questions be dealt with by correspondence between the Departments of Foreign or External Affairs of the countries concerned, it has been found convenient to have representatives of one State present in the capital of other States and get these questions settled by and through such representatives. That it is mere convenience and utility that has brought about such representation is proved by the fact that ancient States that had few or no contacts with other States did not have them and it is only as international intercourse increased that the institution developed. In the mediaeval States of Europe these representatives were at first temporary, appointed from time to time for the settlement of some cause of dispute or some question of marriage or exchange of territory. It is only from about the time of the Renaissance and the Reformation when international relations grew sometimes to the point of inflammation that these representatives become permanently accredited and resident. Now it is considered to be a sign of sovereignty and independence for a State to have permanent resident representatives accredited to other States.

They have been known by various names, Envoys, Ministers, Ambassadors; when they are entrusted with full power to act on behalf of their State and so as to commit them to their actions, they are called plenipotentiaries, but it has been an exceptional title. They represent the State at the capitals of other States, are the normal means of communication between their State and the State to which they are accredited and in general act on behalf of their States in all matters that concern them both.

Their chief tasks are:

1. to keep the department of Foreign or External Affairs informed speedily, accurately, and impartially of the facts of the country to which they are accredited. Their reports must be absolutely uncoloured—statements which a fair interpretation of facts such as is possible to an actual and close witness of them;
2. to represent the country abroad, its ideals, explain its policies, make friends and facilitate through friendly contacts the transaction of any business interesting to the two States;
3. to carry out the instructions of the Department and conduct the negotiations entrusted to them;
4. to protect the lives and property of the nationals of the State.

Diplomacy

In the carrying out of these duties the Minister or Ambassador has to practice the great art of diplomacy. That are consists in faithfully representing his State to the State to which he is accredited and the latter to his. He must tell the truth as he sees it to his Department without reserve whether the truth is palatable or not. The well-known description of a diplomat that he is a representative of a country sent to lie abroad is only a jest. On the other hand the Chinese proverb is more to the point "a lie has no legs". He must faithfully record all conversations and interviews, he has with the Head of the Department of Foreign or External Affairs. When he makes representations on behalf of his Government to the Government to which he is accredited he must do it *svaviter in modo, fortiter in re*. He has to advise his Government on the attitude to be taken on matters of dispute between the two Governments. Although he has to obey in the end and carry out the directions of his Government, he is not a mere figure-head or robot. Although the modern inventions of the telegraph and the telephone and air travel and conference making communication between him and his Government frequent and rapid and direct and visits and interviews of the Minister himself place the temptation before the latter of reducing ministers and ambassadors to mere post offices, his duty to serve his State as conscientiously and patiently as possible remains. He has still to point out mistakes or omissions in the instructions sent to him. He still has to make his Government's communications to the foreign Government appear in the best light possible. He has to adapt himself and his speech and conduct to the atmosphere of his environment and the personality of those he has to deal with. The failure of diplomacy by conference, in the period between the two World Wars and by ministerial intervention has reinstated the old diplomacy in its former position of power and prestige. Conceited and interventionist Ministers of Foreign Affairs are soon shown their place by the force and complexity of modern circumstances. They reduce the position and prestige of their diplomatic representatives abroad only at the expense of their foreign policy.

On account of the peculiar and delicate nature of the work of the Department of Foreign or External Affairs special instruments and methods of work are employed. Secret codes and code-words, the key to which are kept most secret, are used in diplomatic correspondence, by letter or telegram. To ensure still greater secrecy special messengers are sent carrying bags of letters and correspondence. As much information can be obtained in the informal ways of social intercourse, entertaining and being entertained fill a large place in the daily life of the diplomat. The entertainment allowance forma a large slice of the budget of the diplomat's office. Money has to be spent in so-called "secret service", the buying of valuable information through spies and other secret agents. All this costs money. The cost of the Department of Foreign or External Affairs forms a large sector of the public expenditure.

But the work of the Department is worth the cost. For it is charged with the duty of maintaining peace between its State and other States, of solving all difficulties and disputes by the methods of peace, argument, discussion, appeals to interest and avoiding the scourge of war. Peace or war is largely in the hands of the Foreign Offices of the world. It is this high mission, the preservation of peace and the avoidance of war, that accounts for the prestige and power of this Department.

The Department of Home Affairs

Corresponding and parallel to foreign affairs are Home Affairs. But the Department of Home Affairs as it is called in England or the Interior as in Europe or the Home Department for short, as it is called in India, is not concerned with all the home affairs of a State. The fact that Home Affairs are restricted to the management of the internal peace and order of the State not only points to the historical fact that this duty was for long the only internal duty of the Government but to the importance of this particular part of Home Affairs. For the maintenance of internal peace and order is necessary for the security of the life, liberty, and the welfare of the people of the State.

The functions of the Home Department or of the Department of the Interior may be grouped under the following heads:

1. the prevention of crime,
2. the maintenance of peace and order and public safety,
3. the administration of citizenship laws including election laws,
4. the administration of justice where there is not a separate department of justice,

5. miscellaneous.

The first group of functions may include the following subjects:

1. police—central and local,
2. prevention of disturbances and riots,
3. administration of criminal justice—care of prisons and prisoners—production of prisoners before courts of law and coroners—appointment of magistrates and other officials of criminal courts—children's courts—probation courts.
4. use of the prerogative of pardon and mercy of the Head of the State.
5. extradition.

The second group would include:

1. Nationality and Aliens Acts.
2. Liquor and Drug control—White Slave traffic.
3. Obscene publications, etc.

For the maintenance of peace and order and the prevention and pursuit of crime and criminals the Home Department has a large force of men to see to the fulfilment of these duties. This force is called the police. What the Army is to the defence of the State against aggression from outside the Police is to the defence of the State against aggression from within. The forces of disorder within a State are never dead. At the best of times they may be asleep. Modern developments like industrialisation have brought large concentrations of men in several places. Economic discontent when it is not allayed breaks out into movements of people that may lead to disorder. Modern political theories make governments peculiarly and frequently liable to attack. The idea popularised by the French Revolution that States and Governments are made by men and therefore can be unmade by them has made revolution constant and continuous and the revolutionary spirit is in permanent session. Modern society, as Dean Inge said, breeds its own barbarians and the barbarian invasions of today come from within.

Force and the instrument of force are open to the exponents of disorder as to the defenders of order. Dynamite, the bomb, massed attacks have to be faced by the modern police. One section of them has to be armed like the army itself.

The organisation of the police has followed different models. In England the Anglo-Saxon tradition of local self-government has made the police mainly a responsibility of the units of local government, like the borough and the country. Even when modern conditions have called for the organisation of a national police, local authorities are still charged with the duty of organizing the police of the locality. Under a recent Act the local authority is responsible for efficiency while the responsibility for the action of the police is shared by the Chief Constable and the Magistrate, but the Home Secretary has the power to issue regulations calculated to secure a high degree of uniformity in conditions of service and in duties, beside also the right of supervision through inspections and has the right of issuing orders and instructions from time to time. In London the Metropolitan Police under its Commissioner is brought directly under the supervision of the Home Secretary. In regard to the English Police system the principle of English common law must be remembered that the ordinary citizen is as much bound to do his best for the maintenance of peace and order and that the English policemen is not so much a servant of the people, as a servant of the law for everyone of his duties and actions is liable to be reviewed in courts of law.

The other model of police organisation is the Roman model followed in European countries where the police is organised on the model of an army and is therefore incorporated in a national centralised organisation. Similarly Ireland under British rule, got the Royal Irish Constabulary which again was the model followed when the Indian police was organised by the British.

Departments of Social Welfare

So far we have dealt with the absolutely necessary departments of Government or departments without which the State could no exist. For long they were the only departments of the administration. But the State is meant not only to preserve life, but to promote good life. Modern political theory conspiring with modern circumstances like growth of poverty, industrialisation, international competition have thrown new duties upon the State. The reply of the merchants of France when asked by Colbert what he could do to help them. *"Iaissez nous faire"* let us do it and Benthanm's motto for governments "be quiet" have been outmoded by modern social and economic circumstance. The State and its instrument the Government have been called upon to promote the welfare of the people. The Welfare State has created a number of new departments. This welfare may be comprised under two chief heads—social welfare and economic welfare. The departments of social welfare—chief are:

1. Department of Education.
2. Department of Health.
3. Departments of other social services like Insurance Old-age Pension, Housing, Town-planning.
4. Department of Labour wherever industrial labour has become important.
5. Department for Backward classes wherever there are such classes which have to be specially looked after an account of their backward or depressed condition.

The names given to these departments explain and describe their work. The Department of Education supplies the whole of the education required by or for a people or gives aid to help and supplement the educational work of voluntary agencies. In the former case the Education Department supplies the teachers, schools, and aids to education, in the latter case the Education Department sees to it that the grants of money and other aids supplied by the State are used for the purposes for which they are supplied. Similarly, the Department of Health, in regard to the supply of doctors and nurses and hospitals and dispensaries and sanitation. In either case these Government departments have to employ a large number of inspectors to see on their behalf that the money and other help are properly spent and the services supplied are efficient. In the organisation of these departments of

Education and Health men and women in the educational and medical and public health professions will be used in the proportion required.

The Labour Department looks after the interests of that important class of modern society, industrial labour, their education, housing, the relations between capital and labour and the administration of the labour laws passed to protect and promote the welfare of this section of the people.

Similarly the department of backward classes in countries where they exist as in the U.S.A. (the Indians and Negroes) the depressed backward classes aboriginal tribes in India and some British Colonies. These departments also require a large number of field officers carrying out or supervising the work done for these classes by these departments.

The importance of these departments of social welfare is shown by the large sums of money spent by them. In England education and broadcasting accounts for 215 millions (one-tenth of the total expenditure). The Health, Housing and Labour and National insurances services cost 541 million pounds (one-fifth of the total expenditure). In U.S.A. the amount expended in 1945-46 on public elementary and secondary schools was 27,95,80,000 dollars, in addition to 11,10,46,000 spent on capital expenditure. This country of individualism is spending about 4,000 million dollars a year on social welfare, health security, housing, and community facilities.

Departments of Economic Protection or Welfare

The usual departments of economic welfare are the:

1. Department of Agriculture (with which go Forestry and Fisheries);
2. Department of Industry and Trade and Commerce;
3. Department of Supplies.

These departments of economic welfare as long as the State is only a Welfare State restrict themselves to the creation or improvement of the conditions conducive to the greater prosperity of agriculture or industry, or commerce. They aim at improving the productive capacity of private enterprise by the promotion and organisation of research, the creation and maintenance of technical schools, model farms, legislative and administrative action removing obstacles to agricultural or industrial production. These departments are not actually engaged in production or distribution, they aid production or distribution.

The services rendered by such departments comprise:

1. thinking about and devising such measures by law or executive action as would promote the productive capacity of private enterprise;
2. ensuring such a measure of control as may be determined by law or executive act over the production and distribution of commodities by private enterprises;
3. preventing fraud in the manufacture and distribution and adulteration of commodities;
4. watching over and protecting the interests of the consumer and of the community as a whole in relation both to the production and distribution of commodities;
5. administering the laws, protecting the interests of labour, i.e., Factory Acts, Mines Regulations Act, Workmen's Compensation Acts;
6. watching the effect of the laws of the State especially the laws of succession, inheritance, property transfer of property, commercial and company law, the law of patents and trade marks, the law of bankruptcy on agricultural and industrial production and devising remedial measures.

These services may be summed up as stimulus, inspection, regulation, prohibition.

A Department of Supplies is called for:

1. to eliminate competition between departments for labour. material, and the services for supplies of goods required;

2. to ensure that the prices paid and the conditions imposed under Government contracts for various classes of work should as far as possible, be arranged on uniform lines;

3. to secure economies in the use of technical staffs (such as contracting, accounting, costing and inspection);

This Department may also be made responsible for:

1. the provision directly or indirectly, of government printing, publications, books, stationery, office requisites;

2. the provision of furniture, light water, and other household articles for government departments;

3. the provision of the other supplies (except those of a highly technical nature required by particular departments like the Public Works Department.)

The supplies required by the Defence Department are big enough to be handled by the Defence Department itself.

Department of Trade and Commerce

With the going of *laissez faire,* a department of trade and commerce is found necessary. The collection of all kinds of commercial information that may be useful in the development of trade within the country and outside along with such other subjects as conditions of local trade and credit, customs, tariffs, foreign competition in markets abroad is only one of its duties. Also, organisation of efficient commercial services like that of Trade Commissioners in countries where foreign trade is to be developed. The development of the home market is also one of its cares in large countries like India and U.S.A. The development of native industries falls with its scope. The establishment of useful relations with the business world is therefore an important duty of this department. Systems of tariffs, licences, permits, quotas throw considerable and responsible work on this department.

Departments of the Business State

Historical and political reasons have brought into being and activity a small number of departments doing work of a business character. Roads have been built by the State almost everywhere. Where private capital for the building of railways is not forthcoming the State steps in, as in India, first by guaranteeing minimum returns with the option of buying up the railway after a period and then building railways itself or it may build railways for strategic reason as in Germany. The Post Office has everywhere been a State concern, because it was intuitively realised that one single body would be better above to organize this means of communication than a number of competing private business.

The success of State Railways and State Post Offices, has encouraged many Governments to enter more and deeper into business. Modern socialist and collectivist theories have fostered this tendency. The State entering business and having to use the usual instruments of administration, the Government department and its methods of work, the question has been raised early in the career of the State in business, whether the methods and instruments used in general administration could be used without modification or whether and to what extent and how they should be modified in the administration of those new departments, that have taken upon themselves the new duties of producing and distributing wealth. Obviously, the reason why the State has taken upon itself the production and distribution of wealth is that it can do it better than individual and private enterprise. It would produce more wealth and distribute it better than private enterprise. Although the private profit motive has been eliminated its place has been taken by the public profit motive. The profit instead of accruing to the private capitalist must accrue to the State which becomes the sole capitalist when the State has become a thorough-paced Business State. Thus the Departments of Administration that conduct the business concerns for the State must adopt as far as possible the methods used by private enterprise. These enterprises undertaken by Government by their very nature have to be managed as Government departments and as business enterprises. As Government Departments they have to be manned by permanent government officials ultimately responsible to a Legislative and Representative Assembly, which has the right to supervise the conduct of Departments of Government and to follow public money to the hands of those that handle it. As in business enterprise they must also be partly managed by business men and with business methods.

To utilize the advantages of business methods and practices and yet to keep the business managed by the State subject to ministerial responsibility and parliamentary scrutiny a new institution has been found. It is the Public Corporation. It has been called by various names, Board, or Commission, or Corporation. But the essential ideas governing its constitution and work are:—

1. its autonomy as a business body,
2. its membership, consisting of representatives of Government, business men and public bodies,
3. its finances consisting of governmental contributions as well as money it can raise itself.
4. its liability to scrutiny by Minister or Parliament only on matters of policy; its actual management of the business being excluded from such scrutiny.

It harmonises the efficiency of private enterprise with the safeguard of the right of control and participation of the Government as representative of the people. Under the title of Mixed Economy, it has been recommended to the European public. For the Public Corporation or Mixed Economy Institute is a business body managed by business men according to the methods of business of exploiting say the Hydro-electric or irrigation possibilities of a river. This Mixed Economy institution has been adopted widely in Germany, Belgium, Switzerland. Especially, in Germany in the period between the two world wars has this institution been used for the supply of gas, electricity, tramway traffic to the public, the development of the water-power of the upper Rhine, of the port of Hambug the navigation of the Rhine and Danube. Switzerland is the country in Europe where this institution has been most effectively used especially in the exploitation of its great hydro-electric possibilities. Even Soviet Russia has been reported to have resorted to this institution finding it more fruitful than the ruinous practices of undiluted Marxim. In

England this institution is found in the British Broadcasting Corporation for the supply of knowledge and entertainment on the wireless, the Electricity Commission for promoting, regulating and supervising the supply of electricity, the Land Board (for city and county planning) the Coal Board for the production and distribution of coal. In India the Railway Board after its finances were separated from the general finances of India in 1924 is a distant approach to this institution as none of its capital is raised from the general public independently of the Government and there are no representatives of business or the general public on it.

The history of these business concerns introduces us to the following principles and methods of works of the Public Corporation or Mixed Economy Institution.

1. the business must have its own capital, raised from taxation or borrowing;
2. the accounts of these business concerns must be kept separately from the ordinary or revenue accounts of the State. These accounts must be kept according to the system of commercial accounts;
3. its personnel should be partly permanent civil servants and partly business men;
4. business methods should be employed as far as possible;
5. there must be much greater flexibility and elasticity than in an ordinary department of the administration;
6. the profit motive should not be overlooked although it may be subject to the general interests of the State;
7. its policy and programme though not actual conduct of business must be subject to the scrutiny of the Minister in charge and ultimately of the Representative and Legislative Assembly.

British experience in the management of such business concerns as the British Broadcasting Corporation the Electricity Commission have suggested the following ideas in regard to the organisation of such concerns.

1. As to the constitution of the authority in charge of the business enterprise some form of Council or Board would

be directly indicated; the members of such a body might be either persons in executive charge of particular aspects of the work or non-executive directors without individual responsibility; in the latter case they might be either whole time or part-time; part-time workers in non-executive parts of the work would be preferable as only the people with the necessary breadth of experience combined with a continuing freedom of outlook and a reasonable measure of independence can be found.

2. The extent of ministerial control should be defined as clearly as possible in the instrument constituting the authority; in regard to matters falling within the Minster's powers of control he should be liable to be questioned in the legislature; in regard to all matters declared to be within the discretion of the authority the Minster should disclaim responsibility to parliament, not only in regard to matters of business administration but in regard to decisions of judicial or quasi-judicial character.

3. The Legislature and Representative Assembly as the ultimate authority must have adequate opportunity for enquiry, debate and judgment, all accounts of public monies must be subject to audit by or on behalf of the Auditor-General and his department; an annual report should be placed before Parliament and it should be debated.

The problem of finding the best organisation of the business concerns of Government is that of devising one that can be relied on under changing conditions to act with vigour, to exhibit in a high degree initiative and enterprise to accept freely such risks as are taken every day by private enterprise and to engage whenever necessary in competitive activity, in a word to run a government enterprise as a private enterprise as nearly as possible for a Government department subject to the control of the Legislature.

The danger of centralisation to which Governments are prone must be avoided in the interest of the success of the business as modern business methods tested by experience have shown. The old experience of the London and North-Western Railways the model on which a great British administrator wanted the War Office administration to be modelled is confirmed by recent American industrial experience. The secret of organising the management of a great service as that of a modern railway system is nothing more than a carefully arranged system of devolution combined with watchful supervision. At the top the whole mass of the business is divided among 6 committees of the Board of Directors; the executive management is vested in 3 officials, the General Manager, the Chief Goods Manager, the Superintendent; the line is divided into 10 sections each under the control of District Superintendents; monthly conferences are held of the principal offices under the chairmanship of the General Manager of Chief Manager, their recommendations being forwarded and presented for the approval of the Board; a complete system of inspection is necessary.

But at present the responsibility for the several business concerns of the State is that of some department of Government under a Minister. As the main work of the concern is in the hands of the Public Corporation, none of them has a whole department or Minister itself. Its charge is entrusted to the department and the Minister called by its nature to be entrusted with it. Thus the British Broadcasting Corporation in England is entrusted to the Department and Minister of Education, the Forestry Commission to the Department and Minister of Agriculture, the Coal Board to the Minister of Power and Fuel.

A final question raised by this new administrative phenomenon is whether it is capable of indefinite extension. The question need not be asked of a collectivist State for its nature demands such an extension. It is asked only in the normal State which takes upon the handling of business only and when need arises. The answer is given by the origin and history of the business career of the modern state. The history of Mixed Economy in Switzerland has shown that is called for when the business requires:

1. The sanction of public authority.

2. The use of public funds.

3. The need for supervision by public authority on behalf of the users, e.g., in hydro-electric works, also in banking. Similarly it has been used in the exploitation of certain salt mines which required the association of the old owners of the mines and the Cantonal Governments, and which has taken on hand the freeing of Switzerland from the domination of production cartels outside the State

The device of the Mixed Economy or Public Corporation is therefore not capable of indefinite extension. It need not be used when private enterprise is adequate and safe to the State as in the motor car manufacturing industry. Nor is it all absorbing or essentially monopolistic except when collectivism uses it. It is called for only when the interests of the State namely of the people of the State require it.

Auxiliary Departments

1. Department of Research and Intelligence—Modern Governments having to perform so many duties and deal with so many and difficult problems that must get all the help they can. Although individual members and departments have to gather all relevant information and do a lot of thinking and foreseeing to make these departments more and more serviceable to the people, the number complexity and difficulty of modern circumstances justify the establishment of special departments devoted to the collection of information, the dissemination of intelligence with a view to the formulation of policy. The time has come said the Haldance Committee, in the sphere of civil government when the duty of investigation and thought as preliminary to action might with great advantage be more definitely recognised. Adequate provision has to be made for the organised acquisition of facts and information and for the systematic application of thought as preliminary to the settlement of policy and its subsequent administration. There is need for such a special department on account of the proved impracticability of devoting the necessary time to thinking out organisation and preparation for action in the mere interval of the time required for the transaction of business in each department.

A department for overhauling the machinery of administration from time to time has been recommended by an English Civil Service Commission. It was the opinion of Sir Joasiah Stamp that office and operating functions are becoming worthy of separate scientific study and specialisation. The National Institute of industrial psychology in London has been consulted on the position of lights, of desks and benches with a view to promoting efficiency. The Department of Intelligence and Research would be used for:

1. Conducting enquiry and research under the supervision of other departments.

2. Conducting special enquiries and researches for the general run of departments.

3. Conducting special enquiries through itself or through sections of departments doing this work; the departments dealing with economic welfare, agriculture, industry, fisheries, forests would especially require enquiry and research, also the departments of education and healthy.

4. A section would be devoted to scientific and industrial research.

5. The record room or Office containing records of use to the Government or a State would also be attached to this department.

A Statistical section would be an important branch of this department. It would organize the collection and study of the statistics required for administration as a whole. Although there would be a statistical section in each department of Government the organisation of statistics and statistical study for the whole government would be located in the Statistics section of this Department of Intelligence and Research. This central statistical section would see to the collection and study of all the information furnished by the statistical sections of the several departments and make them available for use by the Government as a whole. It would observe the rules for ensuring exactitude and accuracy in the collection and arrangement of facts referred to in the last chapter on the use of statistics in administration. In addition this general statistics section as well as any other departmental statistics section will observe the following practical rules:

1. Classification and sub-division of heads of statistics would be kept within limits, otherwise too much time and trouble would be spent on what will be of little use.

2. The questionnaire used for the gathering of statistical information should be as short and as simple as possible and definite rules for guidance should be issued to the collectors of the facts and figures.

3. Care should be taken to check and control the facts and figures furnished by the collectors.

The Actuary office of the Government might be also attached to this department. A modern Government dealing with Pensions, Provident Funds, Insurance requires much actuarial help and advice. Especially the new welfare services of the modern State would require frequent advice and assistance from the Actuary and his office.

Organisation of a Department

The principle and practice of division of labour necessary for making labour efficient require that the work of a department should be divided into several sections according to the different kinds of work that have to be done in the department. The division of a Department into sections must be horizontal that is to say according to the several aspects or stages of a question and not vertical that is to say each subject having a section in which the several aspects, the legal or financial or administrative stages are dealt with in different sub-sections for each subject. The horizontal division has the advantage of promoting specialisation in each section (e.g., financial or legal), of letting the head see the business of the department as a whole, of allowing the focussing of discussion at the earlier stages, of allowing the Head of the department to delegate work and responsibility to responsible subordinates and to reserve for himself only general supervision and ultimate responsibility. The horizontal division creates a real chain of responsibility and allows business to be conducted with efficiency and dispatch and with economy.

The useful Sections are:—

1. Registry and Recording Section—which receives all letters, dispatches, papers, etc, coming from outside, the general public or other departments. A government department is bound to keep more careful records of its correspondence than would be required from an ordinary commercial house, a Government department has to deal with the affairs of the people and it is responsible to them ultimately. This section is therefore one of the vital parts of the department. The work consists in registering particulars of receipt (date, subject-matter) in a book, or docketing, filing or card-indexing the letter or paper in question.

2. Subject Section—If a department is large and has to deal with a number of different subjects, the chief of these different subjects may have a section to itself.

3. General Section—If there are a number of sections there must be one general section supervising the work sections and debating and deciding on questions affecting the Department as a whole. This section would be directly under the head of the department.

4. Finance and Accounts Section—Strict control over the expenditure of a department is necessary for ensuring its efficiency and sense of duty and responsibility. Although over-all control and external control is exercised by the Finance Department, there must be within each Department a section entrusted with the duty of seeing that the funds allotted to it by the Finance Department are spent according to law or direction of superior authority and is responsible for the finances of the services administered by the department. To enable this section to do its work properly an officer of high grade should be placed over it, the head of this section assisted by a financial staff sufficiently qualified and strong to enable him to maintain a constant and continuous survey of the proposals for expenditure within the

department, and he should be regularly consulted before any decision on a matter of financial importance is arrived at by the Head of the Department or the Minister.

The accounts and accounting of the department should be under a special sub-division of this section. Its duty would be to keep a strict and detailed account of the money allotted to and spent by the department.

All that has been said already on the importance of accounts and accounting in the Finance Department applies with even greater force to the Finance and Accounts section of each department, for it is in each of the spending departments that the money of the State is broken up and spent in detail. As a great expert in financial administration says "with the growing volume, elaboration and technicality of the work of the Government. it to the expert and semi-independent financial branches of the great departments that the public look for its substantial protection against waste and loss. External and therefore comparatively inexpert guardians such as the Auditor-General and the Public Accounts Committee and the Treasury, high as the value of their work undoubtedly is and essential to the legal scheme of appropriation, in the practical matter of enforcing economy in administration they can only supplement the work done within the departments themselves.

The chief duties of the Finance and Accounts Branch for each department have been summarised as follows:

1. Preparation of estimates.
2. Financial review of expenditure.
3. Advising or deciding as to transfer of votes.
4. Seeing that expenditure is properly brought to account.
5. Advising in all questions affecting the expenditure of the department; the head of section should not only be made acquainted with the expenditure after it has been incurred but he should be consulted in all matters involving an expenditure of the department's funds.

Establishment Section

On account of the large number of persons employed in a modern department and the consequent cost it is necessary that there should be a section in each department charged with responsibility for securing efficiency and economy in the staffing and working of the department. The duty of the Establishment section is to see that the department has adequate but no more than adequate staff for the performance of its work, suitable, qualified and well remunerated. It is with the aid of the Establishment section that the head of the department administers discipline and on its advice with or without the assistance of special promotion boards he decides on promotion. This section is responsible for ensuring that the staff is not wasted and that the processes of work are as simple and economical as possible. Every item of work should be examined to see how far it can be made more effective and more economical. It should supply the method of Taylorism to office work. Also, it shall see to the accommodation and general welfare of the staff and to the provision of such services as typists, and stenographers, messengers, heating, lighting transport, and act as the link between the department and the representatives of the staff on all questions. The head of this section should be occupied not only with the watching of the staff at work and keeping records of the work of each member of the staff but should be entrusted with the constructive work of controlling and adopting the scheme of office organisation to changing conditions and circumstances. It should have sufficient staff to enable it to keep in close touch with all sections of the departments and should be responsible in co-operation with their respective heads for arranging transfers of staff from one section to another, discarding unnecessary work, adopting labour-saving machinery and generally devising the most efficient organisation of office work, keeping continuous records of all items of work which can be standardised as well as records of overtime, sick leave, etc., not neglecting the costing of each item of work. He would also be responsible for the application of rules in regard to selection of personnel from among lists made by Civil or Public Service Commissions, and see that the rules governing probation, promotion and retirement are strictly applied.

5. Intelligence and Research section

Each department should have a section devoted to this work on the lines laid down in regard to the general Department of Intelligence and Research. It would also contain a statistical sub-section.

Headship of the Department

The principle of Hierarchy and needs of the organisation require that every Department should have a head. Nothing is more dangerous in a State, said Richelieu, than diverse authorities equal to each other in the administration of affairs. But shall it be single or multiple? Although normally, to ensure decision and responsibility a single head is to be preferred there are departments which require a Board to administer their affairs. The business may be multiple, too great to be entrusted to a single individual, and the administration of the department may require frequent discussion and decision. The administration of revenue, of the management of a port, of a railway or forests, of the new Business Departments of the State would require a Board. Or there may be historical reasons as in the case of the British Board of Admiralty. What was said of the British Board of Admiralty is applicable to similar departments: the department is one in which so vast a business has to be dealt with that a division of labour is absolutely necessary and this requires that the different branches of the department shall be under different persons having authority to deal with all the matters of detail. But on the other hand, all this mass of business has one common object and what is done in one branch necessarily affects the business of all the others; nothing therefore ought to be done in one without considering its bearing upon the others and it is requisite that there should be some provision for keeping the heads of the several branches of the department fully cognizant of what their colleagues are doing and for securing unity of purpose among them. Hence a Board of admiralty came into being. The requirements of individual responsibility for each section of the department and of collective management of the whole are met by each member of the Board bringing any important matter especially of policy that arises to the notice of the Board as a whole and getting its decisions thereon. As these departments have to deal often with questions of policy it is not wise to trust the judgment on these questions to a single individual.

Whether single or multiple, the Head of a Department is responsible for carrying out the duties devolved upon him by the Government acting through the Minister the supreme head of the department and subject to the limits of policy laid down by the Government. We have seen this is done by dividing up the duties of a department into convenient branches or sections each under the head of a branch or section. In all this organisation the principle of devolved discretion with no devolving of responsibility is the principle that operates. The head of the department accepts responsibility for all the acts of the sections or branches and within the measure of his function he may allow large freedom of action and wide discretion to his subordinates. He must be answerable to his Minister—the right being reserved to him of dealing with the particular officers whose discretion may be found at fault but the responsibility for what it wrongly or improperly done rests with the head of the department.

Work and Methods of Work in a Department

Ever since writing was invented it has been used in administration. And as soon as Government advanced beyond the primitive or patriarchal state when the words of a ruler and of the ruled were the principal means of communication between them and formed the instrument of administration, writing has come to be the main instrument of administrative work. And in spite of new means of communication like the Telegraph and the Telephone writing has continued to be the chief means of conducting administrative business. And this is so not only because of the comparative cheapness and elasticity and adaptability of this means but it is also necessary to ensure continuity and reliability of record. Especially as modern administration is responsible to the public and its representatives in the Ministry or the Legislature, business transacted in administrative departments must go on record and therefore must be in writing. Although administrative business can be expedited by use of the telegraph or the telephone and shorthand or the spoken word the bulk of administrative business is done by writing. Acts of administration are subject to scrutiny in public print or speech or in representative assembly or legislature. Subordinate servants of the administration are liable to be questioned especially if things go wrong. Hedged and confined as they are by rules and regulations departments of administration have to maintain consistency and play for safety. Precedent therefore plays a predominant part in the discussion and decisions that go on in a department.

As the decision of a department of Government may affect the life of the people, their social or economic activity, their social and political relations, their pockets and even the relations of the State with other States time is of the essence of administrative business. Questions that come up before a department have to be looked at from all point of view from the standpoint of the Government of the people, of industry, of the other States. Information of all kinds must be sought, if it is not readily available with the Government itself. And once obtained this information must be sorted out, taken in by the several sections, studied and digested. And any discussion around it and any decision flowing from it must be examined to see how it affects other departments of government, or the Government as a whole or the general public. A question taken up or sent to one department may have to be discussed with other departments. As so much hangs on the decisions of Government, of weal or woe to the people, care and thoroughness ought to accompany every stage of the administrative process. Detail is a necessity in public administration. "To know affairs well" said Rochefouncald "it is necessary to know them in detail" Capacity for detail is one of the marks of a good administrator for it means taking the trouble to look at all aspects and into all the implications of a question or of its solution, it means following a question and its solution through to the end, probing the causes and following its course to the end.

The discussion that precedes decision in a department has to be done largely in writing. Notes containing relevant information are submitted by the subordinates in the department. Previous papers must be attached, precedents must be quoted, notes increase in number and sometimes in volume; as the paper ascends the upper rungs of the departmental ladder; the notes are crowned by the Minute written by the head of the department or the Minister. All these several papers are gathered into that formidable instrument of the administrative business, the File.

The File

The file may be made up in two ways—the British way or the Indian way. According to the British way each paper as entered in the register is encased and stays in its own separate jacket; the several jackets when wanted would be sent round as a file of self-contained dockets, each bound by a single piece of white tape. According to the Indian way each paper as it arrives is fixed to the top of its own file and these papers are encased in a large folder, any previous papers marked or referred to in the notes or minutes being flagged: the flags containing of tabs of thick scarlet cardboard, marked A, B, C, D, Lord Curzon was so taken up by the superiority of the Indian system which he had learned when he was Viceroy and Governor-General of India that he introduced it into the British Foreign Office when he became Foreign Secretary in the last lap of his official career.

Books or Manuals of rules or office manuals as they are called to guide workers in the several departments telling them in detail what they should do and what they should not do are usual in most administrations. These in some countries as in India go into minute detail the object being to make them fool proof. But in the endeavour to eliminate fools these books of rules may create robots.

Administrative Architecture

Of first importance for the efficiency of work in an administrative department is its housing, that is the place in which the work is to be done. Two extremes would have to be avoided. Housing each department in a separate building would prevent easy communication between related departments and would add greatly to the cost. Agriculture and Fisheries in England, about 1920 suffered when its headquarters staff was distributed over a large area of London in 16 different buildings, obviously the cost in messengers and cleaning and other services alone must have been large. On the other hand housing, all departments of administration in one monstrously large building must reduce costs and make inter-communication between departments easy but this concentration in one place might lead to congestion of business in normal times and be easy for attack and capture in a revolution. The best way of building for departments would lie between these two extremes. Allied departments had best be together; revenue and expenditure might be housed in one building namely the Finance, and Inland revenue, the Customs Headquarters office, the Audit and Accounts Offices. Similarly all the Economic Welfare Departments and all the Social Welfare departments may be lodged in one single building respectively. The police headquarters office should have a building all to itself.

Within each building the portion allotted to a department must be divided into different sets of halls and its chief sections connected by inter-communicating half doors, each section being in one large room or hall working in full view of its superintendent or manager and with the superior heads in the corner rooms. A separate sound-proof room should be given over to the typists. Record and filing rooms should be nearby. A waiting room for the public is a necessary adjunct to every office.

Also, there must be sufficient room for expansion in the original lay out, otherwise congestion would soon be created. The ideal working space for a worker in an administrative office would be about 100 sq. feet. The physical state of the office lighting, ventilation, and in cold countries, heating should be attended to.

They do these things well in the U.S.A. where according to a recent observer, "the Government offices are as convenient and attractive inside as they are impressive outside; there is spaciousness; they are well furnished and have a distinctively right atmosphere in every respect; where one feels that the rooms including the conference rooms have been expressly designed to promote efficient administration, whereas in Whitehall in London one feels that we get good government despite and not because of the rooms in which our senior administrators work."

Office Equipment

To facilitate and accelerate work not only comfortable furniture in the shape of tables and chairs but modern mechanical devices found useful in commercial firms should be adopted in Government offices. Mechanical enumerators, accounting machines, filing cabinets, card index system need not be despised just because they are used in commercial offices. Steel furniture seems to be more useful for housing files and records.

Abuses of the Methods of Work in Departments

Writing, so necessary in modern administration can be abused, and its abuse has led to a number of evils. The chief of them are:

Circumlocution—It is the temptation of literate men, given pen, paper and ink to write about and round a subject at length. And the official required to write all that he knows about it writes round it especially as and when time is given him, for official decisions must be preceded by deliberation and thought, and that deliberation and thought has to be done on paper. And as so many people have to deal with a question, it gets bandied about from one person to another, and if more than one department has to deal with a question it journeys from one department to another backwards and forwards. If these questions are decided by word of mouth, there would be less opportunities for indulgence in this evil.

Circumlocution has been the subject of classical satire by Charles Dickens in *Little Dorrit.* He called circumlocution the whole science of government as it was in his time.

He put it all in one office called the Circumlocution Office but it was the artist's way of describing what took place in every department. Great events and actions like the discovery of the Gunpowder Plot would have had to wait until there has been "half a score of memoranda, half a bushel of minutes, several sacks of official memoranda and a family vault full of ungrammatical correspondence on the part of the Circumlocution Office. The great art taught in that office and by the method of circumlocution was how not to do it. Prime Minister, Minor Minister, Civil servants of all grades learnt this art. All kinds of people—mechanicians, natural philosophers, soldiers, sailors, petitioners, memorialists—and all kinds of subjects—wrongs, projects for the general welfare, all the business of the country went through the circumlocution office and method—except the business that never came out of it and its name was legion."

A modern actual example of this evil is what is said to have taken place in the war Office in London during the 1914-18 war. The practice in the War Office, we are told used to be when a question came up, to collect the largest possible number of opinions about it from everyone who had even the remotest connection with the question before any attempt was ever made to arrive at a decision. Whereas in the fields of France they tried to get the question straight to the man who could decide and to get him to do so. This evil is described by another, a foreign observer. The British, he says, had an elaborate system of passing documents from one department to another, the legal department in forwarding a brief account of a court martial might offer a few remarks with the concluding comment: this department can advise about law, but the case in point includes subjects which are respectfully submitted to the Director of Military operations, that official would heavily underline "the time of this department is amply taken up by directing, military operations; respectfully submitted to the assistant chief of staff; he in turn would suggest the matter was more for the police than for the military; it should have the attention of the chief of staff to whom it is respectfully submitted, the chief of staff will add politely that he had no intention of being saddled with these questions which involved politics and was likely to be brought up in the House of Commons; the person who should really decide would be the Secretary of State for war to whom he "respectfully submitted it."

2. *Red Tape*—Precedent and regard for precedent is a good thing in a Government where continuity and consistency in policy

and execution are essential as all those that come to it for service must be dealt with fairly, justly, equally and impartially—especially in a democratic State. The official defence of precedent is that adherence to system or precedent is adherence to principle, at any rate is a safeguard against the influence of personality which is so real and frequent in democratic governments. Personality versus precedent is how he put the argument for following precedent. But this regard for precedent may be abused. When the questions are decided not on their merits, not in connection with changed conditions and circumstances, not in pursuit of progress but merely to blind following of old decided cases then the public has a right to complain of the abuse of precedent. This evil is described by the expressive name of Red Tape from the red tape with which official papers are bound and kept together. Carlyle in an essay on Downing Street has castigated with his vitriolic pen this particular evil of administration, so also has Balzac in his novel *Employees*.

Routine—The servile obedience to the rules of the past is the safeguard of mediocrity. It helps the average administrator to play for safety. Uniformity is the pet device of the administrator. Everybody, everywhere, every time, doing the same thing is the ideal of the mechanical administrator. It is as old as unified centralised administration. Saint Simon said of Louis XIV that his timetable was that of a clock and everybody knew in Europe what Louis XIV would be doing at any particular time of the day.

Delay and Detail—Wise delay, no doubt, helps questions to ripen and to be settled when they are ripe for decision. But it is possible to indulge in undue and unnecessary delay. How often, exclaimed a great British statesman and administrator Lord Chancellor Sankey, have we seen endless minutes, departmental disagreement, even departmental jargon delaying and frustrating plans which depended for their success upon the speed with which they were carried. He was of the opinion that the system not the men was at fault and that the code of the civil service is not fitted for despatch but for delay. That is the experience of observers everywhere and not in recent times either. A French observer; 45

years ago in Indo-China calculated the total number of orders of the Governor General at 2,500 for Annam and Tonkin and if Cambodia and Laos were added, 5,000; of these 250 could be said to be of any importance requiring the personal attention of the head of the colony, the rest belonged to the category of routine business or detail, it did not require his special attention but he had to sign them, he had at least to run his eyes over them, and that wasted time he would have spent on business that really required his special attention; the orders that he was asked to sign included such small things as acquiring a parcel of 14 acres for the judicial department, ordering delay of 6 days before the use of a bund constructed without authorisation, depriving a man of the concession that had been granted him; these details should have been left to the departmental head or the local representative of the head of the colony.

Formalism—Forms are necessary and useful as means of acquiring exact information, isolating questions and demands, for more convenient handling and disposal. Forms and formality of procedure in administration are required in order to secure on a given question competence of authority which is the principal condition of order in the administrative process. It has been argued that because administration is largely an automatic organ without a central and ever active mind that gap is filled by the multiplicity of forms and formalities that control and check one another in the interests of orderly administration. In times of crisis this insistence on forms and formality may be a danger but in ordinary times it is necessary. But there can be too many forms and their use encourages the idea that adherence to forms and insistence on them is an end in itself and not means to an end and that a question is settled if it can be put into a form. The endless filling of forms and returns especially required by modern social legislation makes the model official lose the wood for the trees. Such an official is described by Begehot in one of his scintillating essays: Entering the office young, he copied letters for 5 years, he made an index of papers for nine months, he made an analysis of documents for 5 years; more when he commenced at last to transact business it was of a strictly formal character and he was upwards of 20 years in the public service before he ever decided on anything of special importance; no wonder, that he was unwilling to decide anything, that he referred everything to somebody else, that he corresponded in his best hand-writing, with another public office; his entries were most correct but the transactions were normally wrong; the book-keeping was admirable but the affairs recorded feeble or inefficient. But this disease of formalism may attack not only subordinates officials but even men at the top, like Ministers. The formalism of one such Minister in high matters of policy was described by Burke in his famous speech on American taxation. Mr. Grenville whose Stamp Act led to the loss of the American colonies was the Minister. Passing from the study of law Mr. Grenville, according to Burke, did not go very largely into the world but plunged into business, the business of office and the limited and fixed methods and forms established there; men too much conversant with office are rarely minds of remarkable enlargement; their habits of office are apt to give them a turn to think the substance of business not to be much more important than the form in which it is conducted; these forms are adapted to ordinary occasions and therefore persons who are nurtured in office do admirably well so long as things go on in their common order; but when the high roads are broken up and the water flows, when a new and troubled scene is opened and the file affords no precedent then it is that a greater knowledge of mankind and a far more extensive comprehension of things is requisite than office ever gave or than office can ever give.

Obscurity and Obscurantism—is another charge levelled at modern administrators. Official language is a class of jargon that has come in for criticism at the hands of men of letters like Quiller Couch. In the letters and the forms departments send out to the public they are said to employ long complicated tortuous verbose and apparently meaningless phraseology. But public administration as a great administrator points out concerns matters which touch the interests of the individual citizens and therefore has to provide for every exceptional and every hard case and administrative orders and regulations, it has to be remembered, are liable to be reviewed and construed in courts of law and construed almost always in defence of the rights and liberties of the individual in a justifiable bias against the department of Government as a wielder and practitioner of power.

Financial waste—This evil is rife in department of Government all over the world. Everybody's money seems to be nobody's money. Most departments think it is their duty to spend all that has been allotted or appropriated to them. In some countries, as in India, there is a feverish rush the last months of the year to use up the money allotted to departments, fearful that if this is not done their appropriation next year might be reduced.

Abuse of Power—Modern administrators are by law and the nature of the things endowed with vast power. And like all wielders of power they have been tempted to abuse that power. A large measure of discretion has to be given to executive officials and they may abuse it to favour members of their family or class or the party in power. Corruption is open to the official who has to deal with permits, licences, concessions, so rife in the modern State of checks and controls.

Numbers—On account of the volume of work done in the department of a modern Government being large, the number employed in them is large. It tends to grow as new duties are laid on the Government and as greater efficiency and dispatch in business are required by the public. Wherever responsibility of the executive power to the representative assembly and legislature obtains and questions on the administration, on its sins of omission or of commission are the order of the day in legislatures, the work in each department has grown to an enormous quantity. Writing is comparatively easy and not only authors suffer from the *cacoethes scribendi,* and it is easier to procure people that can write than skilled manual workers. And as the profit and loss is of little or no account in a Government Department which does not work for profit but for administrative efficiency the temptation felt by each head or Minister of the department to ask for more becomes understandable. In more than one modern State numbers of the civil services have reached the stage reached in the Roman Empire when the poet Claudian at the end of the 4th century complained that those who received public money almost out-numbered those that paid it. In the U.S.A. the Federal Government alone contains 2,109,435. In Italy a recent estimate puts the number of state employees as 1,000,000 whereas in the heyday of Fascism it was only 7,00,000. In England in 1949 it was 706,197, while if Government employees in State industrial concern were included it would be 400,000 more.

Bureaucracy—Bureaucracy is the name given to modern administration on account of the large numbers of bureaus of departments with the large numbers of people working in them. The evils to which we have already referred, circumlocution, red tape, delay, and detail, formulism, are, if not created, strengthened by the number of departments and the numbers in each department. The chief evils of bureaucracy have been summed up by the great French Colonial Administrator Lyautey as control and criticism for these numbers must justify themselves by work, creation of work and multiplication of work. Weakness of will and of intention to press issues to an end, the lack of follow-through—Lyautey described it as anti-solutionism—also comes from the numbers of men and departments in modern administration. And the desire to grasp at jurisdiction is another temptation to which departments are susceptible and which form one of the evils included in the term Bureaucracy. Modern legislation feeds the appetite of modern administration and the appetite grows by feedings. In the French, play *Le Roi* the King attends a party and stays for a chat with his hostess; neither of them had had anything to eat and on suggesting a little supper she directed a servant to bring something left over. "Madam" said the servant "where the bureaucracy has passed there is nothing left over". Time and money, according to De Maistre are the chief things of the world and they are the chief victims of bureaucracy. Omnipotent and omnipresent, modern bureaucracy is an Argus with a hundred eyes and a Briareus with a hundred arms.

Departmentalism—Although it is true, as Lord Haldane argued, if confusion is to be avoided the departments of Government must have their scope and boundaries carefully defined, and delimited and definition of function and apportionment of responsibility are essential, there is an evil which is inherent in the division into departments. And that is for each department to look upon itself as being the only department or the most important department and to forget that there are other departments and that its usefulness lies only in its working in co-operation with other departments and helping them towards the furtherance of the common end. This evil of departments thinking and acting as if they were a law into themselves may be dubbed departmentalism. It expresses itself in the complete absorption of the department in the daily, specially the routine, departmental duties. Questions are regarded not in their entirety or as affecting other departments than itself. If at all any other department or any other aspect, of administration is regarded it is the financial. No question is regarded in its fundamental relations, as the Germans would say, namely as it affects and is affected by numerous other questions. In Germany we are told no political question would be considered without giving due weight to military considerations for which purpose a special department existed for amassing military information. Departmentalism in its extreme form leads to conflicts and clashes between departments, wars between departments are known in almost every administrative system. Viscount Milner has testified that in his time during the war of 1914-1918 a great deal of his time was spent in trying to compose feuds between departments, each department zealous, each determined to save the country on its own terms and at one time he was tempted to issue bulletins of news from the front in Whitehall.

Remedies for the Evils and Abuses of Administrative Methods

This principle that should govern the devising of remedies for the abuses of the methods of administration and for the avoidance of the resultant evils is that these methods are means to an end which is efficiency and progress in administration and as soon as these methods cease to serve that end their use must be limited or modified. Thus Circumlocution—Can be modified by cutting down writing to the minimum as well as the references high and low and across the sections and to and from departments. The old British War Office. method of forcing questions through a succession of officials in increasing rank and perhaps decreasing knowledge should be avoided. The following suggestions of an experienced administrator would be helpful. No official unless charged with duties in relation to a given subject, should be permitted to intervene. Policy should be reserved for heads and details given to subordinates. Correspondence should follow fixed and unchanging lines, should be reduced to a minimum and should never supplant personal conferences. With regard to the style of writing it should be brief, to the point, lucid, concrete and direct. The object of all official writing should aim at answering questions not at shelving them.

Red tape—Much of it could be cut if those that quote precedent bear in mind the reason upon which it was founded. In the disposal of particular cases care should be taken not only to dispose of the particular case but also to see whether it may not help to recast and improve the general rule. Precedent must be countered and balanced by personality. In high and important spheres of action says Taylor "though general rules will be for the most part of great use in evading for setting aside personal questions, yet personal individualities may from time to time be so important as to make it worthwhile to set aside the general rule on account of them."

Delay—Delay in the disposal of business can be reduced by:

1. Fixing and limiting responsibility of each section; for official delegation and devolution in function and duty are a paramount need in administrative departments; nothing should be done at the central office which can be better done locally. Lord Cromer as ruler of Egypt acted on the view that the main thing the man of affairs has to decide is not what he should do but what he shall let others to do for him.

2. Dealing with the most important and the most difficult matter, that which requires "most to be encountered in the blows of novelty with the substantial edge conscious energy."

3. Wise ignoring of unnecessary or irrelevant papers; Gallieni's advice to Lyautey when the latter was sent to govern Tonkin was: Take as little account as possible of frequent circulars, the vague and abstract orders of men living far from the actual

scene of action. Bite directly upon reality was another piece of trenchant advice. Devolve upon others, was Taylor's advice, even utterly neglecting the easy and less important matters and thereby make time for the important.

4. Remembering that some questions or letters decide themselves, if nothing were done about them. Lloyd George used to act on this principle.
5. Avoiding minuteness as it does not always lead to efficiency. In Russia under the Tsars in the 19th century minuteness did not exclude disorder, much trouble being taken to attain unimportant ends and those employed believed they could never do enough to show their zeal.
6. Good administrators must remember the old Roman saying "De minimis non curat praetor."

Formalism—Forms and returns and circulars should be used with discretion and kept down to the minimum. By introducing a specialist on forms into a railway administration Sir Josiah Stamp was able in two years to halve the stationery bill, a very large number of forms being banished from existence; great economies were affected by reducing the classes of papers, the sizes of the cuts and by scrutiny of long series covering a number of different departments resulting in cutting out certain functions and functionaries altogether.

Dependence on forms, circulars, orders must not be too servile. After all, government departments and services must remember that they are dealing with men. Much more can be gained by direct personal approach than by remote impersonal writing, by seeking the co-operation of the public rather than by issuing orders to them. This is especially to be recommended to departments that deal directly with the public like the Police and the Post Office. The success of a safety force organised by the Lancashire police is illuminating. This force consisting of 300 men 92 cars and 50 light-weight motor cycles concentrated on spots where motor accidents and fatalities were the greatest and by depending on advice, instruction, admonitions and on education and inviting co-operation with the public this force was able to reduce accidents by almost twice more than when only prosecutions were relied on.

Financial waste—A well-run department is careful and economical even on small items of expenditure like stationery, light, transport. It tries to keep down the cost of running itself by rationalisation or standardising of official processes. It keeps to the limits of its appropriation, it furnishes accurate and intelligible and timely accounts. It keeps the taxpayer's interest always in view, especially the cost of the department to him, testing the cost of working by sectional statistics, by determining which of its sections or services does not give a proper return for the money spent on it. A financial test of a well-run Department is the small number of audit queries and criticisms that it receives and the reception and treatment its head gets from the Public Accounts Committee of the Legislature.

Although it is true that the work of a Government Department is not susceptible of accurate measurement as to quantity, yet it is necessary that even Government Departments should see to it that they give the administration and the country good value in return for the money spent on them. The chief means of control of work in a Government Department is inspection, frequent, thorough, strict. This is done generally be the Establishment Section, of the department. There are however certain departments of the administration whose work is capable of measurement. In the Post Office for instance there is a large number of operations recurring on a vast scale, and where it has been found possible to calculate the amount of work taken on each of the operations of each kind for a given period, an estimate can be formed of the amount of time taken to do the whole work of the department Similarly time occupied in shorthand, typing, copying, receipt, registration, despatching letters can be measured. The following hints and suggestions for improvement in methods of work and control of work may be worth considering.

1. Analysis of work done.

2. Differentiation of work, e.g., between initiation and execution.

3. Concentration on each kind of work, e.g., in regard to collection of taxes, inspection and actual collection.
4. Investigation of methods and procedure actually in force; comparison with methods in other departments in regard to use of graphs, diagrams, accounting, control with a view to discovery of the best method.
5. Fixing of time or standard for every operation; use of chronometers for mere routine work.
6. Observation of time taken for each process—time wasted, time saved; calculation of number of hours taken by each worker for each piece of work.
7. Grouping of operations according to division and difficulty.
8. Division of total number of work hours in a year by the number of duty hours of work for a year gives the number of men required.

Departmentalism—The evil of isolationism can be cured only by bringing home to every department its relation to other departments, that there is no meaning in its activity, except in relation to other departments and as part of the general administration. A well-devised inter-departmental organisation allowing for frequent inter-departmental conferences is the best remedy for the evil of departmentalism.

Right use of methods of work—Avoiding the abuses of the methods of work in a Government office just pointed out, the good official should set about his work on lines approved by experience. Here are hints and suggestions of two successful English administrators.

1. A. fast as papers are received the person who is to act upon them should examine them to see whether they require immediate attention and should separate them from those that can bear later treatment. And once papers are thus sorted out he should confine himself to one paper at a time, to be disposed of. for the practice of looking at papers and handling them without disposing of them not only wastes time but

breeds an unnecessary impression of difficulty and trouble; moreover, there is a psychological advantage in dealing with the paper while it looks fresh and does not come to you in a dusty, obsolete, and often postponed appearance.

2. Begin at the beginning of the case in the file.
3. Keep carefully to the dates which are the backbone of every long series of transactions.
4. Keep in mind the arguments brought on either side.
5. Never accept a reference or even a quotation without verification—also look to the context.
6. Respect precedent without becoming a slave of it.
7. In taking the aid and advice of subordinates, consider the character, especially the reliability of your advisers.
8. Guard yourself against the bent of your mind and character against your own prejudices and inclinations.
9. Be clear and accurate in your expressions.
10. Do not confuse rules with principles.
11. Divide the subject matter of a case into several sections the arguments in the several sections should come and be presented in conclusions which make it easy for the Head of the Department or the Minister to come to their final conclusion.
12. The final drafting of any document should be one man's work, embodying the corrections and additions made by other men's minds.

The first of these hints looks to a replacement of the English method of business travelling from bottom to the top, business being strained but in upward direction by the continental or Latin method of business travelling from top to bottom from the *chef de cabinet* to the junior clerk.

Business Methods in Administration

Dissatisfaction with the defects of the methods of administration have in more than one country called for an introduction of the methods of business, the methods used in commercial or industrial offices into Government departments. While here and there this or that device used in business administration may be introduced into public administration with good results, a wholesale or large scale adoption of such methods in an administrative department is out of the question. For the ends and purposes of the two systems of administration are different. One has to do with the government of a people, the other has to do with the production of distribution of goods and for gain and profit to those engaged in it. Especially, when that government is a popular and parliamentary system of government does the difference in character and method become apparent. For one thing, consistency in the application of rules of principles so as not to offend the law of equality is imperative in a Government Department. Together with this consistency goes continuity as a distinguishing feature of public administration. Compared with Government a business is a passing show; in business each subject is treated by itself, in isolation. Public administration is a continuing and permanent business. It has to look before and after, to precedent as well as the consequence. It is not free to experiment, to venture, to dare and do, as business. Uniformity is another rule that governs the conduct of Government Departments. They must treat all alike in the same way; therefore, rules and regulations have to be carefully studied, precedents looked up, and application of rules made impartial, hence delay. And then, as a great authority who had experience of administration in business as well as Government said there is the question of magnitude, the vast area and the vast number of people with which a Government has to deal or whom its acts affects compared to the much smaller number of people affected by a business office. A sign of the magnitude of governmental administration is the large number of departments that it consists of. Hence the need for combination, co-operation between them and the specialisation of functional aptitudes in each of them. A business on the other hand is composed of a few sections all dominated by a single head. In wars the "push and go" men imported from business into administration do get things done but they do not take kindly to consultation and some of these things had later sometimes to be undone. From this magnitude of work in Government arises the need to avoid overlapping of one Government Department over the jurisdiction of another. This effort to avoid overlapping requires time, thought and therefore causes delay. There is no such need in business; if it finds itself overlapping other business it draws back and gives up that part of it. Then also there is rigid financial control which operates in a Government Department and which distinguishes governmental administration from business administration. Spending money freely and largely is allowed in business, the only limit being the prospects of increase of business and profit. Audit comes at the end of the year but in a Government Department there is control by the Finance Department and the audit at every step, almost every daily step. Constitutional government requires it, the tax-payers and parliament expect it. Also, a Government Department even when it engages in business undertakings for the supply of electricity, railway or postal facilities may not try to make a profit as a company would in a competitive market. For the business of a Government Department is to supply its services as cheaply and to as many people as possible; although it should not run its business at a loss, it is not its business to run it at a great profit. As the Macdonnel Commission of 1914 on the Civil Services in England said "some advantage to the community as a whole other than pecuniary profit is the object to which departmental administration is devoted; that advantage cannot be expressed in a balance sheet and as the departments are established in obedience to law or public opinion they must be administered whether the result be a money loss or gain". And lastly there is the practice of ministerial responsibility and parliamentary control which puts the conduct of the business in a Government Department out of all comparison with the business office. Questions in Parliament and motions of no-confidence make the Minister and his permanent officials watch their steps in the administration of the departments.

But although a Government Department cannot be conducted as a business office some of the methods and devices used in business offices might be introduced with advantage. Programmes of action covering periods of time and according to the money available, control of execution at every stage, requiring and insisting on tangible profitable results, dividing up work among the several sections, requiring so much quota of work from every individual, the control of individual output are among the practices that may very well be imported from business. Especially, the system of costing used in business by which a fair day's work may be ascertained would be very useful. In Customs and Excise Departments the unit system may be adopted to ensure as far as possible that each worker shall for the varied labour performed give a fair number of units of results per day. Personal talks rather than notes and minutes, reducing the volume of writing would be welcome in Government Departments. And the mechanical, helps of the loose-leaf and the card index, the mechanical calculator account and book keeping machines, statistical tabulating machines, ledger posting machines, addressing and despatching machines may be tried in administrative offices.

Thought in Departments of Administration

No longer is administration a matter of rule of thumb or routine or tradition or empiricism. It has become so complex and has to deal with matters effecting fundamentally and completely the life and progress of the State, Society, and the individual that thought has to be applied constantly and continuously for the solution of the problems that come before it. Even when administration is not a complicated business every progressive administrator must be "un tourmente", as was said of Lyautey who was possessed by the anxiety, the impatience to improve things, for although reason was the mistress of his acts, what he willed he willed with passion, and what he hated he hated with passion. The time has come, thought the Haldane Committee on the Machinery of government, not only for the organised acquisition of facts and information but for "the systematic application of thought as preliminary to the settlement of policy and its subsequent administration." The business of enquiry and thinking has to be placed in the hands of persons definitely charged with it; whose duty is to study the future and work out plans and advise those responsible for policy or engaged in actual administration. Some organisation, it was realised even early in the 19th century, was needed "with the excellent suggestions that are now flying about."

Whether there should be a special department of thought for the whole administration as the Haldane Committee suggested is open to doubt. For such a department would have to be so large and have so much time on its hands as to be tempted to indulge in uncalled for and ambitious plans that it would not serve practical purposes. Such an objection would apply to planning commissions unless they are to be of temporary duration. The best way to provide for thought and thinking in administration is to set apart one man equipped by education and practical experience inside or outside administration, for each of the groups of allied Departments like the Departments of Economic and Social Welfare, and provided with the small statistical and research staff required. He will keep in touch with scientific workers in the fields connected with his group of departments. He may have to call in the aid of advisory councils and the expert and the specialist.

The Expert and the Specialist in Administration

The complexity and the difficulty of the problems by which modern Governments are faced and the need for ensuring useful and wasteless results under Democracy have called the expert and the specialist in increasing number into administration. Agriculture, Animal Husbandry, Fisheries, Education and Health and Defence have required the help of the specialist and the expert in Departments of administration in order to assist the general administrator who cannot be expected to possess the specialist knowledge required for effective administration. The coming of the specialist and the expert into Departments headed by men with only general administrative qualifications raises the question of the relations between the Head and his expert or specialist. Are these to be only advisers of the Heads of the Departments or ought they to be put in a position of executive control subject only to the Minister in charge of his department. Experience as well as theory would lead to the view that the Head of the Department, must always be one who has an experience of administration of the department from the lowest to the highest grade. The specialist or expert, it has been pointed out by a great administrator is likely to be so enthusiastic about his own particular work that he is in danger of lacking that sense of proportion and that recognition of political financial and practical limitations which every administrator must possess. As a general rule the spheres of the specialist and the expert should be mainly advisory. In exceptional cases if a specialist is found to possess great administrative capacity he should not be barred from executive headship but as a general rule the danger of executive responsibility and pre-occupation preventing scientific study and research of the specialist ought to be avoided as many a specialist has been lost to science and research by his appointment to an administrative department. To avoid this danger it has been suggested that scientific advisers should as far as possible be found outside, in universities and other research institutions, rather than be recruited into and subsequently mummified in administration. Sometimes it may be necessary to have the opinion of expert or specialist checked by the opinion of fellow-workers in the same subject, although the proverbial disagreement among doctors does not give hope. Jenner's difficulties in convincing medical contemporaries of the value of vaccination, Owen and Sedgewick's opposition to Darwin, Simpson's refusal to see any merit in Lister's discovery of antiseptic surgery, Pasteur opposed by medical men do not encourage confidence in the expert. Mussolini had a way with experts and specialists. He would summon two rival experts to sit in two chairs in a room and expound their proposals against each other.

But if the expert and the specialist are to fulfil their ends in administration they are entitled to ask that certain conditions should be fulfiled and their advice must be sought on all matters within their competence. Not that the advice tendered should always be followed, for the administrative head has to see to the wider interests of the department and the interests of the subjects in his charge. As to the best technical method of carrying out a policy the advice of the specialist or expert ought to be decisive. For instance, the advice of the legal adviser of a department on the interpretation of an Act of Parliament can hardly be traversed by the lay head of a department.

In Local Government, as we shall see the need of separation between the specialist and the expert and the general administrator is neither possible nor necessary.

INTER-DEPARTMENTAL ORGANISATION

"The evolution of business and government functions" according to Sir Josiah Stamp "is throwing up matters of specialised treatment in such a way that the old simple principle of departmental autonomy plus permanent specialised service departments is no longer adequate for all purposes and a new type of auxiliary control, criticism and ad hoc special service as an addition to that principle is now justified not as a criticism of the past but to meet the developing needs of the future." Apart from modern developments to which this great authority refers even to prevent and minimise friction and lack of understanding and co-ordination between departments which are absorbed each one in its own work some kind of organisation which regulates inter-departmental relations and makes them work for a common end is required. There must be a department of supreme control, superintendence, and direction. This department would act as the connecting link between the several departments, the *liason* between them. It would arrange for periodical inter-departmental conferences or meetings where Ministers Heads of departments and the principal officers concerned would meet and discuss questions of policy or execution affecting more than one department. This department would also act as a court of appeal on disputed questions between departments. It would also be entrusted with the duty of overhauling the machinery of the administration from time to time. The amount of generalised experience available to an authority outside and above the other departments of administration would be large, especially in the matter of the machinery of administration. What Sir Josiah Stamp called a "flying arm" of co-ordination and criticism attached to this office of supreme control with the right of entry to all departments and criticism and examination would subject departments to constant improvement.

While inter-departmental and supra-departmental activity is necessary and useful, normally the autonomy of each department must be respected. Otherwise, the best cannot be expected of it. And undue interference from outside may be dangerous. Documents which are now coming to light of Nazi and Fascist record in foreign policy and diplomacy show how aggression and the approach to war was facilitated in Germany and Italy by the conduct of foreign policy being taken out of the hands of the Foreign Offices and their official advisers and servants and handled by the Heads of the Government in pursuance of their intentions or pet ideas. Interlace not business except of necessity, was the advice of that great administrator, Bacon.

This inter-departmental organisation must naturally be attached to the Supreme Executive of the State.

The Supreme Executive

At the end of every system of administration there must be a supreme executive body charged with the ultimate responsibility for the government of the country. Its origin or the principles or methods governing its composition have nothing to do with its powers. Whether the system of government is a despotism as under the ancient regime of France or the modern regime of Soviet Russia or a constitutional Monarchy as that of modern England or a democratic republic as that of the U.S.A. and supremacy of its position and power is the same. The old *conseil de roi* of France was beside being the supreme court of justice the supreme administrative tribunal and the supreme council of government, it possessed the power of proposing, drafting and making laws ordinances and decrees, fixed and divided the taxes, fixed the general rules of administration and sent directions to the officials of government at the centre and on the circumference and supervised them; everything in administration proceeded from it and was referred to it. Similarly the Cabinet of England is the supreme executive of England. The only difference being that the French *conseil de roi* was the council of an absolute ruler and therefore performed legislative and judicial functions beside administration while the English cabinet is bound and limited by the law and custom of the constitution of a limited monarchy. But in the field of administration it is supreme. As for the composition of this supreme executive it may be in the hands of the Head of the State as in the case of a despotic monarchy or entrusted to the chief or prime minister under a constitutional monarchy, or to the elected President of a Republic. But even in a despotic monarchy, Richelieu held that members of the supreme executive should be approved by the general public for if they had the support of the people they would be more able to do well in government. This supreme executive is known by the names of Cabinet, or Council of Ministers. It is therefore the apex of the administration and therefore forms a capital part of any study of administration.

The main functions of a modern Cabinet under the system of constitutional Government have been enumerated thus:—

1. The final determination of the policy to be followed by the administration.

2. The supreme control of the country's administration in accordance with the policy laid down by it.

3. The continuous co-ordination and de-limitation of the activities of the several departments.

Constitution of the Cabinet

For the efficient performance of these functions the following conditions governing its constitution and activity have been approved by experience.

1. The cabinet should be small in number not more than ten or twelve.

2. It should meet frequently.

3. It should be supplied in the most convenient form with all the information and material necessary to enable it to arrive at expeditious decisions.

4. It should make it a point to consult personally all the Ministers whose work is likely to be affected by its decisions.

5. It should be assisted by a Secretary charged with the duty of collecting and putting into shape its agenda, of providing the information and material necessary for its deliberation, of drawing out records of its decisions for communication to the departments concerned.

6. It should have a systematic method of securing that its decisions are effectually carried out by the several departments concerned.

The Cabinet Secretariat

The Secretary of the Cabinet requires a Cabinet Secretariat England which from the beginning of Cabinet government had never had a Cabinet secretary or Secretariat has been obliged by the increase of administrative business, by the complexity of the problems which come before a modern Cabinet for discussion and decision and by recognition of the advantages of order, method, and record in the transaction of business to organise a Secretariat for its own cabinet. Such a Cabinet Secretariat is required not only to help the Cabinet to transact its business but to enable the Cabinet to fulfil its function of co-ordinating, superintending, directing, and controlling all the departments of the State. Such an organisation is necessary to keep all the departments of the State working in accord with one another towards achievement of a common end.

Such a role is played by the Prime Minister's Council (Presidence du conseil) in other countries. In Italy before the last war this preponderant role was given it by an organic article of the constitution itself. Under Mussolini it received and exercised unusual strength and energy. In France in 1917 an administrative Secretariat of the Presidence du conseil called later the Secretariat General of the Presidence du conseil was formed. More and more in all countries, says a French authority on administrative organisation it appears that the presidence du conseil corresponding to the English Cabinet Secretariat has to play its administrative role of co-ordination of the work of ministries and departments.

This Cabinet Secretariat also on account of its commanding and overseeing position might be entrusted with the charge of investigating the organisation and operation of all the departments and other agencies of the Government and recommend changes that would promote efficiency and economy. Better than periodical commissions or committees of enquiry would be a permanent department of Government that would do this work of watching and improving the machinery and methods of work in the several departments of government. The Department of Intelligence and Research might be placed under it. It would act as a permanent Hoover Commission studying and making recommendations on such questions as improved administrative practices and procedure, elimination of overlapping or duplication of powers and duties, simplification and co-ordination of the organisation of structure. It its work could lead to results—the recommendations of the Hoover Commission which only partially adopted have already produced an annual saving of two billion dollars out of a total saving indicated by the commission of 5.4 billion dollars a year—it would be worth any additional cost. It would be the Organisation and Method section of the British Treasury on a large scale. And being directly under the Prime Minister in the Cabinet Secretariat, it would command the necessary prestige and power.

Ministers and the Administration

Each Minister of the Cabinet is in charge of one or more departments of the administration. He in subordination to the Cabinet as a whole is charged with the duty and responsibility of framing the policy of the Department and passing it on to his Department for execution. But although he is charged with this responsibility and duty, it would be a stupid or conceited Minister who would think and act as if he needed to help from the head and other officials of the department even in the framing of policy. Compared to him, says an English authority, the permanent head of the department is a person distinguished for general knowledge and ability and likely to have an amount of special knowledge which it would take many years of official drudgery for Ministers to obtain. Speaking from personal experience as civil servant and as Minister, viscount Milner has testified how the Minister comes in the office very often knowing nothing at all about the business; he may have his policy and his ideas but when he comes across the practical difficulties, with the new facts, the vast amount of accumulated knowledge and experience which the permanent officials can bring to bear upon the subject, his ideas almost invariably undergo considerable modification. While the Minister, he goes on to say, may think that all powers rest with him and he has to undertake the defence of the department and its acts in the Legislature and may resent the knowledge and information of the permanent official, he would be wise to realise early in his career in the department that he cannot know as much as the officials. If he were a small-minded man he may be tempted to think that unless he makes many comments and objections to the proposals of his official advisers he may be supposed not to understand the business at all; the wise Minister would look to his officials to give shape and substance to his ideas. The chief duty of civil servants of the upper ranks says Viscount Milner is to give shape and substance to the vague aspirations of the Minister. The misty attitude of the politicians and the service that the good civil servant can render Ministers are described for us from Milner's personal experiences. "I remember" he says not a few ministerial discussions in which I took part myself which followed something like this course. We met together to discuss some rather urgent and burning questions of policy; we were perhaps fairly agreed when we met about the direction in which we intended to go, but as the discussion proceeded, first one difficulty and then another cropped up on points of detail; one these we learnt a good deal from one another and then the debate got off to side issues and after an hour and a half or two hours we were all in a muddle and we were getting tired and everybody's hair was ruffled and the prospect of arriving at a conclusion was gloomy; then the attendant civil servant would quietly slip into the hands of the Chairman an insignificant little piece of paper with a few tidy resolutions which pulled the whole thing together and omitting what was immaterial or impracticable, so to speak, explained us to ourselves and embodied the greatest common measure of agreement between us; these resolutions were readily adopted and we went away, having after all done something." Happy the administration which has Ministers and civil servants helping one another to such fruitful ends!

A Minister should superintend rather than work at matters of detail. He should judge and control rather than elaborate, must learn to make the amplest use of subordinates and their knowledge and experience. He would be like the English statesman reported by Helps and admitted by all to be one of the best administrators of a great department, of whom it was said that days and even weeks sometimes passed without his ever writing a line himself. He was nevertheless one of the most industrious men, he confessed he was all day long engaged in seeing what his people were doing or could do. The statesman was probably Sir George Cornwall Lewis who had said that the most successful minister was one who did not do things himself but saw that things were done by his officials.

However that may be with the Minister, the Head of the department and his subordinates are expected by the nature and duties of their office to place all their knowledge and experience at the disposal of the Minister on any question that may come before him. As J.S. Mill an administrator himself testified, good public servants aid every Minister by their experience and inform him by their knowledge of business. It is their duty to place honestly all the objections and difficulties in the way of any proposal. Of course, they would use tact and management so that their ideas and proposals may appear to be those of the Minister himself. Like Le Tellier, Louvois, Colbert and Lionne in the reign of Louis the XIV of France, they should make their Head believe he was the ruler while they make him accept their ideas. It is not their business or duty to humour or please the Minister to find out what the Minister's views are and play up to him. The true composition of a counsellor says Bacon, is to be skilful in his master's business then in his nature, for then he is like to advise him and not to feed his humour. He owes the duty of service not only to the Minster but to the Government and the State and country. And in the interests of State and country it is his duty to put his Minister wise and not lead him astray. But once the Minister has taken the decision, it is the duty of the Head of the department and other officials to carry out loyally and effectively these decisions however much he may dislike them. As Punch put it once "the head of a department must be on tap, not on top."

And the Minister on his side may follow the great Napoleon who, while he resented criticism in public welcomed and even provoked discussion and objections to this plans and policy in the Council of State and among his advisers and subordinates. And, although the constitutional master of his department, he may not interfere with the day to day administration of the department. Otherwise, the leadership of the Head, the activity of the officials and discipline within the department so necessary for its efficiency would he broken. The Minister should confine himself to laying down the policy and general directions and leave the carrying out of that policy and these directions to the head of the department. Otherwise, if he took part in the routine of his department he would have neither the time nor the mind nor the energy for his real job which is the thinking out and framing of policy and programme for his department.

The Administration and other Bodies

Relations between Administration and the Legislature:

To start with, the character and composition of the administration must correspond to the character and composition of the Legislature. A monarchical constitution would have an administration appointed by and dependent on and responsible to the monarch, an aristocracy would have the chief offices of administration filled by members of the aristocracy. A democracy would have its administration representative of all classes and communities. Otherwise harmony, peace and concord between the legislature and the administration cannot be ensured. As Burke put it, every sort of Government ought to have its administration correspondent to its Legislature, otherwise things must fall into a hideous distraction.

As we have already indicated the Administration is as important a part of Government as the Legislature. Each has a right of its own to exist and operate, however much the constitutional doctrine and practice of Responsible Government may disguise the truth and mislead political innocents. Although by the law and constitution the Legislature can lay down the law for the administration its control and check may be only ultimate and general. This check and control may not descend into interference with the day-to-day administration. The suspicion no doubt comes natural to a legislative body that when legislation is not effective it is because the administration has not acted in full accordance with the letter of the law and the spirit of its enactments. Also "the vanity, the diseased activity, the desire of prominence of individual members of the legislature" may call for this undue interference. The abuse of the right of representatives of the people in the

Legislature to enquire about and take interest in the administration causes waste of the time of departments. Needless questions call for needless returns and question time in the Legislature accounts for a, large part of the size and cost of the administration. More, public offices are hampered, worried and weakened by a sense of their double responsibility to their chief and the Legislature. Of course, the permanent officials are not directly responsible to the Legislature—it is the Minister who is also the spokesman and defender of the department in the Legislature. So far as the Legislature is concerned the official is like the good child who is seen and not heard. Just as and because the official may not defend himself in public against any criticism or censure passed on him or his work in the Legislature, so no member of the Legislature may criticise or censure any individual official. To the Legislature it is only the Minister that is responsible and he must take the blame for anything that happens in his Department. And the members of the Legislature must also remember that captious or excessive criticism of administrative departments defeats the very purpose of criticism which is correction. What Dr. Johnson said of a married couple applies also to the relations between Legislature and Administration. "Wretched" he said "would be the pair above all manner of wretchedness who should be doomed to adjust by reason every morning all the minute details of a domestic day." Trust by the Legislature in the departments is necessary for vigorous action by the Administration.

The Executive Legislating—Delegated Legislation

Modern legislation on account of its quantity and its incidence and its long reach has to content itself with laying down the principles of the law and leaving the details especially concerning execution to be provided for by rules and regulations made by the administration. This has arisen largely out of modern social legislation "In any statute, it has been pointed out which gives to any administrative authority the power to regulate the relationships of human life a certain degree of elasticity is desirable if just and efficient administration is to be secured. The Legislature has neither the time nor the ability nor the foresight to provide for possible contingencies and necessary details. Legislatures, have to content themselves with the formulation of principles and the creation of necessary administrative machinery leaving matters of detail to regulations by the administration. It appears the British National Insurance Act of 1911 was rendered almost unworkable by the attempt to meet every exceptional and hard case in the statute itself.

This duty cast upon the Executive has found expression in the modern phenomenon known as delegated legislation. The grave constitutional danger of such delegated legislation has been presented graphically and described trenchantly as the New Despotism by a former Chief Justice of England. Here we are concerned with the new work thrown upon modern departments of administration. How much it is can be shown by the fact that in countries that have taken to social or welfare legislation the annual output of rules and orders is much greater than that of statutes and laws. Not only does this rule making power involve the providing for the details of administrative machinery, sometimes it goes farther and includes the power to amend in the light of experience the substantive provisions of the law passed by the Legislature. Many modern Acts give the Minister the power when any difficulty arises in connection with the application of the law to overcome the difficulty by order and any such order may modify the provisions of the law so far as it may appear to the Minister, necessary or expedient for carrying the law into effect. This discretionary power branded as the Henry VIII clause is tolerable only so far as it is designed solely to improve matters of machinery and give no power to modify and substantial provision of law. Modern governments it may be said are not so much governments of law and order as governments of laws and orders. This development has thrown new duties and burdens on the departments of administration, they must learn the art of legal draftsmanship. Each department especially a Welfare Department must have a legal section with one or two persons trained in the art of legal draftsmanship.

Relations between the Administration and the Judiciary

As the Judiciary is charged with the duty of guardianship of the laws of the country, it has necessarily jurisdiction over all acts of the administration, and of administrative officials if and when these acts are brought to its notice. In a free country everybody is bound by law and no administrator can plead exemption from its jurisdiction. The Rule of Law therefore is essential to every free Government. But what this Rule of Law involves, whether it should mean as in England that the officials of the administration are not only bound by the laws of the country especially those applicable to them but they are subject to the jurisdiction of the courts of law and cannot claim any special privileges, or exemptions or whether it would mean as in France that the officials should for their official acts be subject to the jurisdiction of a special administrative law *(droit administratif)* and special administrative courts to which not only officials but citizens can resort for redress of wrongs committed against them by officials in the course of administrative business is a result of historical development and national genius and Political circumstances. But that in the French system of administrative law and administrative courts, officials are made responsible for their acts and that individual freedom is guaranteed against administration, there can be no doubt.

In point of fact there are certain advantages in the system of administrative law and administrative courts that both the official and the citizen enjoy. The chief are:

1. The procedure being simpler and more rational and not the result of long history, justice in an administrative court is obtained much more expeditiously and at much less cost than in ordinary courts.

2. As administrative courts have only this business it is another cause for expedition in the disposal of suits.

3. Composed as they are of men experienced in administration the interests of administration which are not alien to the interests of the country are given as much consideration as the rights of citizens whereas in ordinary courts of law especially in England the bias is against the administrative department.

4. Provided the trials in these administrative courts are public, helped by the chief safeguards that operate in a court of law like a defined and ascertainable law, judicial procedure, the assistance of the Bar there is no reason to fear that justice will be obtained at the expense of liberty.

The record of administrative courts of France and in other countries that have adopted this system prove its merits.

Judicial Functions of Administrative Departments

Even where the system of administrative law and courts does not obtain there has set in a tendency to charge administrative departments with judicial or quasi-judicial functions—that is to say they have been given powers of judging and deciding in cases of conflict between the Government and the citizen. Thus in England under the Housing and Town-planning Act of 1909 it is provided that the power to enforce the closing of premises which had previously laid with the magistrates with an appeal to the Court of Quarter Sessions is now entrusted to the local authority with the right of appeal to the Ministry, the Local Government Board. Similarly under the statutes relating to patents and designs and trade marks a complaint that a patent has been refused or has been revoked contrary to law is heard in the first place by the Controller General of Patents and on appeal by another administrative official the Solicitor General and the Controller General is empowered to refuse to grant a patent of which the use would in his opinion be contrary to law or morality. In view of the growth of the judicial powers and functions of the administrative departments and officials in England the question has been raised why England should not straightforwardly and wholly adopt the system of administrative law and courts.

Administration and the Public

Administration like other branches of Government is the servant of the people. This has been recognised even in monarchical ages as in the time of the Enlightened Despots of the 19th century. But with the coming of democracy the people have to be made to see that the administration in fact serves them. And in this age of advertisement and propaganda an administration that does not make its work known to the people goes unrecognised or condemned by default. Information about the administration and its activities and the results of these activities must be broadcast if the administration is to receive the support of the people that is necessary for its efficiency. This information has to be made available to the people if it is to serve its purpose. But this information must be conveyed to the people in a readable form. Not dull reports helped out by tables and figures which can impress only their makers but readable reports and guide books helped out by illustrations would convey interesting instruction to the people. Annual reports to be useful should be issued without delay soon after the expiry of the official year; this might involve the omission of detailed and accurate statistics but such statistical information is of little concern to the general public and could be made available to those that need them in a later supplementary publication. Wireless until it becomes a nuisance can be used for publicity work. Advertisement is as necessary to Government as to business. The day when the good deeds of a Government could shine in a naughty world is gone.

Not only information but service has to be made available to the people. The impact of administration on the life of the people is so great and the contacts of people with the administration are so frequent in modern times that a new service of administration called Public Relations has been organised. This new service allows the general public to have access to government apartments and get information or help in regard to their duties to the State or in respect of the duties of Government to the people.

And information must be sought by Government from the general public. The Legislature and its members must not be their only source of information. Officials of Government must be open to interview by the members of the general public. They must welcome letters from the members of the general public. They must give time and opportunity to the general public to express its opinion on legislative and administrative proposals.

To administer all these new services of information, of publicity and public relations most modern governments have a general Department of Information, Publicity and Public Relations or each of the major departments has such a section. Among the duties of this Department or section would be:

1. Maintenance of good relations with the Press and supply to its representatives of full information regarding the Government's or Department's policy, acts and activities.
2. Arranging of annual exhibitions or weeks or similar functions designed to extend public knowledge of and interest in the work of the Government or Department.
3. Production and exhibition of films, booklets, leaflets, posters and other materials showing what the government or department is doing.
4. Organisation of lectures, meetings, talks, debates, lessons in educational institutions, adult classes, with a view to interesting these audiences in the work of Government or Department.
5. Provision of an information bureau.
6. Radio talks.
7. Handling of all complaints, criticisms, requests made by individual members of the public, associations, groups, newspapers.

Such a department or Section of Publicity and Public Relations uses the following means of serving the public.

1. Correspondence.
2. Interviews.
3. Telephone conversations.
4. The other means and methods of publicity referred to already.

Promptness in answering letters and other communications is courtesy to the public. Not so much the results of complaints as a knowledge that complaints are being attended to is reassuring to the public. Hence intermediate letters of acknowledgement before the final decision is sent would be appreciated. Addressed envelopes and the reply envelope and card used in business would be welcomed. The style used in communications of the public ought to be short, precise, and polite. Official jargon should be avoided. Interviews are much more satisfying than letters. A waiting room for callers and visitors with useful and relevant literature on the table would be appreciated by the public and smoothen public relations. The partition counter between the enquirer and the official as obtains in the revenue, the customs, and post offices is a bar to pleasant relations between the public and administration. The great principle that should govern public relations is that administration and the public are not natural enemies of each other, but are partners in the great business of government.

Between the Circumference and the Centre

Smaller Focuses of Government—To every modern State its political or administrative life is concerned, as De Tocqueville said of the United States of America, in three focuses of action which may not inaptly be compared to the different nervous centres which convey motion to the human body. One is the Village or the Town and the other is the County or District or the State, when there is a union of States called a Federation. The amount and extent of free action allowed to the smaller parts of the units of a State, depend upon the constitutional character of the State. If the State is a unitary State, that is a State with only one centre with large political powers, the extent of freedom and self-government allowed to the units is not as great as those allowed to the larger units in a federal State. And even in unitary states the autonomy of the parts is greater in a decentralised State like England than in a centralised State like France. And the character of the government of the units is taken from the character of the government at the centre. If there is divided and distributed government in the centre there is divided and distributed government in the units. If there is concentration of power in the one there is concentration of power in the other. Thus the concentration of power in the hands of the monarch and his council in the ancient regime of France was reflected in the concentration of local power in the hands of the Intendant. Law the Scottish Controller of Finance in the time of Louis the XV who with his speculative financial policy contributed to the downfall of that regime was struck by the fact that this kingdom of France was governed by 30 Intendants without parliaments or estates of government; on these 30 Intendants depended the happiness and misery of the provinces of France, their prosperity and their sterility. Whereas, the parliamentary government of England at the centre is reflected in the self-government of the counties, the towns and the parishes.

As to the number of units of local government apart from historical causes and the needs of self-government the cost of the organisation of the units is a prime consideration. If the administration is to be rationalised, that is to say made as useful and as cheap as possible, and its organisation rationalised, the question has to be asked whether old historic divisions and sub-divisions ought to be continued when abolition of some of them and a re-grouping of those left would bring down the cost of administration. Parishes and villages no doubt served a useful purpose in the old days when communications were few and far between. Although villages are worth preserving in the interests of local self-government and for promoting the effectiveness of democratic government, every village, however small and few its inhabitants, need not be provided with a full and separate set of institutions and services. Could not a number of small contiguous villages connected by roads and forming a minimum population of say 3—5 thousand be grouped together so as to form an administratively economic self-governing unit. Under such an impulse of economy the French Government in 1926 replaced the Conseils de prefecture by inter-departmental councils and suppressed 106 sub-prefectures and 70 secretaries-general as well as tribunaux d' arrondissements. As communications become developed such economic regroupings of local units become progressively possible. Such rationalisation of political divisions also would benefit the national budget which would have to finance a smaller number of local units; the people would have quicker and better services; and the administrative services themselves, being reduced in number would be better paid. The administrative map of a country might thus be modified in the interests of economy and efficiency.

The importance of work of the local government units may be seen from an enumeration of the activities of such local authorities in England, the list though not complete is formidable and include.

1. Watching and prevention and detection of crime.
2. Administration of justice.
3. Street lighting.
4. Fire service.
5. Cleaning of streets and the removal and destruction of household refuse.
6. Provision and maintenance of sewers and drainage systems.
7. Provision of wholesome water supply.
8. Construction and maintenance of roads and streets.
9. Prevention and removal of nuisance.
10. Prevention and treatment of infectious diseases and for that purpose the erection and management of hospitals, dispensaries, etc.
11. Provision and management of maternity and child welfare homes and clinics.
12. Provision of parks, open spaces, recreation grounds.
13. Provision of libraries.
14. Relief of the poor.
15. Education.
16. Provision of burial grounds.
17. Care of lunatics and the mentally defective.
18. Manufacture and distribution of gas and electricity.
19. Provision of tramways, buses, etc.
20. Provision of harbours and docks.

21. Provision of slaughter houses.

22. Provision of dwelling homes for workers and destruction of slums.

23. Administration of large numbers of Acts of Parliament and departmental orders thrown on the local authority.

Not all of these subjects are administered by all grades of local bodies, the village council, the town council, the district or county council, but the list gives one a notion of the number and importance of the work of the local units of Government in a modern State. The modern characteristics of the work of these local bodies is the supply of those public utility services, water, gas, electricity, transport, housing which Bernard Shaw in one of his early political pamphlets summed up as Municipal Socialism.

Special Characteristics of Administration of Local Units of Government

Although the organisation, instruments and methods of work in the administrative offices of a local unit like a country or district council or a municipal council are similar in most respects to those of the Central Government, there are a few characteristics differences due to the smallness of the unit. These differences are due to the fact that the smaller the unit of government the less easy is it to maintain the separation of powers, the separation between legislature, administration, and the judiciary. Not only is it less easy but a rigid separation may be detrimental to the interests of popular government, for the smaller the unit the more easy is it for the people or the representatives of the people to take part in administration and the judgment of their peers. That is one of the merits of decentralisation.

Varieties of Systems of Local Administration

The following are the most notable:

1. Elected Council and Committee system—the governing body is an elected council and it administers through committees elected by and from among itself; it prevails in England and in countries that derive their political system from England.

2. Professional administrator system—it prevails in Germany, the Head of the local administration being a Burgomaster appointed by the Government; the City Manager of the U.S.A. is another example of this system for though he is appointed by the City Council he is an administrator in his own right.

3. Presidential system—corresponding to the President of the U.S.A. is the Mayor of a large city who though elected by the people is Head of the Administration and responsible to the people although he would have to carry the council with him as the President has to carry the Congress; the mayor of certain French towns is another example of this system.

4. Ministerial system—which allows of a kind of Cabinet government in local bodies the members of the Cabinet being elected by the Council; it obtains in Holland, Belgium, Denmark, Switzerland, and the commission form in some local bodies in the U.S.A. is a variant of this system.

But the most notable of these is the elected council and committee system because it combines democratic government with effective administration. Administration by the council and its committees prevails in all countries which derive their political system from England. Local Government in such countries is largely government by committees. This is how it is done—

1. The Council or deliberative and legislative body of the local unit takes part in the administration of the county or district or town through a number of elected Committees. These Committees have considerable delegated powers but for matters of principle, policy and finance they must get the approval of the Council; they also have to resort periodically to it on all matters of substance which they have dealt within the delegated powers; most of the work of the Council is done through committees.

The committee performs such administrative functions, as selection of staff, opening of tenders and choosing the operative tender, visiting and inspection, selection and order of material.

2. Each committee has a chairman whose personality often decides whether he rules the committee or the committee rules through him.

3. Besides education, health and other committees whose names are given by the subjects they deal with the most important is the Finance Committee which like the Finance Department of the Central Government watches the expenditure of money sanctioned by the Council to the several Committees beside being charged with the duty of collecting the revenues of the Council.

4. The actual work of administration the execution of resolutions and other decisions of the council and its committees is done by the officers of the council, the Education Officer, the Health Officer, the Engineer and so on. The chief of them is the Chief Executive Officer called in England the Clerk of the Council and elsewhere the Commissioner, all the others working under him.

5. Members of the Council and the Committees do not interfere with the day to day administration and officials do not concern themselves with the deliberations and decisions of the Council or the Committees except to help them with information and suggestions whenever called upon to do so.

6. In the administration of District Boards or County or Municipal Councils on account of the character of the services they render to the people there is not the separation between the general administrator and the technical expert or specialist that there is in central administration. Education, health sanitation, roads electricity are in charge of technical experts and specialists who are not only technical advisers of the Council and the Committee but heads of their respective departments, an additional reason for this arrangement is that the departments are not large enough to warrant the addition of a head with general administrative qualifications involving additional cost and as policy is made by the Council and its Committees there is no need for a general adviser on policy; and the Clerk of the Council in England or the City Managers of the U.S.A. or the

Commissioner elsewhere is enough general policy adviser for the whole of the local administration. But as a technical specialist does not always make a good head of administration the local authority or its committee should have the power of choosing the administrative Head of a Department from among the technical officers of that department for his administrative qualifications and capacity. A provision might also be made for special training and courses in general administration for eligible officers of the department.

Relations between the Central Government and the Local Government:

In a Unitary State:

In countries with a large measure of local autonomy or self-government the administrative control of the Central Government is not extensive and at the most it is restricted to.

1. Seeing that the laws governing the activities and services of the local authorities are observed; in recent times the Parliament in England has thrown the duty of supplying certain educational and health and social services on counties and boroughs by legislation like the National Health Service Act of 1946, the National Assistance Act of 1948 and the Education Act of 1944.
2. Seeing that the County or District or Municipal Councils administers Act like the English Public Health and High Ways Acts and exercises power under the Housing Acts.
3. Financial control and supervision in regard to the use and expenditure of money granted by the Central Government to the local authorities; by the British Local Government Act of 1949 the old block grants have been replaced by equalisation grants designed to produce a measure of equalisation of rate burdens by giving a greater measure of central assistance to the local authorities who are financially not well off; under the same Act the function of making valuations for rating purposes is transferred from the local authorities to the Commissioners of Inland Revenue.

4. Although there is a wide extension under recent Acts of the local authorities, e.g. in power to provide entertainment and to incur expenditure for such purposes the tendency towards centralisation in recent times is unmistakable in England.

5. Through inspection and audit the control of the Central Government on the local authorities is made effective and real.

The Instrument of Inspection:

Inspection is the method of control used by a superior authority to ensure that subordinate authorities are exercising their powers and responsibilities according to law and orders governing their activity. The nature and degree of this control varies according to the constitutional system that prevails. In a highly centralised system the inspection exercised by the Central Government is close and continuous. The age of centralisation is the golden age of Inspectors-General. Gogols' satire of the *Inspector-General* was written of an official of the Tsarist regime. When a large measure of local autonomy or self-government obtains, the inspection would be that which is just necessary to see that the laws are observed by the local authority and that the monics granted to it by the Central Government are spent for the purpose for which they were granted. This inspection may be permanent or intermittent. When the inspection is permanent it is generally exercised by inspection officers stationed in the locality inspected; intermittent inspection is exercised by inspecting officers proceeding from the capital and who start out not and then at irregular intervals, sometimes suddenly, without notice given, for the locality to be expected.

Inspection requires certain special qualities in the inspector. Knowledge of the subject whose administration in the locality he is inspecting is fundamental, especially knowledge of the Acts and Regulations under which the administration is carried on. Tact, discretion, sympathy with the workers in the field are a great help. An efficient inspector should be looked upon by the local authorities whose work he inspects as their confidential adviser and friend. He would go on his inspection not so much to find fault as to help to improve the administration. He should so regulate his conduct as an inspector that the local authorities readily consult him on difficulties and emergencies. It is a practice in many areas of public assistance administration in England to send copies of all minutes and agenda of the public assistance committee and sub-committee to the inspector.

In a Federal State:

In addition to and superior in power and autonomy to the local units of Government like county, district or town, there are in Federal States large autonomous units called States. These have jurisdiction over a large number of important subjects like education, health, agriculture, forests, industry, the Central Government being charged with fewer subjects concerning the country as a whole. The autonomy and self-government of a State in a federal State is large and extensive and a federal constitution being a written constitution the spheres of the Federal and the States Governments are defined and limited by the constitution. The autonomy and self-government of a State in a federal constitution is therefore more secure as it is wider than that of a county or district or town whose autonomy and self-government is subject to the ordinary legislative powers of superior authority. But even in a federal State the tendency towards centralisation brought about by modern needs like those of the Welfare State or by modern dangers like war has now set in. We see this tendency illustrated in the recent activities of the Federal Government of the U.S.A. undreamt and unpredicted by the fathers of the constitution.

Methods and Instruments of Federal activity in the U.S.A. These are:

1. Use of the taxing power and the power to regulate interstate commerce granted by the constitution to enter upon policies and programmes of administration which are remotely connected with taxation and inter-state commerce.

2. Activities of a general nature authorised by the wording of the preamble of the Constitution which, according to it, purports "to form a more perfect union, ensure domestic tranquility and promote the general welfare"; provided there

is nothing in the constitution to prevent action in regard to such purposes the federal government has gone ahead in activities which aim at the realisation of these objectives.

3. By constitutional amendment of which the eighteenth amendment which introduced prohibition is the most memorable.

4. By grants in aid and subsidies and the resultant control and supervision by the Federal Government over the activities of State Governments. These grants or subsidies have been defined as payments made by the Federal Government to State and local Governments subjects to certain conditions for the support of activities administered by the States and their local sub-divisions. They may be either permanent or recurring and emergency or temporary or extraordinary. In 1950 there were 25 aided functions and activities. These grants or subsidies are made on certain conditions, the chief being that the State must match the federal contribution with a State contribution on a dollar for dollar basis or more or less. Administrative control by the Federal Government varies greatly. Strict supervision is exercised by federal road officials over the construction of federal-aided State highways. The amount of control by federal authorities over educational and agricultural services aided or subsidised is almost nothing.

An illustration of the manner and extent to which federal activity has operated in the U.S.A. in such a primarily State subject as Agriculture is the number of agencies set up by the Federal Government to promote the welfare of Agriculture—the Forest Service, the Weather Bureau, the Bureaus of animal husbandry, plant industry, chemistry, soils, entomology, biological survey, crop estimates, market and public roads, the Horticultural board, Insecticide board and the division of Home economics.

But it is in the field of police administration that the most sensational development of federal activity in a primarily State matter has taken place. The Federal Bureau of Investigation known all over the world as F.B.I. under the leadership of Hoover (not the ex-president) has drawn popular notice to itself by its successful campaign against gangsterism, organised and scientific crime with which the State authorities had not been able to cope, its nationwide record keeping and identification technique and inter-state and intra-state activities have served to integrate the police organisation of the U.S.A. In the pursuit of crime the latest developments show that the Federal Government is pushing the States into the background and that the States have almost been deprived of their traditional control of crime. The Federal Government has now jurisdiction over obscenity, prostitution, rape, assault, indecent exhibitions, kidnapping, mayhem, blackmail, extortion, racketeering, criminal libel, murder, robbery, burglary, grand larceny. There more than one thousand federal police officers operating all over the country.

The Commerce power of the Federal Government extends to every sort of transportation and communication, also to manufacturing, mining, and other industry that affect inter-state commerce; through its taxpower the Federal Government justifies not only the grant in aid of the tax, offset and expenditure for research and information services in the states but for regulatory purposes as well, e.g., taxing State bank notes out of circulation and bringing dealers in narcotics under federal control.

The New Deal policy and programme of the late President Roosevelt have also extended this sphere of federal activity. Although in the Supreme Court State rights have found a watchful and vigorous defender, the tendency towards increase of federal activities is defended as being called for by the needs of the State. The States have had to pay for it in increased federal influence if not control on State legislation also, for in return for federal grants and subsidies they have had to act on legislation which the federal congress is neither expressly nor by implication authorised to enact.

But if the tendency to central control and influence is to be resisted in a federation, the States must fulfil their constitutional duties with efficiency and success. Their governments must give their people the services in regard to the promotion of education, health agriculture, industry, that the constitution expects them to give. Confining ourselves to administrative organisation this must be so effective as to enable the State Governments to fulfil their obligations to the people. The defects noted in critical studies of the administrative organisation of State Governments in the U.S.A. must be avoided. The large number of State executive authorities beside the Governor and similarly elected by the people and with overlapping jurisdictions, the rule by elected Boards and Commissions lowering the authority of heads of departments, the lack of budgetary control and of continuous and constant financial supervision by an officer directly responsible to the Governor, the short period of the Governor's term, two years in half the States, are defects in State administrative organisation that militate against administration efficiency. And the reform and reorganisation of State administration already undertaken by progressive States like Massachussets, Maryland, California. Michigan and which aim at making the Governor with a term of four years, the real and sole and responsible head of the administration and with a Cabinet composed of heads of departments, all making the head of the department responsible for the work of the department, the abolition of conflicting jurisdictions, the establishment of a finance department with budgetary financial and personnel control will make for administrative efficiency in the States.

Even so the warning of De Tocquevile is still in place and in time. "A centralised administration" he warned "is and tends to enervate the nation in which it operate by incessantly diminishing public spirit. Such administration succeeds in crystalizing at a given movement or at a given point all the disposable resources of the people, it impairs the renewal of those resources. It may ensure a victory in the hour of strife but it gradually relaxed the sinews of strength. It may help admirably the transient greatness of a man but it cannot ensure the durable prosperity of a nation".

4

The Nature of Organisation Aims

Men often submit willingly, even cheerfully, to authority when they believe it to be exercised well and responsibly in the pursuit of ends of which they approve and in whose benefits they will justly share. The rulers have "power," no doubt, but there is at least a "myth" to the effect that this power is exercised in the public interest and that the purpose which the "powerful" satisfy in their capacity as public servants is not one that sets them in competition with their "weaker" brethren, but one which can be shared and in the name of which men can reasonably work together. Even the realists observe that the semblance of such disinterested devotion to a common cause must be preserved if morale is to be maintained.

The administrator like any other creative artist works in and through a distinctive medium. But in his case the medium has three facets. It is a composite of the activities of the organisation as such, of the human beings who compose it or relate to it and of the total environmental setting in which both of these carry on. A going organisation brings into being a real, if subjective, entity which has identifiable traits and which is at once affecting and being affected by all who are under its influence.

A going organisation arises out of a deliberate association of persons desiring to accomplish something together, to realize certain defined objectives, which as individuals the persons either could not do for themselves or could not do as well. These persons as they continue to associate create a small society or community or "social system," as some have called it, which has many of the characteristics of a larger society.

Indeed, certain aspects of an organisation's activity are to be understood largely from this point of view or frame of reference. And today a sociological and social-psychological approach to what goes on when people are associated in this purposive way has become one of the fruitful approaches to administration which to a considerable extent will be found also to underlie this study.

As small societies or social systems, our typical organisations—factories, stores, banks, schools, hospitals, government departments and others—artificially bring together individuals who have already been formed by many influences. These individuals are thus already products of a larger society. Also, certain spontaneous groups tend to arise within the organisation, influenced by factors of contiguous workplace, age, sex, religious or fraternal affiliations, education and other common bonds. And these groups have a certain life of their own, have certain accepted standards of conformity, have informal leaders who emerge, agreeable personal ties that develop. All of this interplay of personal sentiment gains a vitality which the wise administrator does not ignore.

A customary outcome of these intensive human relations is the development of sentimental ties arising out of common wisecracks, anecdotal allusions, nicknames, amenities surrounding the recognition of weddings, funerals, births, amusing recitals about anniversary dancers and picnics—a satisfying camaraderie. And this greatly enhances the pleasure of the association, which the individual comes to prize for its own sake. Those who have never experienced it would be astonished at the value placed upon this *happy sociality,* which almost spontaneously grows up through and in the corporate setting. To help this sentiment into full flower is, indeed, a mandate of administrative skill. The fact that all this bears only indirectly on job performance and yields satisfactions separate from those intrinsic to the work itself does not lessen its importance. At the least people will rightfully strive to feel happy and congenial while at work. At the most is the hope that they may come to some measure of satisfaction in the work itself.

The dominant characteristic of the kind of small society or corporate body with which this book is concerned is obviously its *purposiveness.* It exists to get something done. It has certain aims and ends in view to be realised by people in association. Hence, a basic question at once emerges: Are the nature and character of the aims such as to predispose individuals to find satisfaction in striving to realise them? What kinds of aims will be appealing to large groups of individuals? Once some answer on this score is forthcoming, there arises the further problem of discovering the ways to assure zealous acceptance of the aims established.

Beyond this, and integral to meeting this challenge, account has to be taken of some general view of human nature which recognises its persistent search for certain satisfactions, as influenced by prevailing social and cultural forces. For my assumption is that when people in association accept some common aim, it is because they believe that in so doing they are advancing the satisfactions they believe they may rightfully expect out of the activity. Corporate aims are good, other things being equal, if efforts to realise them by individuals yield them satisfying outcomes. These are the issues which are elaborated in this chapter.

An aim, end, purpose or objective—the words will here be used interchangeably—of organisations gives expression to a controlling desire for specific outcomes shared by a group of individuals. These group desires may be of great variety and thus in one organisation or another comprehend the whole sweep of human interests. We find, for example, the desire of an inventor and his associates to produce and sell for a profit some new gadget; the desire of a group of bankers to combine and operate certain railroad properties; the desire of the people of the United States to have railroad rates regulated; the desire of a group of citizens to protect civil liberties; the desire of a group of doctors to own and operate a hospital; the desire of parents in Public School XYZ to function through a parent-teacher association; and so on and infinitum.

The interested individuals, having identified a common purpose arising out of a common need, difficulty or opportunity, proceed to organize into some formalised body, association, institution, or corporation. Whether or not the form of legal incorporation is employed depends on numerous factors of size, amounts of money involved, desired permanency, etc. And even the type of corporation may differ with the purpose, since society recognizes in law nonprofit corporations of various kinds (educational, charitable, governmental, etc.). Nor is the fact of incorporation the key factor, for there are partnerships and voluntary associations for all of which administrators are necessary.

Thus in the initiating phase the aims of organisations derive from the shared desires of those who bring them into being. For them the purpose is fresh, clear, appealing, important, worthy of their best collaborative effort. The common intension is obvious, and common action results. The enthusiasm and zest with which new organisations of all kinds get under way are familiar facts.

But just as soon as there has to be, for effective realising of the agreed aim, an enlistment of persons beyond the small initiating group, complications of an administrative sort begin to arise. That enlistment may be by the most varied devices. We naturalise citizens who are not born into citizenship privileges. We may invite new members into our golf club. On the one hand we sell shares in our stock corporation and on the other hire individuals to fill salaried positions to start the company into operation; and those individuals in turn help to build up a working force, all of whom are one step further removed from firsthand concern with the aims the company is organised to realise.

As time goes on and organisations become going concerns with an established pattern of purposes and activities, a certain momentum is usually achieved; and administrators often tend to assume that the agency will "go ahead on its own steam." By this it is too frequently meant that those who are administering believe that they know and those becoming newly associated with them will somehow know what the associated aims are. And they may even assume further that "it goes without saying" that all involved are anxious to carry out those aims.

This human frailty is perhaps the basic cause for the familiar natural history of organisations, which all too often evidence a life cycle of eager birth, rapid growth, successful middle years, decline and liquidation. Statistical evidence regarding the life span of industrial corporations which we tend to think of as relatively stable reveals a remarkably short life for a majority . Read the listings of the corporations whose stocks were traded on the New York Stock Exchange in 1915 and see how many of these no longer exist.

Aims as Primary and Secondary

There is another complicating factor about the realising of aims. It has to be assured that those who initially organise with specific aims in view and who seemingly have the power to command the means necessary to realise them will in fact know the requisite ways and means. There are many, said a wise philosopher, who, knowing that they have laid down the ends, believe that the means thereto will take care of themselves. I do not here refer to such means as technical facilities and processes, for which skill can readily be enlisted. I allude rather to such means as the attitudes, outlooks and motives of those who are successively brought in as members or as employees.

And it becomes important for the administrator to distinguish between major aims and minor, or primary and secondary aims, and between long-run and short-run aims. For in order to realise any central purpose it is vital to have in mind those subsidiary aims which must be given effect if the central purpose is assuredly to be attained.

If we ask how successful going organisations retain their vitality and unity, a clearer sense of he importance of these subsidiary aims emerges. Look at the processes utilised in joining a fraternal lodge or a church or entering a college, where systematised initiation and induction have had extensive historic testing. There is marked identity in the means employed.

If we examine these means in detail, we see clearly the essential role of secondary aims. There is careful selection of neophytes; there is prolonged indoctrination as to aims; there is the evocation of a variety of symbolic supports to stimulate the emotional zeal of the newcomer (the flag, the college songs, the ritual of worship or of fellowship, the building up of a sense of unique value in the special mysteries, traditions, and glories of the institution). Nothing is left to chance in the effort to inculcate in the individual the significance of his affiliation and the high seriousness of his coming to share in the pursuit of the common objective. For each new member to know what the organisation seeks and why, how, and where he shares in its efforts and benefits is an immediate and continuing concern of the organisation's leaders. So important are these measures of orientation that they have to be come secondary aims if the primary end is to be realised.

In the examples just cited the relation of newcomer to institution is one of membership and not that of paid employee. But this fact does not substantially alter the underlying psychological problem to be faced when recruiting employees. For the challenge is almost identical except that, in the case of the employee, managers are hopeful that the degree of loyalty to the organisation may become even greater, more sustained and more informed than a often true of various membership affiliations which may require less of the member's time and energy. For nothing less is ideally sought than the growing intellectual and emotional commitment of each newly enlisted employee to as many as possible of the aims which the corporation is striving to realise.

I never cease to marvel at how ineffectually the whole industrial world acts in contrast with avocational groups when it puts employees "on the payroll." Compare prevailing practices here (there are exceptions) with the entire body of procedures by which a lad becomes a good army private, or a devoted son of dear old Siwash College, or a "confirmed" member of a strong church body. Such a comparison highlights the emotional poverty, the intellectual bleakness and the imaginative sterility of the typical processes of perfunctory initiation into corporate, or hospital, or public departmental employment. Why our expectation should be so much less for the employee and why we have not asked more insistently whether the usual notions of employee status and outlook are good enough both for the employing organisation and for the worker—these are important questions for the administrator

The intent of this analysis of aims is to point out two facts. One is that the single-minded pursuit of any one aim as central by an administrator would represent a serious shortcoming in his understanding of his problems. And the second is that in actual practice organisations are found to have a number of more or less controlling purposes which had better be explicit in order that they may be properly evaluated and effectively implemented. Further analysis of these plural aims should thus help to suggest their relative importance and appeal under different circumstances.

Aspects of Organisation Aims

I shall consider these several aspects of aims as: (1) legal, (2) functional, (3) technical, (4) profit making, (5) personal, and (6) public.

1. The legal aims of an organisation are those which are set forth in its charter, constitution, declaration, etc. These are sometimes exceedingly general, sometimes quite specific. It is here that the central aim would usually be made explicit. The governing body presumably addresses its own efforts to this end more closely than do all the other individuals or groups involved. And if, as is true in business, the governing body, namely, a board of directors, is responsible to a body of stockholders on the one hand and is responsible for a body of hired employees on the other, the top administrators are presented with a problem, if not of dual allegiance, at least of dual solicitude in realising the legally stipulated objective. Or, to put it differently, if the central aim is primary to those who are stockholders but is only of secondary or even indifferent concern to employees because their direct connection with the aim is far less obvious to them, the task of administration is obviously increased in complexity.

   Clarity and preciseness about the legal aim are essential. Only so can all involved begin to see the extent to which the means employed are proving to be a contribution to the end legally articulated.

2. Functional aims are those centering on the performance of a social function, or the fulfillment of a social need, or the

supplying a recognised demand for production of goods or services. Increasingly in economic life the pronouncements of executives in published statements of corporate objectives make explicit reference to the aim of securing a fair profit from the *supplying of products or services needed by consumers.* The idea of service through business widely publicised by the Rotarians may not always be interpreted in the most profound way, but it represents an emphasis and a moral justification for which businessmen seem more and more to feel the need as an acknowledged part of their total motivation and objective. Pride in the total corporate effort—in turning out a good product, fairly priced, with favourable consumer reception, and with cordial labour relations—this is an increasingly influential administrative aim of almost professional quality which cannot be ignored or minimised. It is an aim of good *functioning.*

Creative, constructive and imaginative capacities of the highest order are thus invested in organisation efforts by thousands of executives. And it is never easy to draw a line and say where creative drives for good social functioning dominate and where acquisitive and other impulses are controlling. More and more administrators themselves are testifying that pride of administrative workmanship is often a greater influence than amount of salary or rate of profit.

In short, the functional aspect of corporate aims not only cannot be lost sight of, but it deserves greater prominence than it usually receives in any true understanding of the controlling factors in executive motivation.

3. By the technical purposes are meant the more specialised, planning and engineering efforts to assure the maximum utility of technological equipment and process requirements. While this obviously is only an implementing or subsidiary purpose, it may assume large proportions in the minds of certain executives. Especially in those business organisations where trained engineers are largely in control, pride in technical superiority often looms large in administrative thinking.

The whole problem of technological obsolescence and the introduction of newly invented improvements is one fraught with great administrative consequences, especially where the displacement or replacement of large number of the working force may be entailed. The proper balancing of technological and of humane considerations in such situations is crucially important. For in the past all too often professional engineering pride has weighed so heavily in administrative thinking that blind spots to other aspects of the total operation have meant a total eclipse of human relations interests. Such professional preoccupation can be so dominant as to become a controlling purpose, even if its efforts are only means to the central end.

Indeed, this precisionist concern about process is to be found in other than technological areas, wherever a prescribed pattern as to the ways of getting the job done is rigidly held to by administrators preoccupied with methods they may have learned and become thoroughly habituated to in earlier years when they occupied lower rungs on the executive ladder.

4. Profit making is an explicit, central and legal aim of many organisations, including virtually all privately organised business corporations. Also, to operate without loss within a given budgetary situation of available financial resources is a necessary secondary aim of most non-profit organisations. But the extent and influence of this aim in business requires careful analysis because the facts are more complex than the theory.

The making of profit in each fiscal year is by no means achieved by every business. The figures of the first few years in the 1940's show on the average that only about two-thirds of the active corporations made a definite profit.

The concept of profit needs careful scrutiny. Here it means the net surplus which is earned by a corporation after all legitimate operating costs, fixed charges, depreciation and obsolescence costs are met. Some of this surplus is typically paid to stockholders as "earnings on their investment"; and some of it is usually retained in the business to give more liquid resources, to provide for expansion, to help pay dividends in less favourable years, or in other ways to meet the unforeseeable contingencies. To the extent that surplus is devoted to plant expansion or is otherwise held in the business, it adds to the value of the shares owned by the stockholders.

The *rate* of profit not only varies greatly from company to company and from year to year, but there is no fixed rate which is generally regarded as the right, just or socially defensible one. The line between what is adjudged to be legitimate profit and what may be criticised as "profiteering" is a fine one; yet to invoke any universally acceptable standards is all but impossible. The climate of public opinion affects decisions here in ways that on occasion curb business practice and outcomes and even lead to some effort to disguise or minimize the facts of a high profit showing.

It is thus necessary, in considering profit as the end, to see its two separable functions. Profit is, first, the index of the survival possibilities of an enterprise under current, accepted standards of corporate operation and accounting methods. And it is, second, the measure of the extent of net monetary gain which has resulted.

As to profit as an index of survival possibilities, if our economy is viewed as a whole, and if no companies showed a profit, there would be no resources available for capital development or plant expansion, unless they were taken from public revenues secured from taxation. And failing some such outside source from which losses could be recouped, the companies would be bound sooner or later to liquidate. In an economy of public industrial operation, as in Russia, all surpluses earned in producing units are turned in to the national treasury and from there are allocated into the desired new channels of capital development or other use. And if no surpluses result, the administrators are presumably "on the carpet."

As to profit as the measure of gain which is acceptable to owners or tolerated publicly, our economy has no absolute standards. We do, however, invoke accepted methods of corporate taxation including on occasion "excess profits" taxes. Both of these are designed to put some check on what may publicly be regarded as "excessive" earnings. In short, the avowed purpose of making a profit today is qualified and modified for administrators by recognised social controls which the people as a whole have seen fit to impose. Indeed, if we look at those companies defined by law to be "public service companies," we see an even more stringent and explicit imposition of limits upon the profit which may be earned.

However central and single the profit-making motive and aim may seem to be, it is thus increasingly a *qualified* aim—qualified by a public opinion which is variously expressed, no less than by the outlooks of individual administrators, to say nothing of labour union officials and workers. There thus arises in ways not as yet completely formalised a disposition to pose tacitly through one or another more or less public channel such questions as: How much profit; for whom; and by what means? It is of prime operating importance for the enlightened administrator to be aware that these questions are much in the air and have on occasion to be specifically confronted by him before one or another tribunal. Such awareness increasingly acts as a modifying influence upon the singleness of his aim in the direction of profit.

Another modifying factor has also to be reckoned with. Stockholders and top managers are generally no longer the same persons. The head executives of a large number of businesses have small holdings of the stock of the company which they manage. They are themselves, at least legally, in the position of hired aides and not owners. Their connection with the stockholders is not close, usually confined to the reporting of results at annual meeting. And if these results are on the black side of the ledger, if a reasonably good showing is being made, few, if any, stockholder questions arise. The pressure upon the salaried administrators of a business to keep a single-track mind which subordinates all else to profit making is thus considerably tempered. Significantly, the exception to this statement is usually in those cases where an executive bonus tied to profit amounts is in effect. But to lay it down as an unassailable dogma that considerations of profit making constitute the all-controlling and simon-pure aim of administration is just not the truth. Motivations are far more complex and plural.

5. The personal aspects of organisation aims are an actuality which is often slighted in the effort to understand motivating forces in organisations. The desire to be accorded prestige for a job well done, or to have a status of recognised eminence, or to have the reputation for being a conspicuous success in some or all phases of management, or even just to exercise power because ego-maximisation is a satisfying experience (see Chapter 8)—all of these are possible manifestations of the administrator's *personal* objectives. Every experienced executive and observer have known numerous instances where such personal influences have proved to be stronger motives than all the rest which might have weight. True, it is frequently impossible to separate these personal preconceptions, ambitions, outlooks and vanities from the rationalised pretexts set forth by executives as to their aims in advancing certain policies. And such personal predilections of interest or prejudice can become so controlling that organisations are actually hampered and weakened in their effective operation. Instances come readily to mind of top executives who have taken such a "die-hard" view of dealings with organised labour, for example, that it has taken the corporation years to overcome the attitudes of conflict and hatred that they have thus been responsible for creating.

On the more positive side, also, top executives with strongly personalised aims and special interests will spend money on their pet projects out of all rational relation to other expenses or to demonstrable benefits. Instances of this are a passion for immaculate factory house-keeping, the maintenance of an elaborate company hospital, the conduct of a splendid company lunchroom or motion picture theater at an operating loss.

Supporting evidence for this view, if such be needed, is interestingly presented by that discerning student of administration, Chester I, Barnard, formerly President of the New Jersey Bell Telephone Company, when he says:

In the broad sense that no business can escape its balance sheet, it is true that the economic or money motive governs the administration of business. Nevertheless my observation in several different well-managed businesses convinces me that business decisions are constantly being made that are not based on economic motives. This is something that businessmen seldom admit, and of which they are frequently unaware. Prestige, competitive reputation, social standing, philanthropic interests, combativeness, love of intrigue, dislike of friction, technical interest, Napoleonic dreams, love of accomplishing useful things, desire for regard of employees, love of publicity, fear of publicity—a long catalogue of non-economic motives actually condition the management of business, and nothing but the balance sheet keeps these non-economic motives from running wild. Yet without all these incentives I think most business would be a lifeless failure. There is not enough vitality in dollars to keep business running on any such scale as we experience it, nor are the things which can be directly purchased with money an adequate incentive.

So important is it for all of us, including administrators, *to stand well in the eyes of those whose approval we desire* that if one can know the type of people with whom a given administrator hobnobs and "compares notes," one will have a good idea of the general line which his decisions are likely to follow. Tell me whose commendation the executive seeks, and I will tell you in which way his purposes and policies will be slanted.

It is because of this truth, also, that the selection of the business, industrial, commercial and trade organisations with which companies and executives become associated is of importance. For the policies and platforms of such associations can readily color the individual thinking of members and give them moral reinforcement on behalf of those policies which the association supports. Enlightened leadership in all types of business associations can thus have a far more beneficent influence than will ever appear on the surface or be recorded in its reports.

All of this is simply the recognition of what should be the obvious fact, namely, that scientific objectivity and a disinterested balancing of all possible aspects of corporate aim on the administrator's part are an ideal which organisations may hope to approximate but rarely achieve. The capacity to weigh evidence and to generalise, unaffected by one's personal interests, is not a common attainment. But there is reason to believe that this is a capacity which education directed to this end can develop much more generally. Indeed, if collegiate schools of business did nothing more than inculcate this disinterested and objective problem-solving capacity in their students, they would be passing on a priceless boon.

6. A final and potent factor in the modifying of aims is the influence of public sentiment from various sources. To adjust to recognizable and important influences, demands and claims has thus become one aspect of aim which has now attained a new significance.

Among such influences is consumer opinion. But because it is a fairly familiar and recognised factor, it will not be here further elaborated upon.

Rather, certain other less emphasised public influences merit more explicit treatment. For it seems certain that these will increase in vigour and in range as time goes on. Mention has already been made of the regulative aspect of taxation over corporate financial operations. Labour laws of all kinds, social security legislation, antitrust laws, fair business practice requirements, financial reporting requirements for "listed" securities—these at once come to mind as instances of public rules within which the game of business has to be played. The corporation is a creation of the state, and the state properly specifies certain provisions requisite for retaining a franchise. And if the public conscience and public standards are more sensitive and more inclusive than formerly, these are facts to be reckoned with before rather than after offenses against these standards have been committed. Such matters, also, as adequate old age pensions, employee "welfare funds" and an annual wage are further examples of outside pressures for policy alteration which it will be impossible and undesirable to ignore. And when such pressures become imperious, they do in fact qualify present corporate aims. Indeed, to reckon with an anticipate the various changes in public, consumer, labour union and worker reaction—reflected in law, administrative decree or collective agreement provisions—becomes a major administrative responsibility. Only in the full acknowledgement of these interposing influences does the work of administration proceed intelligently. In fact, a stage seems to have been reached in public attitudes about numerous aspects of corporate operation where open resistance by corporate heads may lay them open to adverse sentiments harmful to their organisations.

There are still other less sharply focused sentiments abroad in the land of which it will be shortsighted for the administrator to be oblivious as he shapes his policies. One example of this, elaborated upon in a later chapter, is suggested by the recent comment of a prominent executive that "it is the job of management to make democracy work." If in important particulars our corporate agencies operate in what is publicly felt to be undemocratic ways, that fact can have adverse consequences. The American people may not yet know in any widely agreed and specific terms what they mean by "industrial democracy," but that somehow *corporate and other organisational controls and procedures have to be more democratic in nature* is a sentiment which is gaining unmistakable momentum in the American community. And it is a sentiment, no matter how crudely it may today manifest itself, to which corporate administrators surely have to become more sensitised. For many new expressions of desired changes in policies—legislative on the one hand and voluntary on the other—which otherwise may seem to some executives arbitrary, irrational, selfish and threatening to their customary freedoms are in reality manifestations of a groundswell of concern for an extension of democratic influences and of a kind of freedom which seeks to attain the general well-being of more and more citizens.

Another growing attitude which conditions managerial purpose is that it is necessary to reconcile so far as practical the personal desires and satisfactions of individuals with the announced aims of the agency which employs them. Persons have a justifiable integrity and worth in their own right; the fulfillment of personality potentials is a valid demand. What this means in terms of rounded life activities and its implications for the needs and desires of people at work has still to be spelled out. *But the purpose of such a reconciliation of personal and corporate goals in increasingly being recognised as imperative.* And it is a purpose, call it primary or secondary as you will, which requires a growing place in administrative thinking.

How these plural organisation and managerial aims come into being and how they are tempered by forces within and outside the organisation is what we have just been considering. The conclusion is clear that the so-called "legal" or "central" aim is rarely as absolutely in control as is often assumed. Other secondary, supplementing and supporting aims do and should have varying weight. And for the administrator to realise and be mindful of these other aims, without which he cannot achieve the primary one, becomes more and more crucial to wise strategy.

A second conclusion which emerges from this analysis of the several corporate aims is that not all of them are likely to have the same appeal for the rank and file. In fact, the workers may even oppose certain of these aims as they work out in practice. Or even if the purposes as such are not opposed, the going ways of realising them may give rise to conflicts of point of view or interest. Indeed, real divergences of outlook as between management and men may grow out of mistaken understanding, first, as to what purposes are in control and, second, as to what a specific group's true interests really are.

In short, if there are to be the necessary efforts toward a harmonising of purposes and reconciling of interests, if purposes are to be broadly shared and special group interests subordinated to larger loyalties, there has to be further exploration of the appeal of different purposes and of the ways and means of assuring their more inclusive acceptance. It is to this phase of the problem that we now turn.

5

Staff and Auxiliary Agencies

The traditional organisational pattern of the administrative branch of the government is departmental. But due to increase in departmental work and also due to the impact of the principle of specialisation, the departmental pattern has branched off into two new directions. This new trend is towards the development of Staff Agencies and Auxiliary Agencies as distinct from the 'Line' Agencies.

Staff Agency

In Public Administration, the top management, specially the Chief Executive, is burdened with diverse types of functions. Although it has to delegate the actual performance of many of its duties, yet it cannot delegate the responsibility of overhead management and general direction. It is vitally concerned with the formulation of policy, the duty of command, the problems of organisation and co-ordination, with finance, personnel and public relations. These functions can, in no case, be delegated. And yet all these cannot be performed by one man single-handedly. Hence arose the need of an expert staff, attached to the offices of the Chief Executive and the heads of Departments, to whom the executive may look for information and advice and for taking timely and considered decisions. Such services are called "Staff Agency".

The need of the Staff Agency is felt in two principal areas, namely, one, in management problems like organisation of jobs and personnel, smooth operation of interrelated functions and removal of frictions and differences, and two, in substantive problems of policy formulation e.g. the fixation of price of sugar cane. Now, these are highly technical and complicated functions which need considerable research and verification of facts and figures before a decision can be taken. Therefore, in every country there are legal statistical, financial, planning and other staff agencies attached to the Chief Executive and departmental heads.

Its Functions. The main functions of the Staff Agency have been very nicely summarised by Dr. L.D. White. They are:

"1. To ensure that the Chief Executive (and other officials at the top) is adequately and correctly informed.

2. To assist him in foreseeing problems and planning future programmes.

3. To ensure that matters for his decision reach his desk promptly, in condition to be settled intelligently and without delay; and to protect him against hasty or ill-considered judgments.

4. To exclude every matter that can be settled elsewhere in the system.

5. To protect his time.

6. To secure means of ensuring compliance by subordinates with established policy and executive direction."

Thus, the main functions of the Staff agency are to furnish to the head all relevant information regarding the case, to put up the case at the proper time and to offer its own advice on the matter. But beyond that it should not go. There sometimes develops a tendency either on the part of the operating head to assign operating duty to the staff or on the part of the staff to take power in its own hands. This is a very undesirable tendency. It divides responsibility within the department and causes jealousy among the subordinate operating officials. The staff agency is, really speaking; outside the direct line of administrative hierarchy. The line of command, authority and responsibility does not pass through it. It is an adjunct to, and not a part of, the office of the operating head.

Qualities of a Staff Officer. In view of the fact that the main duties of a staff officer are to plan, advise, suggest, and assist rather than to operate, qualities of an expert and not those of an administrator are required of him. So he must have the following qualities:

1. He must have a sound general knowledge of the whole administration rather than an expert knowledge of any one department. Of course, a departmental staff officer must have an expert knowledge of that department or branch of department.

2. He should have the capacity to negotiate rather than command.

3. He should prefer to work from behind the scene. In fact his duty is to tender his best advice to the chief and then to withdraw so as to give the chief time to take his own decision.

4. He should accept the decisions of his principal officer. His sole function is to give his advice to the best of his lights. It is no business of his to see that the principal officer accepts that advice or not. The officer is not bound to accept the advice of his staff. Therefore, if the officer does not accept the advice of his staff, he should not grudge even though the officer turns to be wrong. After all, it is the officer who is to shoulder the responsibility in either case. So the staff should ungrudgingly go on helping the officer in every matter irrespective of the fact whether his advice is being accepted or not.

Examples of Staff Agencies in the Central Government. The best example is the British Treasury which is not an operating agency in spite of its name. It merely acts as an agency of general direction, supervision and control over other services.

In the Government of India, the main staff agencies are:

1. Budget and Economic Affairs Department in the Ministry of Finance which not only formulates the financial policy of the Union Government but also exercises a sort of supervision, and control over the operating services. This control, however, is not as great as that of the British Treasury.

2. The Cabinet Secretariate has now become a very effective and dependable agency for the performance of staff duties to the Cabinet as a whole and to the Cabinet Committees.

3. The National Planning Commission, above all, has come to occupy the primary position in the staff agencies of the Indian Government. It not only plans but even supervises the implementation of the plan to some extent.

In U.S.A. the general Staff agency is composed of the President's Executive office which is composed of two parts, namely:

1. The White House office consisting of Presidential secretaries, administrative assistants, personal secretary and an executive clerk.

2. The Bureau of Budget which, though formerly was under the Treasury Department, has now become administrative research and planning unit of the Federal Government.

Besides these, the National Resources Planning Board which was appointed in 1933 functioned till 1948 as a general Staff Agency. Similarly the War Department during the time of war, functioned as a general staff agency.

The Auxiliary Agency

Till recently every department or administrative agency used to be a self-contained unit. Like the family it performed all the activities necessary for its maintenance. But since recent times through the process of specialisation, the primary activities of the department began to be differentiated from its secondary activities. And as the house-keeping activities are almost similar in all the departments, they began to be organised into separate, single purpose, and specialised offices. They are known as Auxiliary or Institutional activities.

This tendency of organising the secondary or subsidiary functions of the line agencies into different agencies has grown due to two main factors. First was the rapid expansion of public business in volume which began to overtax the top management of the line agencies. The second was the fast developing tradition of specialisation. So, while formerly each department used to keep its own accounts, handle its own funds, purchase all its supplies and equipment, hired and fired its own employees and made its own contracts, now these functions are separated from the primary responsibility for which the department came into existence, and are organised under separate agencies, thus enabling the line agencies to maintain themselves as working organisations. The first agency to develop on these lines was the Central Accounts and Audit Department, the second was the Public Service Commission for the recruitment of personnel, the third was the Central Purchasing Agency; then came the Central Department of Printing and Stationery and so on.

Distinction between Auxiliary and Functional or Primary Activities: Willloughby defines Functional or Primary activities as "those which a service performs in order to accomplish the purpose for which it exists", and Institutional or Auxiliary activities as "those which it is necessary that a service should perform in order that it may exist and operate as a service." For example, the primary activity of the Home Affairs Department is to maintain peace and order inside the country, while its auxiliary activity is the recruitment of employees, the purchase of furniture and stationery, the keeping of accounts etc. The efficiency and economy in an administration depends upon the proper performance of the auxiliary activities. Therefore, it will be in the fitness of things to analyse this distinction.

1. Functional Activities are an end in themselves, while the auxiliary activities are only a means. They are necessary to maintain the department as an institution.

2. Functional activities, being an end in themselves, are represented by a product in the form of work performed. Hence the question of economy does not arise in their case. So long as the returns received are proportionate to the expenditure made, it may be desirable to expand, rather than curtail, the operations. But such is not the case with auxiliary activities. They are performed purely with an idea of bringing economy in the department.

3. The whole problem of administration—its efficiency, economy etc., depends upon the proper performance of institutional activities. The qualities of the employees will depend upon how they were recruited and trained, how the services are organised and the efficiency of work will depend upon their personal qualities, upon the way in which their services are employed and their work is managed.

4. In case of functional activities, the problems of organisation and procedure are different in each case. The organisation and procedure of the Foreign Affairs Department have to be of a different type from those of the Home Affairs department. But they are similar, if not identical, for all the auxiliary services.

5. Functional Activities are meant for rendering some service or the other to the public. But institutional services have no relation with the public. They only cater to needs of the various departments.

Distinction between Auxiliary Activities and Staff Activities: The Auxiliary Activities should be differentiated from the staff activities. They differ in the following respects:

1. The auxiliary services are operating services, whether they are recruiting boards, purchasing agencies, stationery stores, they perform some operation. But staff services are only thinking, observing, planning and advising agencies.

2. Auxiliary agencies are not concerned with major substantive policies, while the staff is concerned with the formulation of major policies and even with matters of reorganisation etc.

The two services are, however, similar in one respect. Both exist to facilitate the work of the main operating agencies, namely the Line Departments. They do not have a locus standi of their own.

Need of Special Organisational Units for Auxiliary Activities. As the nature of these activities is different from that of the Functional activities and they are all of a uniform nature, they should be put under separate organisational units. This will have the following advantages:

1. The operating officers will be relieved of duties regarding these secondary activities and thus will be able to pay full attention to their main duties.

2. This system will ensure specialisation of functions and placing them into the hands of experts.

3. It will have the advantage of increased scope of operations and reduced unit costs, such as in large scale purchasing, common godowns, storage etc.

4. It secures the advantage of closer supervision of these functions and more rapid introduction of the most improved methods as each service will be concerned with only one type of activity.

5. It secures economy in administration as it avoids duplicity of work in different departments.

6. The Chief Executive may give special attention to the enforcement of economy through auxiliary activities.

While grouping of auxiliary services into separate organisational units is now a general tendency and to a certain extent a desirable one too, we should not forget that the nature of auxiliary work is primarily facilitating rather than controlling. This tendency, if carried too far, may really result in a definite harm to the administration. The main defects that may occur by this process are:

1. .There is the danger lest "the process of tearing the departments apart in order to establish auxiliary functions may go beyond the point where efficient and responsible administration results." After all, the auxiliary services belong to the department in which they occur and hence they do have some sort of peculiarity which differentiate them from the similar activities of other departments.

2. There are inherent dangers of encroachment by the auxiliary agencies upon the responsibilities of the line agencies and therefore an undercurrent of conflict begins to run between them. This happens specially when the Central Personnel Agency is given certain authority in disciplinary matters.

3. The separation of these functions from the parent departments tends to complicate the organisation and to create additional points of friction in the administrative machinery. And if the Chief Executive does not keep sufficient supervision over these activities, they may lead to departmental rivalries and frictions.

In conclusion, we may say that organisation of Auxiliary Agencies may be useful for large scale organisations but not for small ones. "While, therefore, the auxiliary agencies have," says Dr. White, "ample justification under favourable circumstances, there is a point of marginal utility beyond which the unity and sense of full responsibility of the line department becomes the greater good."

Willoughby has suggested a standard scheme of such an organisational unit which will comprise of the following divisions:

1. Office of the Chief Clerk (i.e. Secretary).
2. Division of Mails and Files.
3. Division of Personnel.
4. Division of Supplies.
5. Division of Accounts.
6. Division of Printing and Publications.
7. Office of Superintendent of Buildings.

Willoughby further suggests that there should be a Bureau of Administration in each Department to supervise and co-ordinate the work of different units. This would mean that "there will be in each department a single service presided over by an officer of high rank having direct responsibility for the performance of this distinct category of administrative duties and constituting in effect, the general or business manager of the department." This officer-in-charge of the bureau should be a Deputy Secretary who should be an expert in this branch of administration.

Such a scheme, according to him, will have the following advantages:

1. Responsibility will be definitely located at one point.

2. Appointment of an official of higher rank to head this branch will lay the basis for the establishment of uniformity and standardisation.

3. It will facilitate formulation of budgetary estimates.

6

The Department

The traditional form of the 'line' agency is departmental. A department is the fundamental organisational unit of administrative which actually carries on the governmental operations. There are various problems involved in the departmental structure. The more important of them, which we shall study here, are the basis of organisation of department, the location of authority, the problem of Field Establishments and the problem of co-ordination.

Principles of Organisation

There are four different principles or bases of organisation of departments, viz., (1) The Financial or Purpose Principle, (2) The Process or Professional Principle, (3) The Clientele or Commodity Principle, and (4) The Geographical Principle.

1. *The Financial Principle.* Where administrative business is organised on the basis of the nature of function of purpose, then the system of organisation is called Functional. Thus, for the regulation of trade and commerce in the country, there may be a Department of Commerce, for the development of Industry, a Department of Industry and so on.

2. *The Process Principle.* Where administrative business is organised on the basis of process of nature of the activity, then the system of organisation is called as the Process or Professional Principle. Thus for the legal activities of the Government, there may be a Law Department, for the medical and other health activities, there may be a Health Department.

3. *Clientele or Commodity Principle.* Where administrative business is organised on the basis of the clientele, the class

or classes of people for whom the service is meant, then the system of organisation called Clientele Principle. Such a department looks after all Department for Schedule Classes and Tribal Areas are examples, in question. Instead of a class of people, a department may be based upon the class of commodity or commodities. For example, we may have a Food Department.

4. *Geographical Principle.* Where administrative business is organised on the basis of geographical area, then the system is called Geographical. Thus we have Foreign Affairs Department which is concerned with all the problems of the country falling outside its national boundaries. A still clearer example is the Damodar Valley Corporation which is concerned with all the development schemes in that region.

It is difficult to discuss the advantages and disadvantages of each of these systems in the space at our disposal. The question has been very beautifully discussed by Luther Gulick, in the chapter entitled "The theory of Organisation" in 'Papers on the science of Administration." Suffice it to say here that much depends upon the exigencies of the time, rather than upon abstract principles. Historical traditions and political considerations also sometimes play a part in determining the basis of organisation. And in actual practice it has been seen that governments usually follow more than one principle in organising their departments. But inspite of all that is stated above, the fact remains that the functional principle is coming more and more in vogue as it has a number of advantages over the others. It has been called the Scientific Principle of Organisation. Its advantages are:

1. It is quite in consonence with the principle of division of labour and speculisation of functions. Unfunctional departmental bring about efficiency, speed and economy is administration.

2. It is based upon expediency. The other principles are difficult to be worked at. In the process principle, it is difficult to clearly evaluate the nature of the activity. Moreover, it will cause unnecessary division of function. For example, even

if you have a separate Medical Department that will require the collection and compilation of certain statistics which will be done by some other Department. Similarly in the other two systems the principle of specialisation does not work at all as the same unit will have to perform different types of functions.

3. Apart from expediency, this system will make possible the concentration in single head of full responsibility for all matters pertaining to general field of endeavour.

Organisation of a Department

Even if the department is a unifunctional unit, it has to perform diverse types of activities. For the maintenance of peace and order—the main substantive function of the Home Affairs Department it has to organize a police force, establish and maintain law courts, keep a watch over foreigners inside the country and so on. Besides carrying on the major substantive function, each department has to keep its own establishment section. Thus each department has to be divided into Divisions and sub-divisions. There are two main methods of dividing departments—the horizontal and the vertical. In the horizontal system, the department is divided according to the several aspects or stages or question, each in charge of a separate head. But in the vertical system, each department is divided according to major subjects and then, each division is sub-divided according to several aspects. See diagram 6.1.

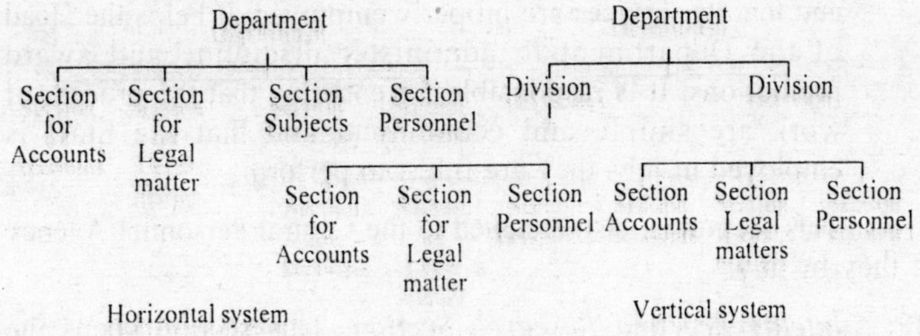

Diagram 6.1.

The horizontal system is to be preferred to the vertical system due to the following reasons:

1. It tends to promote specialisation within the divisions of the department and avoids duplicity of work, while the vertical system has nóne of these advantages.

2. It makes delegation of functions and responsibility to subordinate officials easy and thus avoids too much concentration of work in the hands of the Head of the Department.

3. It allows focussing of discussion at the earlier stages.

4. It enables the Head to exercise general supervision and control rather than the bothered about details.

Usually a Department is divided is divided into two divisions or bureaus—one dealing with institutional activities and the other (there may be more than one under this category) with the Primary activities of the Department. The Division for institutional activities generally has the following sections:

1. *Registering and Recording Section.* It receives, letters, despatches, papers etc. from the public or other departments. Its work consists of registering particulars of receipt in a book and filling on card-indexing the letters etc. and send them, after registration, to the appropriate officer in the department.

2. *Establishment and Organisation Section.* It is concerned with questions of internal Organisation and Staff of the Department. It has to see that the Department has adequate, but no more than adequate, Staff for the performance of its work, that the Staff is well-qualified and well remunerated and that its services are properly employed. It helps the Head of the Department to administer discipline and award promotions. It is responsible for ensuring that the process of work are simple and economical and that the Staff is employed in jobs they are fittest to perform.

This section is, also attached to the Central Personnel Agency if they by any.

3. *Intelligence and Research Section.* This section keeps the statistical records for the use of the department, conducts research and enquirer for the general run of the departments, and also conducts special enquiries regarding the special economic or other problems of the Department.

The Section also is attached to the Central Department of Research and Intelligence, if there be any.

4. *Finance and Accounts Section.* Although over-all control over finances is exercised by the Finance Department, yet strict control and supervision from within is essential for ensuring efficiency and economy in the Department. Hence each Department maintains a Section. The chief duties of this Section have been thus summarised by Sir H.N. Bunhury, himself an Administrator of repute.

    1. Preparation of estimates.
    2. Financial review of expenditure.
    3. Advising or deciding as to transfer of votes.
    4. Seeing that expenditure is properly brought to account.
    5. Advising in all matters affecting the expenditure of the Department. In India, this Section is under a Financial Advisor, who is an officer of the Finance Ministry.

5. *General Section.* If there is a large number of Sections for the performance of primary activities, then there is usually a General Section for supervising work of other Sections, and for debating and deciding on questions affecting the Department as a whole. This Section is directly under the Head of the Department.

For the performance of the primary functions, there may be one or more divisions, each under the charge of a Deputy Secretary. Each Division may be further divided into branches, each under the charge of an Under Secretary. The Branches themselves comprise of a number of Sections, each under the charge of a Superintendent (now known as Section Officer in India).

Besides the Central Office, there may be field establishments if the work of a Department extends outside the H.Q. In the Government of India, they are known as Attached and Subordinates offices.

Thus, the typical organisation of a Department will look like chart shown in Diagram No. 6.2 on p. 150.

ORGANIZATION OF A DEPARTMENT

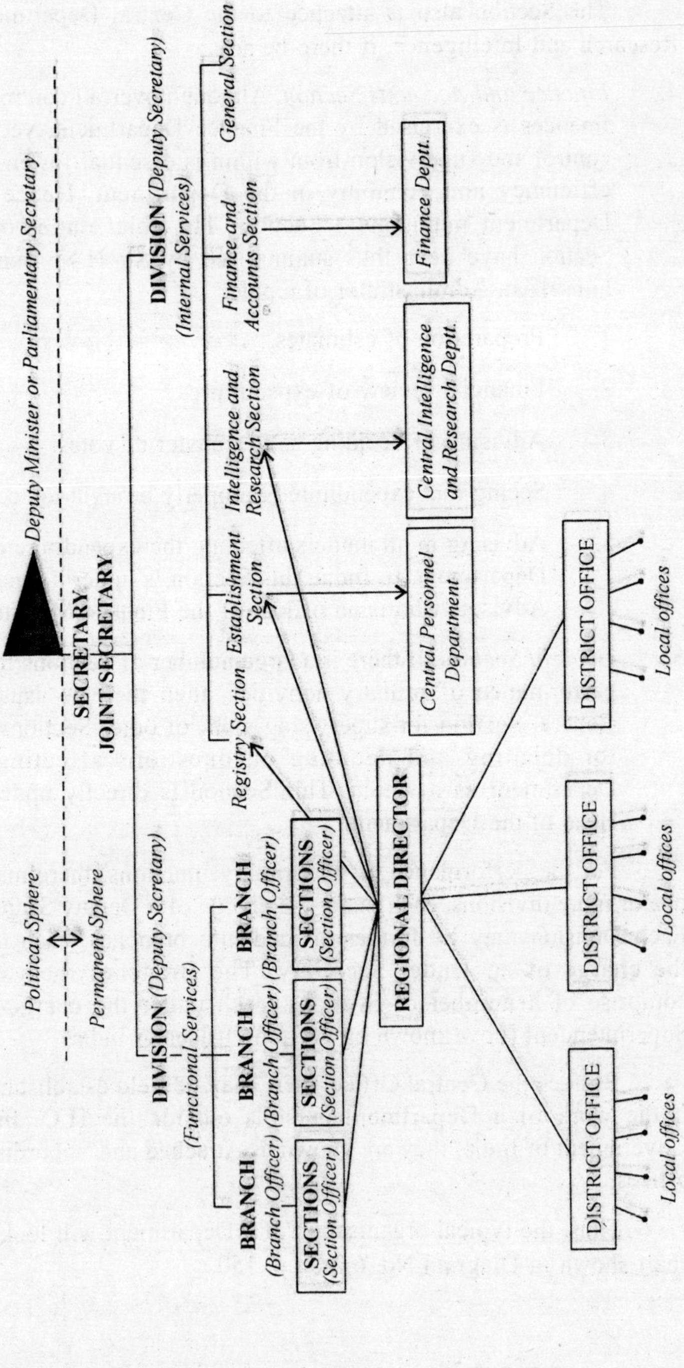

Location of Authority

The next problem with regard to the internal organisation of a Department is that of location of authority. That is, whether administrative authority should be vested in one person or a body of persons? There are two main systems *viz.,* the Bureau system and the Board or Commission system.

Bureau System. If administrative authority within a department is vested in a single individual, then it is called a 'Bureau system'. It is this system which is usually followed in the government departments.

Board or Commission System. If administrative authority within a department is vested in a plural body, then it is called a 'Board' or 'Commission' system.

Which System to be followed and where? Although it is difficult to lay down any hard and fast rule with regard to location of authority, yet certain principles may here be stated without much fear of contradiction. They are:-

1. "As a canon of correct administrative practice it may be laid down that where the work to be done is essentially of an administrative character, the Bureau system should be followed."

This is so because the efficient operation of administrative activity requires unity of command, quickness in decision and promptness in performance. All these things are possible only when authority is vested in a single individual. Moreover, it keeps the cost of overhead administration reasonably low.

2. "Where the duties to be performed involve the exercise of discretion on an important scale in the formulation and adoption of politics (such as, drafting of rules and regulations affecting private citizens), and in the adjudication of claims, the Board or Commission system should be adopted."

Where the operating service has also to perform in addition to its administrative function, sub-legislative or sub-judicial functions, there the Board or Commission system is to be preferred.

In short, Board or Commission system is to be preferred in functions which involve wide discretion, mature views and considered decisions as they can be better performed by a number of individuals combined rather than a single individual.

The Board or Commission system is usually followed in the followed conditions:

(i) Where the function is of a quasi-legislative or quasi-judicial nature, *e.g.*, the Railway Board in the Government of India.

(ii) Where the duties of a service call for wide discretionary powers *e.g.*, the Central Board of Revenue or the Public Service Commission.

(iii) Where it is desirable to have a number of different interests represented *e.g.*, Arbitration Board of Industrial dispute.

(iv) Sometimes, this system is also followed in order to give representation to different political parties. For example, the Tariff Commission of U.S.A. This system is called the Bi-Partizan system there. This system, however, is not advisable and there is no example of this system in the Government of India-whether at the Centre or in the State.

3. There are certain services whose duties are both administrative as well as quasi-legislative or quasi-judicial, for example, Public Health, Public Education, Charities, Police, etc. The legislature generally delegates certain authority to these agencies for making rules and regulations and sometimes also for adjudicating in disputes between the public official and private citizens. In such services a mixed system of organisation is followed. For example, in the Education Department, law provides in some States for a Board of Education as well as for a Superintendent of Education (the D.P.I.). The Board is vested with sub-legislative and supervisory powers, while the Director, with administrative powers. In certain cases, the Board is legally

vested with all the powers, sub-legislative or administrative. But for practical purposes, it delegates administrative powers to an Executive Officer. Thus the administrative officer comes under the supervision of the Board. Such is the case with Executive Officers of Municipal Boards in the Punjab.

Distinction between Board and Commission. Generally no distinction is made between Board and Commission. The two terms are commonly used interchangeably. But acutely there does exist a distinction between the two systems.

Willoughby defines Board thus: "A board, properly speaking, is a group of members who are required to act collectively upon all maters falling within their jurisdiction." That is, whether it is a function of farming rules or of supervising that work of administration, the Board functions as a corporate body. Of course, for the sake of convenience, the Board may function through committees composed of smaller number of members. But the ultimate responsibility is that of the Board as a whole. No member can be individually held responsible for any function of the Board. For example, Municipal Board in India.

But a Commission, again in Willoughby's words "is a group of members having the duty not only of acting collectively as a board, but also of serving individually as heads of organisation units that have been set up for the performance of administrative work that has to be done." In some states of U.S.A. Municipal Boards are organised on Commission basis.

Bureau System. The Bureau or Single Administrator system is to be preferred in fields where broad policies and objectives have been accepted, standards have been developed and public interest has been fully defined and accepted but there remains only the direct performance of work. "Effective performance of work, singleness of purpose and unity of command and direction-these things are possible only in the Bureau system. Alexander Hamilton has beautifully summed up the merits of this system. "It would give us", he says, "a chance of more knowledge, more activity, more responsibility and, of course, more zeal and attention."

Top Management within the Department

The organisation of a large-scale body falls into three well-defined zones, namely, top management and the middle management and the rank and file. Although there can be no hard and fast line of demarcation between them, yet the levels of work and responsibility are well-marked, at least in Britain and Inida. In Britain the services are separately organised for these levels of work. There are Administrative Service for top management, Executive Service for middle management and Clerical Service for rank and file. In India, though the demarcation is not so well-marked, yet the top-management is manned by members of the Indian Administrative Service, middle management by the Secretariat Service and other field officers and the rank and file by the Clerical Service.

The top-management consists of political as well as administrative personnel. In India the political side comprises of Cabinet Ministers, Ministers of State and Deputy Ministers and the administrative side of Secretaries, Joint Secretaries and Deputy Secretaries. We are here concerned with this part of top management.

The top management is mainly concerned with direction and control-direction "in the sense of providing for the right kind of action" and control as "looking toward the attainment of accountability for and in the execution of policy." These terms, in actual practice, include a variety of functions. For example, direction includes planning, co-ordinating and programming, while control involves organisation, supervision, documentation and reporting Besides, there are certain functions in top management which involve both direction and control at one and the same. For example, budgeting is a tool of planning and at the same time a method of accountability. Similarly personnel administration serves both direction and control. Although formulation of policy is, theoritically, the function of the political head, yet actually the top administration has a lot to do in this sphere. Government work is basically a team work. As such, all its functions, whether of policy-formulation or of policy-execution, have to be done by the whole team. The rank and file collect the data, the middle-management arrange it and the top management, on the basis of this systematised material, formulate the policy. Of course, the final word of approval or disapproval is left for the political head. There may be cases where the bread bases of a policy may emanate from an enthusiastic Minister. But they would be, for most part vague and would remain mere dreams unless given a practical shape by the top management. Modern administration is a highly technical affair which is, day by day, going far beyond the comprehension of a lay politician as a Minister is. Therefore, whatever theoretical objections to the growing powers of the public servants there may be the powers and influence of the expert administrators of the top and middle management will go on increasing.

Top management in a large-scale department is a very complex task. Beside the normal managerial functions, it has to prepare notes, reports and information for the legislature, press and the public. It has to furnish the minister with all sorts of information required or likely to be required by him and by the legislators through interpellations, short notice questions and by committees of the legislature. It has to gather information which the Minister concerned has to supply to his fellow party men outside the government, to pressure groups and to his constituents. It has to prepare press communiques, reports and circulars. It has also to supply information regarding legal matters pending in law courts. Dr. White has aptly remarked that "on the normal management job is piled the urgent necessity of dealing with legislators and their communities, party leaders high and low, the press, and important organised, often highly vocal, groups affected by the work of the agency. Questions of legal authority, cases before the courts, perplexities of inter-agency co-ordination, and problems of public opinion all complicate the task."

Above all, the top management has to co-ordinate the various inter and intra-departmental agencies. On the one hand, it has to serve as a link between the Cabinet and the Civil Service and on the other, it has to co-ordinate the activities of the various departments, commissions, boards and divisions. Further, it has also to assimilate the activities and energy of the various technical agencies into the general administrative business of the state. In Britain they are called as "intelligent amateurs" and according to Mr. T.A. Critchley, an ex-Civil servant of Britain, "they are concerned with policy, with directing the business of whole departments, with preparing new legislation and drafting regulations and circulars, with assisting and advising Ministers in the conduct of their parliamentary business, and above all with constructive long-term thinking and the co-ordination of the activities of government." Continuing his description, he writes, "They weigh technical against financial and economic arguments, and balance the results against political expediency."

For discharging these highly responsible and diverse types of activities, these officials must possess high qualities of mind and heart. "Their essential quality", to quote Mr. Crithley again, "is open-mindedness, with the ability to see all sides of a question." "Vision, imagination, drive, a capacious intellect, and a wide experience of men and affairs are part of the equipment of the men at the top…"

7

Middle Management and Field Establishment

While the top management is a narrow zone, the middle management is a wide and well-populated one. And as its area is wide, so are its functions varied. It forms a liaison between the policy-formulating part-top management-and the operating part-rank and file-of the department and as such its functions are partly supervisory and partly exceptional. Britain gives it a commendable name. "Executive Service" as differentiated from administrative on the one hand and clerical or operational on the other.

In India there is not one service for the performance of middle management functions. Each Ministry and Department has its own service recruited on different principles and under different conditions. But in spite of this diversity, there is one common factor to be traced in all these services. It is this that they are mostly recruited by the Civil Service Commissions under set rules and standards. And while India does not follow the rigidity of Great Britain in matters of educational standards, promotion and classification rules, the draws a fairly efficient staff for the middle management jobs. Moreover, India does not maintain rigid demarcations between the Clerical, Secretarial and Administrative services, although unlike U.S.A. it is highly difficult in India for a person recruited in the clerical service to rise to an administrative position. But he can certainly progress to the middle management post. Since independence it has also been possible, in the Education Ministry at least, for a lay man to occupy the top administrative post.

Middle management, in general, includes these posts: Branch Officers (Under-Secretaries), Section Officers, Heads of Attached and Subordinate office and departments, officers of field establishments, Heads of departmental auxiliary agencies, liaison officers *e.g.* budget and accounting officers, personnel officers, Public Relation Officers, Managers of Public Corporations and institutions and a host of intermediary supervisory posts.

Functions. "The task of middle management is to supervise direct and control the performance of business within the scope of law, policy and regulations already established, and to keep the financial and other records incident to the performance of work." Although it is not responsible for the formulation of administrative police, yet it is directly concerned with programme planning and the direction of operations. And as such, it does modify the details, if not the principles, of the policy to make it workable. Prof. F.M. Marx has rightly held that to a certain extent "the middle managers is always a policy-maker". "Not only does he take part", he observes, "in policy formulation by translating strategy into tactics, by tracing out top determinations into line activities, by framing operating policies under his own responsibility. He is also a policy-maker indirectly-by implicit or explicit reference, in his reporting function, to existing weaknesses in the administrative approach, inadequacies in current policies, and emerging problems and issues that warrant top-level consideration."

The main concern of middle management is the control and direction of operations, to get the job done. It involves matters like production standards, provision of personal, supply and equipment, good working conditions, the spelling-out of particular assignments, the definition of standards of performance, the establishment of recording and reporting requirements, the designation of appropriate methods and techniques, the determination of the most expeditious flow of work, the review of the end products, co-ordination of operations, maintenance of morale and with constant regard to improvement of operations. These matters call for skill, fidelity and capacity for leadership. These are the persons in administration who come in direct contact with the field-workers-the civilian army, who collect taxes, maintain law and order, regulate trade and business, and carry out various types of social and economic welfare activities for the public. Therefore, it is unto them to decide matters of what, when, where and how, to persuade the employees to give their best and utmost to the public service, to co-ordinate the related operations, and to seek the co-operation and sympathy of the public. They are experts in various parts of the administration activities, some in financial, some in commercial, some in public utility, some in educational, some in administrative and so on and thus make the backbone of administration.

The importance of middle management cannot be minimised, as it is here that the state objectives come to fruition, it is here that the citizens deal with the government after passing their first contact with the employees and it is here that the spirit and temper of the public service and efficiency and reputation of public administration are made. Moreover, middle management is a training ground from which a large part of the top management is drawn. As a matter of fact, middle management represents the most of the length of the "chain of command" and occupies a position wherein he is well acquainted with both the arts of giving orders and of obeying them. So serving his way up steadily, be usually makes an ideal commander.

The Problem of Delegation. Due to the fact that middle management occupies a central position in the hierarchical structure, it is engaged in a two-way traffic. On the one hand, as the agent of the policy-makers *i.e.* top management—it has to give a practical shape to the policy and pass it on to the base of the hierarchy-the field operators. On the other, as the master of operations, it has post convey the needs and difficulties of the operations to the top. So while his internal position in the hierarchy, compels him to look for the signal from above, his operational responsibilities compel him to face downward, towards the detailed transactions at the base of the hierarchy. His attention, is, therefore, persistently drawn in two opposite directions. The impact of these two opposite pressures taxes his energies very greatly.

But as he is the person on the spot in-charge of the operations in whose technique he is an expert, certain top-managerial powers should necessarily be delegated to him. Moreover, the top-manager himself cannot go beyond the "span of control." This delegation of powers, however, is not so spontaneous in actual practice. The top-managers, conscious of their responsibility to their political master, and the political head, in turn, conscious of his immediate responsibility to the Parliament and ultimate responsibility to his electors, do not want to shift the level of decision-making down. Specially in a period when the State is rapidly changing from a regulatory pattern to a social welfare pattern, as in India at present, the machinery, designed in and for the old set-up, fails to bear the pressure of the new set-up. Hence the informal delegation of functions no longer serves the purpose. Radical reforms in organisation and procedure are, therefore, called for and formal rules of delegation are required. In fact, in a dynamic and developing situation, the need is to have a permanent organisation to look after the working of the administrative machinery constantly and to keep maintaining the balance in the relationships of the different parts of the machinery. In a developing state more and more powers will have to be delegated to the middle management. And because of this, besides others, the top management will have to be more vigilant—vigilant not in the sense of keeping greater control over the operational activities but of getting greater insight into the working of the administrative machinery, so that they may understand the needs and requirements of the middle management.

In India the greater difficulty, it seems to the author, has been the lack of the proper understanding of the problems of middle management by top management. No doubt, the facts that the deterioration of "the quality of personnel and supervision" and "the natural desire of the new Ministers, conscious of their responsibility to the Parliament, to be consulted or kept informed before the issue of orders even in comparatively unimportant matters" in the post-independence period, as Shri S.B. Bapat points out, are responsible for the tendency of shifting decision-taking to the higher level of the hierarchy, are true. But there is a greater cause of the development of this tendency and that is the lack of understanding of the managerial problems of the modern welfare administrative activities on the part of the top administrative officers who were trained only to supervise the activities of a dominion government. The whole system of departmental and inter-departmental relationships will have to be changed and so will have to be the Manual of Office Procedure. The latter has been partly reformed. Through the efforts of the O and M Division, certain powers have been delegated to the Section officers in the Central Secretariat. But the main problem is with the regional agencies, and newly constituted Officers, Institutions and Corporations. Here the relations between the Secretariat and the Agencies have to be put on sounder basis.

Principle of Delegation. The concept of unity of command requires that every activity within the department must emanate from and must be controlled by, a single leader. But the principle of "Span of control" lays down that no control is practicable beyond a certain span. Hence we get a general principle of administration that *administrative policy should generally be centralised and operating policy decentralised.* That means that leaders at various levels of administration must delegate to subordinates the power to make operating decisions.

The success of administration depends mainly upon a sound system of delegation. Prof. J.M. Pfiffner states some human causes of failure to delegate which are generally at work in public administrative organisations. They are:

1. Persons who rise to positions of hierarchical leadership have more than normal egotism.

2. They are afraid that others will not make the proper decisions or carry them out in the desired manner.

3. They fear that disloyal or subversive power centres will develop among strong subordinates.

4. Strong, vigorous, and highly motivated persons become impatient with the slower pace and indecisiveness of subordinates.

5. In public administration, political considerations often make delegation difficult.

6. The cultural heritage of man has been one of authoritarian, patriarchal leadership; thus the practice of delegation is partly dependent on cultural change.
7. The act of delegation requires an emotional maturity which apparently is rare, even among successful persons.
8. The symbols of leadership (those personal qualities and traits which attract the attention of others) are inconsistent with the philosophy of delegation. Those striving to succeed must make themselves prominent.
9. Persons who desire to delegate do not know how.
10. They do not know how for at least two reasons: (i) the science of organisation and management is immature; and (ii) their work experience has not taught them to delegate because most organisations fail to practise delegation."

The causes noted above are of two types, *viz.*, personal and organisational. Hence the methods of developing a sound system of delegation also must be two, namely, changes in the personal traits and environments of man and certain reforms in the organisational set-up of public administration. For changing human behaviour, clinical psychology and psychiatry can do much by way of reducing anxiety and apprehensions among executives. Psychological tests may be employed to discover the emotional malad justments. This may be done both at the time of recruitment and of promotion. Similarly Psychological training may help much in developing superior-subordinate relationship.

On the organisational side, certain structural and procedural devices will be very helpful in developing a sound system of delegation. The first of these devices "is to spell out the authority and responsibility for each position in the management group." Each operating service should have an Organisation Manual and also an Office Procedure Manual, in which the *"sphere of descretion"* of each position should be fully described.

Second device is "the standardisation of operations" Standardisation when combined with "exception principle", makes delegation easy and automatic. For example, the incoming dak is distributed by the Central Registry Office of a Department to Section Officers on the basis of function and the Section Officers are given discretionary powers to decide as to which dak should go to the higher officials and which should be dealt with by himself. Thus only the selected important dak will go to the Branch Officers and higher officials of the Department.

In order to force the unwilling subordinates to accept responsibility in taking their own decisions, development of performance standards is a good device. This device requires the subordinate officials to plan and programme their own work. Thus he will be forced to determine how much work his section has to perform, how many man-hours would it take, and how should he arrange the performance of that work within time etc..?

Sometimes, officials feel that they cannot control a certain work effectively unless they are personally present. But the procedural device of internal checks and reporting can make it quite possible. Through specification and cost accounting, the head may prepare a budget of the scheme quite early and through the help of inspectors may supervise the whole work from the headquarters.

FIELD ESTABLISHMENT

It is popularly believed that the business of the government is carried in the capital of the nation or state. But actually hardly twenty-five per cent of the work of the modern government is centred in the capital seat, called Headquarters. More than seventy-five per cent of its work is carried on in wide areas scattered all over the country, called 'field'.

The problems of Operating Services having field establishments are in various ways different from the Departments having their activities centred in the Headquarters. There arise, in them, various questions of internal organisation of the field establishments and their relationship with the Headquarters.

1. Legal status of Field Stations. The first question is whether the existence of the Field Station is to be provided by a statute or by only an administrative order of the Executive. Upon this will depend the position and authority of the Station. If

established by the Legislature, it will enjoy greater security and freedom than if established by the executive.

Both the systems seem to be extreme. A better plan would be where the establishment and control of the Field Stations is left in the hands of the Executive but the Legislature should keep control over the determination of their number, location and grade through the system of grants. This will have a number of advantages, namely:—

(i) This relieves the legislature of overburden of work. The legislature can not legitimately decide technical questions of location, relations and organisation.

(ii) This will avoid rigidity in administration as statutory regulation usually creates.

(iii) The Executive, being in the know of things, may provide better arrangement. After all, government activities are of different nature, and hence each calls for a different system of organisation and relationships.

2. Grading and Classification of Field Stations into a Unified System. Operating Agencies whose operations are carried on wholly by field stations scattered all over the country, like the Railways and Post and Telegraph Departments, have to face a gigantic problem of finding a unified system of control and direction. All the stations are not of equal importance. So obviously they cannot be governed by one uniform standard. And yet some standards have to be laid down, otherwise the Headquarters may find it impossible to control these stations. Therefore, these stations are graded according to their to their importance and are classified, according to such grades, into a hierarchy of offices. Thus a single unified service emerges out of what otherwise looked like a heterogeneous sort of growth. Thus the Railway Stations, for example, may be graded, accordingly to their importance and volume of work, into stations of first, second and third importance. And thus we can put all the stations of first

importance into class A. of secondary importance into class B, and of third importance into class C.

The classification of field stations will serve a number of purposes, such as:

(i) It would make it possible to build up a hierarchy of offices constituting a single unified service.

(ii) This will help the government in prescribing a uniform system of work for all stations of the same grade.

(iii) In financial matters also, it would help the government in making allotments of money to these stations according to their grade. In the absence of such a system, the government would find it difficult to evaluate the needs of each station individually.

(iv) It would check extravagance, as it would be quite possible for the headquarters to get in idea as to the expenditure required in a particular class of stations.

(v) It would help the government in determining pay and allowances of the employees of the field stations of various grades as positions can be graded according to the grades of the stations.

(vi) Similarly, transfers of officers and employees from one station to another of the same grade can be easily made.

(vii) It would also help in the establishing of a proper system of promotions as officers and employees can be promoted, in consideration of their efficient work, from low grade stations to higher grade stations.

(viii) Likewise, if some officer or employee has to be demoted for inefficiency etc., he can be sent to a lower grade station.

3. Sub-Station, Another problem affecting the establishment of a proper system of relationships between the Headquarters

and the field stations is whether there should be sub-stations. If so, what should be their functions and relations to the station?

It should, first, be understood that sub-stations are not the same thing as lower grade stations. Although there may be no difference in the nature and importance of work between the two, yet there is a marked difference in respect of the status and authority. In case of sub-stations, the line of authority runs through the station of which they are a part, while in case of stations, whether of high grade or of low, the line of authority runs directly to the central office.

The system of establishing sub-stations under high grade stations in important areas has a number of advantages:

(i) It makes possible the development of more effective co-operative relations between contiguous stations.

(ii) Secondly, it makes it possible to decentralize responsibility and thus lessen the burden of the Central Office.

(iii) In many cases it would lessen the expenses and work involved in furnishing sub-stations with supplies and in subjecting them to physical inspection.

This system cannot be adopted, with advantage, in each and every department. For example, it cannot be adopted in the Railways Department but can be every usefully adopted in the Post and Telegraph Department. The latter needs decentralisation of responsibility but not so the former. Hence the Government of India employs this system in the latter not in the former.

4. Centralisation vs. Decentralisation. The next problem of field establishments is of determining as to how much power is to be given to field stations. In a centralised system, the field stations would work only as executing agencies. They will have no power of initiative or control over their activities or even their internal administration. But in decentralised system, the field stations are given authority of taking their own

decisions in certain type of matters and have full control over their establishment. An appeal may, of course, lie to the Central Office. How much power of initiative and control is given to a station depends upon the question as to how far the activity and authority is decentralised.

The centralisation or decentralisation of authority within an agency depends upon the following factors:-

(i) The factor of Responsibility,

(ii) Administrative factors,

(iii) Functional factors, and

(vi) External factors.

(i) The principle of administrative responsibility is deterrent to decentralisation of authority. According to this principle, every agency head is answerable for all the administrative activities of his department to the executive, and is responsible to the control budgetary, according, auditing and personnel agencies for the institutional activities of his agency and is responsible to the law courts for the integrity and legality of his agency's operations. As a result of this, agency heads hesitate to delegate wide discretionary authority to the field officials.

(ii) The second category of factors which effect decentralisation is administrative in character. It includes age of the agency, stability of its policies and methods, competence of its field officers, pressure for speed and economy and above all administrative sophistication. Age of the agency is basic to all other factors in this category. Every institution takes time to have a set organisation, a well qualified staff, set methods and technique and a uniform police. Passage of time gives wider experience in all these institutional problems. Moreover, time creates expertness and an exprit de corps among the personnel of the organisation. Therefore old agencies are more prone to delegate authority to their field officials. Then, the competence of the field officials themselves is another factor favouring decentralisation.

Similarly, demand for economy and speed work also demand decentralisation, as field establishments are nearer to their clientele than the officers at the Headquarters.

Lastly, administrative sophistication, that is, a professional approach to the question of delegation, is the most important factor influencing decentralisation. If the agency heads bear intelligent understanding and constructive approach upon field problems like the respective roles of functional experts and general administrators, the techniques for closer co-operation between the Headquarters and the field stations, the appropriate distribution of functions and authority etc., then there would be no hitch to decentralisation.

(iii) The third category of factors which influence decentralisation is functional in characters. This involves answers to questions like what different types of functions the agency performs? Do its function call for specialisation and for national uniformity or diversity in different regions? Multiplicity of functions within an agency is deterrent to decentralisation, because the different divisions-incharge of the different functions usually do not come to any agreement on the problems on the problems of field establishments. Hence they prefer to keep all powers to themselves. Similarly, the technical services dislike decentralisation because they would not like to delegate their functions, which, they feel, require expert knowledge to the field officials who usually are general administrators rather than technicians. Then, if the agency function needs uniformity in standards or results or in both, for example, income-tax collection then, centralisation is preferred. But if the function needs diversity, such as in agriculture, forest, water-resources activities, then, decentralisation is preferred.

(vi) Finally, there are external factors which influence the problem of centralisation *vs.* decentralisation. The more important in this category are factors like the necessity of bringing the citizens into the administrative process (as in development programmes) collaborating with other federal, states or local agencies (as in educational, public health and irrigational activities), and adapting field activities to political pressure.

The last factor, through not desirable, does sometimes affect the owner and authority of the field stations. The Ministers, in order to place some party leader or his own group of supporters, may sometimes delegate more powers to certain field stations in his department.

Merits and Demerits of the two Systems. Coming to the advantages and disadvantages of the two systems, centralisation has the following advantages:

1. It provides for a maximum of control by the Executive.
2. It ensures uniformity in policy, methods and technique.
3. It makes more difficult administrative abuses in such matters as employment and handing of personnel, purchase and use of supplies etc.

But the disadvantages of this system overbalance its advantages. Firstly, it delays in taking prompt decision and quick action. It creates red Taoism in administration. Secondly, It increases the cost of administration, because centralisation means large staff for inspection, control, reporting and auditing. It increases the travelling expenses and others. Thirdly, the Central Office has, for larger part, to act without the knowledge of local needs and conditions which local units can very easy get. Lastly, it makes administration very rigid. A government by procedure and precedents is, in this fast-changing age, a clog to progress and reform.

Decentralisation obviates all the above defects from administration. It given it flexibility, efficiency and economy. It democratizes administration and brings it nearer to the citizens. Further, it creates a field of training for the raw officials. This may be called an age of decentralised democracy. The more public welfare activities the States takes to itself, the more will its administration stand in need for decentralisation.

5. **Field-Headquarters Relationship.** The field-headquarters relationship is a major problem in Field Establishment administration. The connection between the Central Office and the field station may be organised in either of the two

ways, *i.e.* Functional a Multiple and Territorial or Unitary. If organised in Functional or Multiple way, then each functional division of the field station is directly responsible to its counterpart in the Headquarters, as in figure A, Diagram 7.1 on page 171. But if organised on territorial or Unitary basis, then each functional division of the field station is responsible through the station officer to the central officer as in Figure B. Diagram. The main difference between the two systems is that while in the Unitary system the head of the Station is "the general manager of the station in the fullest acceptance of the system", in the Multiple system "The station is looked upon as an assembly of units which are only loosely held together for matters of general administration by the authority of the head of the station." In the unitary system there is a unity of command. That is why this systems is also called as the Military system. In this system every instruction, order or communication passes from the agency head to the operating field units through the head of the field station. This, in a way, means the supremacy of the general administrator over the functional experts. It has a number of advantage:

Firstly, it avoids the general tendency to concentrate too much authority in the Central Office and thus to become unwieldy and unmanageable.

Secondly, it ensures enough flexibility to enable any arrangement to be made of the whole or any part, which may be found necessary or advantageous for reasons of policy, business or law, without affecting the business. The head of the station make any modification in the method, technique etc to suit the needs of his area without much affecting the agency work as a whole.

Thirdly, it ensures sufficient autonomy to each division of the field station from its central counterpart. This given life and responsibility to the administration of every unit.

Fourthly, under this system officers would be able to get good training in the technicalities and theories of the business by taking responsibility in lower units and will thus be able to move

Diagram 7.1 A

MULTIPLE SYSTEM

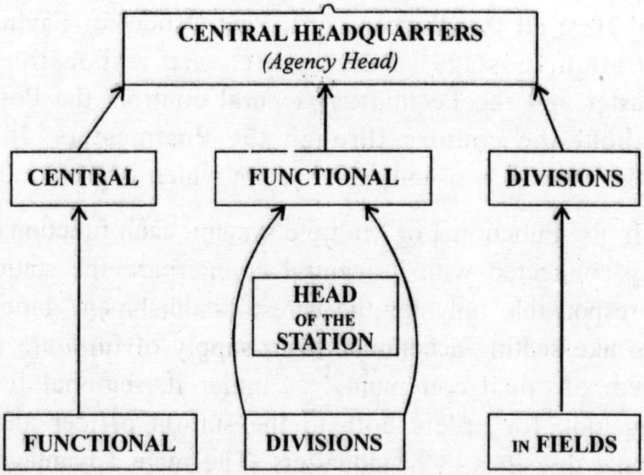

Diagram 7.1 B

UNITARY SYSTEM

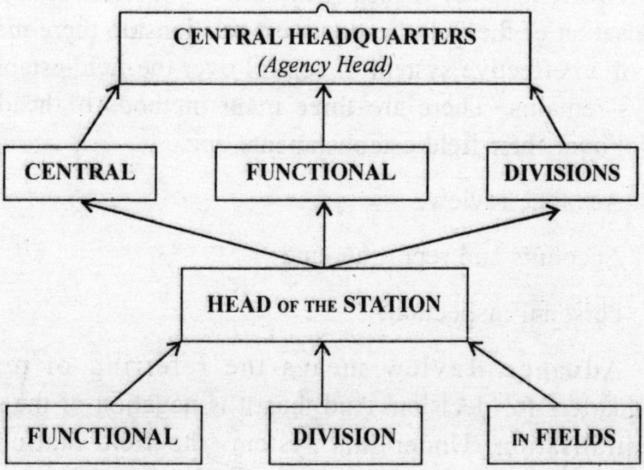

upward in the hierarchy. Thus there would arise a body oftrained men from whom the executive may choose at any emergency.

Lastly, this system is indispensable in agencies whose operations call for diversities in policy and programme according to the needs and requirements of the regions. Then, it is very useful for department whose functions are varied in nature and scope.

The Post and Telegraph Department in India follows this system. Here all the divisions of a Post Office for Saving Bank, Registration, postage, Delivery etc., are responsible to the Postmaster and the Postmaster-General controls the Post office throughout the country through the Postmasters. In Public Administration, it is usually this system which is preferred.

In the Functional or Multiple system, each functional unit is directly connected with its central counterpart, the station chief being responsible only for the barest establishment duties of the station, like seating accommodation, supply of furniture etc. It is a system of "dual command," as under it, regional functional experts look for orders both to the station officer and to the functional divisions at headquarters. The main advantage of this system is that technical operations in fields come under the direct control and direction of the central experts.

Control over Field Stations. Whichever system of organisation of the field-headquarters relationship there may be, the need of an effective system of control over the field establishments always remains. There are three main methods of headquarters' control over their field establishments, viz.

1. Advance review.
2. Accounts and reporting, and
3. Personal inspection.

Advance Review means the referring of matters to headquarters for decision. And thus it is negation of the system of decentralisation. Under this system, the field station will be concerned only with the investigation of a case arising in its area and then referring the case, with its recommendation and supporting data, to headquarters for the factual decision. Thus the central office gets full control over budget, personnel transaction, space allocation and other managerial facilities. It leaves practically no initiative to the field officers. Hence it is too reactionary a method of control and can be advised only in very exceptional cases, such as in periods of grave emergencies or crises.

Accounts and Reporting. Is a very effective method of control if properly organised. To be more effective, this system should be such as may secure the same data complied in the same form from all the field stations. Of course, very much will depend upon the fairness of the officials preparing the reports, because they will be the same persons who staff the field stations. The form and content of the reports should be so prescribed may go beyond the ability of the field officials to escape self-revelation of his errors. The data, thus collected, will enable the central office to compare the organisation, personnel, and operations of like stations and of the same station over a period of years. For this, the central office should maintain recording and reporting office. This would ensure an effective control.

Inspection: is essential to effective central control and hence must be adopted together with reporting. The Central Agency must maintain a Central Inspection Service. And if the Agency is very large, then it should maintain regional inspection services as well because it would be more effective and less expensive.

Field officers, however, feel irritant of inspections and tolerate the visits of inspectors with some distaste. Therefore, the inspectors should be unusually skilful. They should have the insight to enter into the interior working of the field activities but also have a fact as not to injure the feelings of the field officer. The inspector should go more as a counselor and less as a reporter. Instead of control or authority, he should try to keep stimulation and encouragement as the massif of his inspection visit. Another method of preserving the field officer's dignity is to let him see the inspector's report and let him submit his own comments upon it.

Problems of Multi-level Field Organisations. Agencies which have a very large clientele and a very large volume of field work, have to maintain different levels of field organisations. They may have regional sub-agencies, district and local offices. Considering the span of control, the Central office, in such agencies, cannot keep control, over all these areas. Hence many controlling and inspectional powers have to be delegated to the regional offices. So here arises a question of the relationship of the Central Office with the regional office and of the Central Office with the local office.

Strict hierarchical principle demands that the regional sub-agency should have exclusive inspectional authority over the local office in its region. This would mean that the Central agency will have control only over the regional sub-agencies. But it would be harmful to separate the policy-makers at the headquarters from the operators at the local levels. Hence a via-media should be found and that would be different in different agencies.

8

Management and its Tasks

"The heart of administration is the management of Programmes designed to serve the general welfare."

—Paul H. Appleby

The above statement is particularly applicable to India in the context of our planned economy geared up to achieve 'socialistic society' and 'welfare state'. Management is significant to every organisation, public or private, government or business, because it deals with a natural function of human society, namely, the fundamental endeavour of achieving objects. Business and complexity of the modern government have made the study of public management imperative.

Meaning

The term "Management" is used in many senses. It should not be confused with a person, a group of people, an economic, social or political class. Management is a process made up of definite function; those who perform these tasks are managers. No standard terminology has yet been evolved in this would satisfy everyone. Thus, Management is sometimes confused with Administration and sometimes with Organisation. Some writers equate the terms Administration and Management; others go further and susbordinste Administration to Management. The widely prevalent view, however, is of Meyer according to whom Management, in contrast to Administration, is a purely internal concept "characterizing and activity discharged within the framework of an organisation unit." There is a similar confusion as to the relationship between Organisation and Management. Some writers regard Organisation as merely one of the many functions of Management. Others use Organisation is a wide sense to comprehend Management. The fact, however, is that Organisation is the anatomy or the structure while Management is the physiology or the process. Drawing a distinction between the two terms, Seckler-Hudson says, "In this volume, Organisation will be regarded as the division and unification of effort towards some goal or policy. Management will be regarded as the collective utilisation of human rescourse and material in an effort to reach the known goal."

In other words, Organisation is the framework or apparatus of administration, while Management is the running of it. In the words of Milliett, "Public Administration is an instrument for the exercise of political power. Administrative organisation in the formalised structure for exercising certain power of government and Management is the group of person and the process by which organisation is animated to accomplish these ends." Management, thus, is a process of achieving a desired goal. However, Management is not doing things, but getting them done. Management achieve objectives through the efforts of others. According to Terry, "Management is the accomplishing or predetermined objective through the efforts of other people."

Nature

Some of the main characteristics of Management may be described as follows:

1. *Universality of the Management Process.* It means that the fundamental functions of Management are a sort of distinct skill and are performed by the manager regardless of the type of enterprise, the major activities or the level at which the manager works. Management, according to this view, is a technique which can be studied, and training in its application acquired. Such skill can also be transferred from one field to the other. The concept of generalist administration is predicated upon this assumption. There is a growing trend towards the transfer of personnel at the managerial level from public to business field and *vice versa.* It is in this sense that Management may be called a science.

2. *Management as Team Work.* Management is more than a single manager; it is collective endeavour by a team. The process of Management is not confined to one particular step or level in an organisation. It is present in the organisation at many different hierarchical level of authority and responsibility. In the words of Fayol, "Management is neither an privilege nor a particular responsibility of the head or senior members of the business; it is an activity spread, like all other activities, between head and members of the body corporate." According to him, the work of each class of employees in an industrial concern requires some managerial ability. The difference between types of activities is, thus, one of degree and not of kind; it may range from 5 per cent in the case of worker to 50 per cent in the case of manager.

3. *Management as Profession.* A profession has been defined as "a calling in which one profession to have acquired specialised knowledge which is used either in instructing, guiding or advising others." The present managerial class fulfils these conditions. Complete professionalisation, however, is not possible. There is greater possibility of it in staff positions than is operating ones. Again, management cannot be a profession in the sense of accreditation by a third party similar to admission to the bar or lilcence to partise medicine. However, professionalisation has its advantages. Apart from giving the managers a professional pride in their job, it also helps in the acceptance of the functions of management.

TASKS

If management is a process, it can be broken up into a number of tasks or functions. Gulick summed them up in a self-coined word POSDCORB-planning, organizing, staffing, directing, co-ordinating, reporting and budgeting. According to Terry, the four fundamental functions of Management are planning, organizining, actuating and controlling. To Fayol the process involved planning, organizing, coordinating and controlling. Seckler-Hudson takes a more comprehensive view and includes in this process policy formation; securing, locating and utilizing authority; planning: budgeting; staffing; operating; reporting; leading; directing; and controlling.

Millet distinguishes between the 'substantive or peculiar' problems of Management and the 'technical or common' problems. Substantive problems are peculiar to each agency of government and are related in the nature of service it renders. Thus, there are differences between the Management of education and police departments. On the other hand, technical problems are common to all large-scale organisations, and embrace the threefold task of work direction, work operation, and internal services. Work direction includes the problems of leadership, planning, communication, supervision and public relations. The common problem of work operation are organisation, personnel, budget and legal service. Internal service include 'house-keeping' functions like provision of physical plant, stores, record-keeping, etc. In brief, among the more important tasks of Management are: Leadership, Policy formulation, Decision making, Planning. Co-ordination, Communication, Delegation, Supervision and Public Relation. These functions of Management are discussed in the following chapters. Other function of Management, like Organisation, Staffing and Budgeting are dealt with elsewhere in the book. It should be borne in mind that no rigid lines can be drawn between different phases or Management process. Not are these tasks performed in a particular order. It is also possible to perform these tasks, or some of them, simultaneously. In practice, these functions are inextricably interwoven.

Participative Management

'Participative Management' is a currently fashionable phrase in Management circles. The term means participating by the employees in the decision-making process of the organisation they serve inso far as it affects their interests immediately or remotely. This is part of recent demand for 'democratic leadership' in organisation and 'human factors' in administration. It is said that 'participative management' tends to-

1. increase -the degree of 'we' feeling or cohesiveness that participants have with their organisation;
2. provide the participants with an overall organisational point of view instead of the traditionally more narrow departmental point of view;

3. decrease the amount of conflict, hostility, and cut-throat competition among the participants;
4. increase the individuals' understanding of each other which lelads to increased tolerance and patience towards others;
5. increase the individual's free expression of his personality which results in an employee who stick with the organisation; and
6. develop 'a work climate' as a result of the other tendencies in which the subordinates field opportunity to be more creative and to come up with ideas beneficial to the organisation.

It should, however, be remembered that 'participative management' is no magic formula to solve all employer-employee problems. Its successful introduction in an organisation depends, according to Argyris, on factors like the nature or organisation, structure, the informal groupings within the organisation, the personnel policies of the organisation, and the attitude of top management towards it.

TESTS OF FOOD MANAGEMENT

It is not easy to evolve a universally accepted test of good management. Standards devised to measure the quality of performanace are bound to very from item to time, place to place, and community to community. Yet it is accepted, by and large, that the true test of good administration is effective performance. Most persons are prone of judge this effectiveness by the extent of accomplishment of target. They are interested primarily in result but results may be attained at tremendous costs in men, money and materials, and by the use of wrong procedures and iniquitous means. Attention must, therefore, be given to means as well. According to Herbert Simon, "Rational behaviour in administration is primarily a calculation of means reasonably expected to realize a given end." Luther Gulick regards effecience as the "single ultimate value in administration." Similarly, Waldo regards efficiency and economy as 'twin beacons' of administration. But what is efficiency? It is a compendious term and may include varied attributes like swiftness in action, economy in cost, proper procedure, maximum utilisation of resources, etc. Efficiency is said to have three aspects-physical efficiency which is the relationship between physical quantities consumed and produced; business efficiency which is the relationship between amount of money spent and income received; and social efficiency which is the relationship between the human costs incurred and human satisfactions produced. In other words, efficiency is the relationship between the input and output in terms of materials, money and men. There is still another aspect of efficiency, namely, the state of personal relationship within the organisation. In fact, no administration agency can give a good account of itself unless there is harmony and shared understanding among the employees of the organisation. Physician must cure himself before trying his hand on others.

To these tests; Millett adds three values-satisfactory service, responsible performance, and good government. 'Satisfactory service' means fair and equitable service, that is, equal treatment to all citizens on the part, of administration; timely service, that is, service to be effective must be in time; ample service, that is, the right quantity at the right place and at the right time; continuous service, that is, service unobstructed by "rain, snow, sky or dark night"; and progressive service, that is, "a service which improves in quality and performance." "'Responsible performance' of the public service means that Management provides direction for administrative effort by working with and through those institutional devices which exist to express the will of a democratic society." An arbitrary and irresponsible administration can hardly fill the bill in modern time and that is why the administration today has to be democratic and responsible, and not bureaucratic and irresponsible. 'Good government' has been the goal ever since the times of Plato and Aristotle, but throughout history, the term has been differently interpreted. To the Americans 'good government' has come to mean a limited government within limits and a government in which the people participate. The Communist interpretation of 'good government by a single party.

Gulick makes the tests of effective Management still more comprehensive. To him the true goals of Management are to make the conduct of affairs technically sound, politically responsible, publicly acceptable, professionally approved and socially constructive.

9

Coordination and Supervision

Whereas it is essential, for the sake of convenience and efficiency, that government departments should have their boundaries and scope clearly delimited, their functions and responsibilities properly defined and their activities sharply divide, there is an evil inherent in this division. The evil is that each department begins to look in itself as an end and take its own functions as the most important. The curse of 'departmentalize' is the unhappy off shoot of the system of functional division in public administration. It creates departmental rivalries, constant friction and consequently delay and inefficiency.

Therefore, a sound system of organisation is that which, side by side with specializaion, provides an elaborate machinery of coordination and control. If the components of an organisation are not welded together, the programme will limp along, no matter how efficient most of the individual parts may be. An organisation without a proper machinery of coordination and control is like an automobile whose front wheels are going forward but whose rear wheels are going sideways.

COORDINATION

Nature. Coordination means the bringing about of the consistent and harmonious action of aspersions with each other towards a common and. Every collective activity, however simple, needs coordination. There is coordination in space and coordination in time. Administrative activities have to be coordinated in both. Friction arise in the actual execution of policy, that is, at the inter-departmental level, because no system of classification of work among the various departments can make them entirely self-sufficient. The primary interest of one is the secondary interest of the other. To take an example, the primary interest of the Education Department is to provide means of education to the children. But while doing so, it has also to look after their health. And to look after the health of the people is primarily the business of the Health Department. Hence, howsoever clear-cut the classification system may be, some sort of overlapping is inevitable.

Inter-departmental disputes usually arise when two or more departments claim exclusive jurisdiction over a given matter. The child health may become a done of contention between the Health and the Education Departments. Sometimes, a dispute may occur when all the Department decline jurisdiction over a matter newly arisn. This is known as "passing the buck". The use of atomic power, for example, may create a new problem for a particular region which due to its novelty every existing department may decline to handle. Then, sometimes dispute occurs over matters in which a number of departments have legitimate interest but they give contradictory decisions over it. Thus, the Ministries of Health, Society Welfare, Planning and Housing may have legitimate interest in the site of a clinic but they may hold different views on the matter.

There is another class of matters which needs effective coordination—namely, the field of supplies and services. Two or more departments may have legitimate and for the purchase or control of a certain kind of supply or skilled personnel. They may compete for its purchase and may thus force the price up.

Frequent occurrence of fruition is a consequence of the adoption of the uni-functional system of classification for government department. Under this system, one department must act on behalf of another. To build up a house, the Planning Department will clear the site, the Commerce Department will supply material, the Labour Department will provide labour, while the Housing Department will construct the building.

So, all these kinds of matters need a proper machinery of coordination. The Cabinet certainly cannot look to these matters as they arise, not in the formulation of policy, but in the execution of the departmental policy. They need a machinery at the departmental level itself.

MEANS OF COORDINATION

Coordination, to be effective, has to be concerned with policy, programme as well as personalities. And its achievement may require, as Dr. White has said, "the most delicate insight, the most mature wisdom, and perception of a truly artistic quality." It has to depend not on formal media but also on informal. In fact, the informal means are often more effective than the formal. Among the formal means of coordination, the more important are:-

1. *Planning:* In large-scale operations, planning of the programme, personnel and operations before-hand is very important. It is said of Napoleon that before winning his battles on the battle-field he used to win them on a piece-of paper in his drawing-room. A well-chalked-out plan will pre-determine the places of friction and disputes and will make adequate provisions for coordination. Thus pre-planning of programme and operation is in itself an effective means of coordination by way of working as a preventive of disputes and frictions.

2. *Sound organisation:* The positive means of coordination begin with structure and organisation. A sound system or organisation is in itself an effective check upon frictions and disputes. "An organisation characterised by clear lines of authority, adequate powers, well-understood allocation of functions, absence of overlapping and duplication of effort and proper delegation of work in itself reduce the necessities of coordination".

While a properly organised machinery of administration minimizes the need of coordination, it cannot altogether do away with it. Every large-scale organisation needs a machinery of coordination and needs it at every level of organisation.

3. *Cabinet and Cabinet Secretarial:* During the previous centuries when administrative work was less and simple, most

of the inter-departmental disputes were resolved by the Chief-Executive. Even now, disputes of a very grave or fundamental nature are referred by the departmental heads to their respective Ministers who first try to resolve them amongst themselves: and if that is not possible, then put it before the Cabinet. The Ministers, or the Cabinet, as the case may be, may either resolve the dispute in toto or may agree to a procedure of resolving the along the dispute and may instruct their permanent secretaries to resolve the dispute line provided in the agreement. The latter course is adopted more usually.

This is super-departmental means of coordination. Since the timeout the Cabinet Secretariat has developed as an adjunct of the Cabinet, it has been relieving the Cabinet of much of its routine and less important work. And as it is a body directly functioning under the Prime Minister, the person charged with the general supervision and control of the government is a whole—it has been discharging the function of coordinating the activities of the various Ministries. It discovers precedents, prepares rules and works towards manual understanding for revolving the disputes. In the official Directory of the Government of India, it has been specifically stated that among others, the Cabinet Secretariat will attend to matters of "general coordination of important administrative measure of the Government of India which affect more than one Ministry", to "measures necessary for resolving difficulties or delays which may arise in the administrative field whether between Ministries of the Government of India or between Government of India and State Governments, and to matters of "coordination of all economic and statistical works of the Government of India". For these, the Secretariat maintains a separate Divisions of Coordination.

4. *Inter-department Committees:* While the super-departmental means of coordination are employed only in more important cases, the departmental and inter-departmental methods are the usual means of coordination. The task of coordination within agencies is born by the top and middle management officials. The work of section is coordinated by Branch officers, of Branches by Division Chiefs and of Divisions

by Secretaries and Joint-Secretaries. But the inter-departmental conflicts are resolved by inter-departmental committees which may be composed of officials drawn from the top or middle management officials of the departments concerned. These committees are made use of at different levels of administration. They serve a very useful purpose and thus, relieve the Executive and the top officials of much headache. They can, however, be useful only when the members come together with a sense of urgency and compromise. If they come with a dogged attachment to their own pet plans and notions, then "a session of an inter-departmental committee tends to be a place where departmental representatives come well prepared to defend their positions and leave more convinced than before of the correctness of their attitudes." There may be agreement between different departments without surrounding any part of the policies of the departments, but there can be no agreement when persons are blindly attached to their own views.

5. *Regional Councils*: Sometimes regional councils, representing different field organisations working in a particular region, are formed to coordinate the activities of these field organisations. These councils may serve a useful purpose by way of exchange of information and interrpretation of policy and programme, for coordinating the operations of services working in the same sphere and combining their auxiliary activities, such as, joint purchase of supply, or arranging legal advice etc.

6. *Staff Agency:* Staff officers, who are attached to the Chief Executive and the top officials, render very useful service by way of supplying information regarding the personnel and other questions of the agency and furnishing advice to coordinate and control its activities. The financial and personnel advisors are very effective agencies of coordination. The Civil Service Commission, the O. and M. division and the Central Purchasing agency may be very useful means of coordination.

7. *Informal Means of Coordination*: are usually more unifying elements in Public Administration as in private life. Public officials are human beings like ordinary citizens and therefore, meet fellow officials in clubs, restaurants and other meeting places and have family and neighbourhood relationship like all other people. It is, therefore, natural that they must discuss, among others, problems of departmental conflicts and find some solution for them. In the British Civil Service there has developed a "tradition of Civility" as Sir Ernest Barker calls it, which enables them to resolve the interdepartmental conflicts with ease. and patience. Speaking about the effect of this tradition on British Administration, Prof. S. E. Finer says, "The long term cumulative effect of informal collaboration—ringing up, calling at lunch, "dropping in to see"-is prodigious. Least visible publicly, it is the most powerful cement in the whole executive structure." Such a spirit existed among the I.C.S. officials in India during the British rule and it is hoped that it would continue even now. There is, however, a feeling that the I.C.S. men keep somewhat reserved from the I.A.S. men. Mr. Gorewala also has pointed out this fact in his report. This is undesirable. In fact, there should be closer personal contacts between the higher and lower officials. It is wrong practice to have separate clubs and canteen for different grades of officials. Mutual contacts higher and lower officials will be beneficial to both of them and ultimately to the administration.

SUPERVISION

Supervision may be defined "as the direction, accompanied by authority, of the work of others." In is one of the most indispensable parts of the dynamics of administration, as it is the top-to-bottom chain to supervision which gives coherence to organisation. Supervisor at the lowest level is called first-line supervisor in public administration and foreman in industry.

Phases of Supervision. There are three phases of a supervision's job, *viz.,* (1) Substantive or technical, (2) Institutional, and (3) Personal.

The substantive part of his work consists in knowing the technique, the 'know-how' of the work. He has to plan the work set standards of quality and quality of work to be expected and make specific assignment of duties. But while he must know the work, it is not necessary that he should be an expert in the field.

Institutional Aspect. This aspect of a supervisor's job involves a knowledge of policies, procedures, and practices of his agency. In matters of personnel and procedure he has a great responsibility. Although personnel are selected by the Public Services Commission, yet he may refuse to accept a particular employee in his unit. He is responsible for assignment of duties, for attendance, punctuality and personal conduct of the agency and for the conservation of equipment and supplies.

Personal Aspect. This is the most important aspect of his work. Work cannot be taken by use of authority alone. To get good work from the workers, enthusiasm and interest in the work has to be created. Real authority flows from within, as Miss Marry Parker Follett has said. "Authority should arise," she held, "within the unifying process. As every living process a subject to its own authority evolved by, or involved in, the process itself, so social control is generated by the process itself. Or rather, the activity of self-creating coherence is the controlling authority." So that such an authority may arise from within an organisation, the supervisor must be a master of the art of human relationship and must fully know the art of supervision.

Requirements of Good Supervision. Prof. J. M. Pfiffner has laid down following requirements of good supervision in his monograph entitled "Introduction to Supervision":

1. Command of job content—the know 'how' of work.
2. Personal qualifications—ability of the cooperate, to attract others, to motivate, enthuse and unite others to work.
3. Teaching ability—by this he means the ability to keep oneself perpetually at the process of self-education, to lead in conferences and to teach groups of workers.

4. General outlook—He must love his job. Only then can be enthuse others in the work and create in them an *esprit de corps*.

5. Courage and fortitude—these will give him the stamina to take action decisively.

6. Ethical and moral considerations—moral standards set good example among the workers.

7. Administrative technology—it refers to the supervisor's ability to organize and co-ordinate.

8. Curiosity and Intellectual ability—An inquisitive mind goes a long way in making a leader. Therefore, it is essential for a supervisor to have fertile and inquisitive mind so that he may be capable or grasping a situation well in time and take prompt action to meet it.

Books For Further Study

1. L. D. White: *Introduction to the Study of Public Administration* Parts II and III.

2. W. F. Wileoughby: *Principles of Public Administration,* Chapters II to XII.

3. J. M. Pfiffner: *Public Administration,* Parts II & III.

4 F. M. Marx (Ed.): *Elements of Public Administration,* Part II Chapters 6 to 12; Part III, Chapter 16, 18 and 19.

5. Herbert A. Simon: *Public Administration,* Alfred A. Knoff, New York, Chapters II to VI.

6. E. N. Gadden: *The Essentials of Public Administration,* Part III.

10

Public Undertakings

The crucial importance of public sector undertakings to the economic development of our country hardly needs emphasis. The Industrial Policy Resolution of 1948 enunciated for the first time the Government's policy in regard to the setting-up of public undertaking.

The Industrial Policy Resolution of 1956, which replaced the earlier one, expanded the role of the public sector, and as a result, industries of basic and strategic importance, or of the nature of public utility services, or which required investment on a scale beyond the capacity of private enterprise, but which nevertheless were essential, were to come under the ownership and control of the Government. By the mid-eighties the number of public undertakings increased to nearly 200 involving a total investment of Rs. 30.000 crores and employing slightly less than 2 million people. In addition to these Central Government undertakings, the State Governments too have set up a number of undertakings in the public sector

Their number has steadily increased with every plan, and by the end of Third Plan period, various State Governments owned or held majority shares in about 175 public undertakings with an estimated total investment of nearly Rs. 2,000 crores.

Public enterprises in our country cover a range of activities that is at once vast and varied. They are engaged directly or indirectly in advancing loans; regulating trade; organizing promotional and development activities; manufacturing heavy machinery, machine tools; instruments, electrical equipment, chemicals drugs and fertilizers; prospecting and drilling for oil and refining crude oil; operating air, sea and road transport; mining of coal and mineral ores; smelting and casting of steel and other metals; production and distribution of milk, trading, markets, hotels, etc.

A public undertaking, for purposes of examination by the Estimates Committee, was defined by the Speaker of the Lok Sabha as, "A Public Undertaking means an organisation endowed with a legal personality and set up by or under the provisions of a statute for undertaking on behalf of the Government of India an enterprise of industrial, commercial or financial nature or special service in the public interest and possessing a large measure of administrative and financial autonomy." This definition obviously is concerned only with the public undertakings under the Union Government and leaves out of account public undertakings in the States. A more comprehensive definition has been given by Khera: "By State Undertakings is meant the industrial, commercial and economic activity carried on by the Central Government or by a state Government or jointly by the Central Government and State Government, and in each either solely or in association with private enterprise so long as it is managed by a self contained management."

Types or Kinds of Public Undertakings

Khera, analyzing public undertakings from the point of view of ownership, divides them into four types, namely—(1) Central Government enterprises, like Hindustan Steel, the State Bank of India and Life Insurance Corporation; (2) State Government Undertakings, like Electricity Boards and State Transport Corporations; (3) Enterprises under joint ownership and management of both, the Central and the State Government, like Damodar Valley Corporation and Bhakra Nangal Project; and (4) Undertakings born out of association between Government and private enterprises, like Singareni Collieries and Oil India Limited.

According to William A. Robson, public undertakings may be divided into seven categories so far as the scope and nature of the undertakings is concerned, namely—(1) Public Utilities, like water, gas, electricity, ports and harbours; (2) Transport and Communication, like railways, airlines, shipping telephones, posts and telegraphs, buses, etc.; (3) Banking, Credit and Insurance, like Bank of England, Reserve Bank of India, Life Insurance Corporation of India and Finance Corporation of India; (4) Multi-purpose Development Projects, like Tennessee Valley Authority in U. S. A., and Damodar Valley Corporation in India; (5) Basic established industries, that is, industries or services of importance to the economy which had been established by private enterprise and then taken over by the government, namely, coal-mining iron and steel, oil production, etc. (a good example in India would be the Hindustan Shipyard which has been bought over by the Government from the private owners, Scindia Steam-Ship Company); (6) New industries or services, like Hindustan Steel, Indian Telephone Industries, Hindustan Machine Tools and the State Trading Corporation; and (7) Cultural activities like Arts Council in Britain and Film Corporation of India.

Growth of Public Undertakings in India

Increasing intervention by the State in the economic field has been a characteristic feature of the 20th century, particularly after the end of the First World War in 1918. This trend got accelerated after the termination of the Second World War in 1945. Today State intervention of a positive kind in the ownership, operation or regulation of industries and services has become a vast movement of world-wide dimensions.

In India also this general trend has been in operation for quite some time. It was at its Karachi Session, in 1931, that the Indian National Congress, for the first time, attempted to define the economic and social content of the Swaraj it was striving for, and it its resolution on economic and social programme, among other things resolved: "The State shall own or control key industries and services, mineral resources, railways, waterways, shipping and other means of public interest." Herein lay the germs of future nationalisation of means of production and distribution. This resolution was passed at the instance of Jawaharlal Nehru who along with a band of progressive young men, belonged to what may be termed as the leftist or socialist wing of the Congress. Then came the publication, in 1934, by Sir M. Visvesvaraya of a book called *Planned Economy for India*, suggesting a systematic plan for the economic development of the country. Soon after in 1927, the Congress set up a National Planning Committee with Jawaharlal Nehru as its Chairman and K.T. Shah as the General Secretary. This Committee appointed two sub-committees in 1940 to report on principles of national planning and administrative machinery for India's National Plan. However, due to the outbreak of the Second World War and Congress involvement in the struggle for freedom, the reports of these sub-committees could become available only in 1948. The National Planning Committee supported State intervention in the country's economy and recommended increasing State control over it including nationalisation of industries. Earlier, even during the war, had been published in 1943 the Bombay Plan prepared by eight leading industrialists of Bombay. All this had set people a thinking about planning and development. These ideas were later embodies in the new Indian Constitution in Part IV of Directive Principles of State Policy. Article 39 committed the Government "to direct its policy towards securing that the ownership and control of material resources of the country are so distributed as best to subserve the common good: and that the operation of economic system does not result in concentration of wealth and means of production to the common detriment."

With Jawaharlal Nehru at the head of the government in free India, it became certain that government would move in the direction of State control and nationalisation of economy, and on April 6, 1948, was published the Government's Industrial Policy Resolution. The Resolution recommended a Mixed Economy pattern for the country, that is to say, a pattern in which both the private and the public sectors would have a place. Under the 1948 Policy Resolution, only three Government monopolies were established, viz., the manufacture of arms and ammunitions, the productions and control of atomic energy, and the ownership and management of railway transport. In six industries, viz., coal, mineral oils, iron and steel, aircraft manufacture, shipbuilding and telephones, telegraphs and wireless apparatus (excluding radio receiving sets), existing firms were to be allowed to continue production at least for 10 years, but new undertaking in this field were to be the exclusive responsibility of the State. Even here, exceptions could be made if national interests were served by securing the co-operation of private enterprise. All other industries, old and new, were left to private enterprise, subject in eighteen cases, to control, and regulation which was subsequently embodied in the Industries (Development and Control) Act of 1951. It was in this way that both public and private sectors were called upon to work jointly as equal partners in the great adventure of building up industrial India.

Meanwhile, the Congress at its Avadi Session, in 1954, had accepted as its goal the establishment of a "socialistic pattern of society". In pursuance of this policy, the Government of India enunciated its Industrial Policy Resolution on April 30, 1956, in the form of a new Industrial Policy which revised and improved upon the 1948 Resolution. The Resolution declared that "the state will progressively assume a predominant and strict responsibility for setting up new industrial undertaking… with a view to reducing economic inequalities and concentration of economic power and monopolisation." It drew up two schedules of industries A and B – one consisting of 17 industries, the future development of which was to be the exclusive responsibility of the State, and the other of 12 industries of great social importance which were to be progressively State-owned. All other industries were left to the initiative and enterprise of the private sector, although it was open to the State to enter any field. Since then, the trend has been towards more and more of nationalisation and the Government has been increasingly entering commerce and trade, when necessary, in public interest.

Our public sector has grown with our plans. From a mere trickle of 5 units at the beginning of the First Five Year Plan, it grew to 21 units at the commencement of the Second Five Year Plan and to 48 at the beginning of the Third Five Year plan, as would be clear from the following:

Year	*Number of Undertakings*	*Total Investment (in Crore Rs.)*
1951	5	29
1956	21	81
1961	48	953
1966	74	2415
1969	85	3902
1974	122	6237
1979	176	15602
1980	186	20000

This number, it must be emphasised, does not include departmentally managed undertakings and nationalised banking institutions.

Reasons For Government Participation In Economic Activities

S.S. Khera gives six good reasons to justify the Government's playing an active role in economic development.

1. Modern economy has to be a planned economy, and it has come to be widely recognised and the prejudice against it is fast dying out even in the so-called capitalist or free-economy countries. Planning is of particular significance to an underdeveloped country like India, where a lot has to be achieved with limited resources and within a limited time. Modern planned economy has, thus, become inevitable; and in a planned economy, the national responsibility of planning is something that cannot be assured or discharged by any authority other than the Government which the people have elected to office to look after the affairs of the country.

2. In a country like India where the industrial base has not been built up sufficiently, and the capital investment funds still need a great deal of building up and garnering, state intervention becomes imperative.

3. A government, such as, the present Government in India, which is committed to the objective of a socialist society, is

increasingly compelled to enter directly into industrial and commercial activity.

4. A government, politically committed to certain social objectives, may well decide that in order to achieve certain minimum per capita income it may be necessary to set up, to evolve and to operate a pattern of prices, subsidies, incentives or disincentives of different kinds in order to influence the consumption pattern.

5. By active participation in business, the Government has sought to tap gold mines of industry and commerce for the funds needed to discharge the new and heavier burdens it now shoulders.

6. Large-scale participation by Government in industrial and commercial activity is bound to augment the national dividened.

Organisation of Public Undertakings

There is no one ideal form of organizing public enterprises. What is even more confusing is the fact that no well-defined principles have been followed in determining the form of such organisation. In general, three main forms of organisation, each with significant variations, are now utilised for the administration of public enterprises, namely, departmental concerns, government companies and public corporations. We shall now briefly outline the characteristics, strong and weak points, of each of these types.

Departmental Concerns

Initially, no distinction was drawn between public enterprises and traditional government functions. Thus, the oldest state enterprises, such as, the postal, telegraph and telegraph and telephone services, and railways were organised, financed and controlled as any other government department. This form of organisation is till commonly employed when the main purpose of the enterprise is to provide revenue. The principal characteristics of this form or organisation, according to the Report of the Rangoon Seminar of 1954, are as follows:

1. The enterprise is financed by annual appropriations from the Treasury and all, or a major share of its revenues, are paid into the Treasury;

2. The enterprise is subject to the budget accounting and audit applicable of other government activities;

3. The permanent staff of the enterprise are civil servants and the methods by which they are recruited, and the conditions of service under which they are employed, are ordinarily the same as for other civil servants;

4. The enterprise is generally organised as a major sub-division of one of the Central departments of government and is subject to the direct control of the head of the department;

5. Wherever this applies in the legal system of the country concerned, the enterprise possesses the sovereign immunity of the state and cannot be sued without the consent of the government.

The great advantage of this type is that it is a well-known form of organisation with set structural pattern and fixed procedure. Staffing poses no serious problem. In addition, it also assures the maximum degree of control by politically responsible officials, which is a factor of great importance. But this form lacks managerial flexibility so very essential for effective operation. The Krishna Menon Report on State Undertakings in India sets out the limitations of this form as follows:

(a) Permanent staff is subject to rules and regulations applicable to civil servants, thereby preventing both promotion on merit and prompt disciplinary actions, where necessary;

(b) Tardy procedures for arranging funds, for instance; the necessity for getting sanction for expenditure and other matters in every single case;

(c) Cash receipts have to be put into government account and cannot be taken out without special sanction;

(d) The complicated system of accounting and audit; and

(e) The department methods of purchase of raw materials and sale of products, etc., lead to delays.

Of course, many governments have attempted to alleviate these weaknesses by introducing new dorms of structure and more flexible procedures with a view to giving autonomy to management; for example, the setting-up of the Railway Board for managing railways and the posts and Telegraphs Board for managing the posts and telegraphs in India. But the problem is more basic, and in the words of the Rangoon Seminar Report. "As long as an enterprise is not clearly differentiated from other types of governmental activity, strong pressures will be brought to make it conform to standard government regulations and procedures, since emphasis on uniformity is a common characteristic of a bureaucratic administration."

Government Companies

The Joint-Stock Company form has been used extensively in recent years in respect of manufacturing activities in the public sector. Both, the Central and the State Governments seem to favour it. This type is also known as mixed ownership companies. It should be remembered that the form does not describe a legal or organisational pattern but an economic concept. It includes various forms of joint enterprises shared between the State and private interests. The latter may be national or foreign. They may represent the shares of individual forms participating in the venture or the subscriptions of members of the public at large.

According to Report of the Study Team on Public Sector Undertakings (or the Administrative Reforms Commission) central and provincial characteristics of this form are as follows:

(a) It has most of the features of a private limited company;

(b) The whole of the capital stock or 51 per cent or over of it, is owned by the Government;

(c) All the directors, or a majority of them, are appointed by the Government depending upon the extent to which private capital is participating in the enterprise;

(d) It is a body corporate, created under a general law, *viz.*, the Companies Act;

(e) It can sue and be sued, enter into contract, and acquire property in its own name;

(f) Unlike the public corporation, it is created by an executive decision of the Government without Parliament's specific approval having been obtained, and its Articles of Association, though conforming to an Act are drawn up and are revisable by the Government;

(g) Its funds are obtained from the Government and, in some cases, from private shareholders, and through revenues derived from the sale of its goods and services;

(h) It is generally exempt from the personnel, budget, accounting and audit laws and procedures applicable to Government departments; and

(i) Its employees, excluding the deputationists, are not civil servants.

There are three major reasons for the adoption of the company form of organisation:

(i) The government may have to acquire shares of an existing enterprise in an emergency, in response to a financial or employment crisis, or in order to maintain a nationally important production or service which has become unprofitable or insolvent under private enterprise, for example, the recent taking over of the Indian Iron and Steel Company Limited and a number of textile mills.

(ii) The State may wish to launch an enterprise in association with certain other interests, national or foreign. Important recent example is Hindustan Steel Limited. A joint venture of the Indian Government and

private interests in India is Hindustan Shipyard Limited in which the Government holds two-thirds of the paid-up capital which it took over from a private enterprise.

(iii) The government may wish to start an enterprise entirely as a public venture in order to put it on its feet, with the intention of disposing of all or part of it to the public, or to specific private interests as soon as possible.

In several recent instances national development corporations have been established in the ECAFE region with a share capital, as a means of enabling them to set up subsidiary operating companies and to acquire interests in them. Examples are the National Development Company of the Philippines and the Industrial Development Corporation of Pakistan. In our own country, of the 70 Central Government undertakings, 64 have been organised as Government companies and 6 have been created by statute. The State Government have also tended to favour the company form. There were, in 1967, about 145 Government companies in which one or more State Governments held either the whole of the share capital or a majority of it.

The Company device, however, has its own limitations. It was once described by no less an authority than a former Comptroller and Auditor. General of India as "a fraud on the Company's Act and on the Constitution." Its main disadvantages are the following:

(i) It evades the Constitutional responsibilities which a State-controlled enterprise has, in a democratic society, to the government and to parliament;

(ii) The use of the Company form and of the law regulating commercial Companies usually becomes a mere fiction because all or most of the functions normally vested in the shareholders and in the management, are reserved to the government by the statute setting up the Company.

A.H. Hansen believes that there is not much to choose between a Corporation and a Company. He says, "My own view is that the State Company and the Public Corporation really do not differ very much from each other except, of course, in the legal status. In matters of operations there seems to be very little difference. The Company is entirely under State control in so far as the State is its sole shareholder. Further, it is usually subject not only to Company Law but, through Articles of Association or Terms of Agreement, to Special forms of governmental supervision which are not really very much different from those which are embodied in the legislative instruments which create Public Corporations."

Government of Public Corporation

During the last 40 years or so, a new form of organisation for managing public enterprises has been evolved in the shape of public corporation which has been described by W.A. Robson as "the most important constitutional innovation" of this century. The principal characteristics of the Public Corporation, according to Rangoon Seminar, are as follows:

(i) It is wholly owned by the State.

(ii) It is generally created by, or pursuant to, a special law defining its powers, duties and immunities and prescribing the form of management and its relation to established departments and ministries.

(iii) As a body corporate, it is a separate entity for legal purposes, and can sue and be sued, enter into contracts and acquire property in its own name. Corporations conducting business in their own names have been generally given greater freedom in making contracts and acquiring and disposing of property than ordinary government departments.

(iv) Except for government appropriations to provide capital or to cover losses, a Public Corporation is usually independently financed. It obtains its funds from borrowing either from the Treasury or the public, and from revenues derived from the sale of goods and services. It is authorised to use and reuse its revenues.

(v) It is generally exempted from most regulatory and prohibitory statutes applicable to expenditure of public funds.

(vi) It is ordinarily not subject to the budget, accounting and audit laws, and procedures applicable to non-corporate agencies.

(vii) In the majority of cases, employees of Public Corporations are not civil servants, and are recruited and remunerated under terms and conditions which the Corporation itself determines.

The principal benefits of the Public Corporation as an organisational device, are its freedom from unsuitable government regulations and controls and its high degree of operating and financial flexibility. In this form, one discerns a balance between the autonomy and flexibility enjoyed by private enterprise and the responsibility of the public as represented by elected members and legislators. In the famous words of President Franklin D. Roosevelt, the Public Corporation "is clothed with the power of government but possessed of the flexibility and initiative of a Private enterprise." However, this form, in its turn, has given rise to other problems, namely the difficulty of reconciling autonomy of the corporation with the public accountability. That the Public Corporations cannot be made immune from ministerial control and direction is universally conceded. But how to do it without infringing their autonomy is a dilemma defying solution. The theory of corporate autonomy had come into direct conflict with the urgent need for bringing the operations of these Corporations into harmony with related actions of the government. Moreover, "Public Corporations do not function in a political vacuum. Removal from the so-called political pressures may mean, in fact, that the significant political power is being placed in the hands of a Small unrepresentative, and, in extreme cases, possibly even a self-perpetuating groups controlling the Public Corporations."

To sum up, each of these three types of organisation has its strong and weak points. Thus, A.D. Gorwala has held the view that the departmental management was in many ways a direct negation of the requirements of autonomy and militated against flexibility and initiative, that is sound "State enterprise tradition". It must, therefore, be a rare exception to be resorted to when dictated by the need of secrecy, strategic importance, etc. He, generally, favoured the Company form substantially commercial functions because of great flexibility. According to him, Corporation form should be used when the undertaking was to discharge what in effect were the extensions of government functions, for example, broadcasting irrigation, etc.

In the opinion of the Estimates Committee, the corporate form combined in it the advantages of suitability both for parliamentary control and internal autonomy. The extent of the accountability of a Corporation and the nature of parliamentary control over it, were invariably indicated in the statute under which it was set up. The Committee therefore, recommended that wholly government-owned undertakings should ordinarily be organised in the form of statutory corporations, and in the form of departmental management only where justified by special reasons; for example, defense, strategic or security needs, or for purposes of economic control. The Company form should be an exception to be used only for organisations of a specified nature, *viz.,* where the government had (i) to take over an existing enterprise in an emergency, (ii) to launch an enterprise in association with private capital, or (iii) to start an enterprise with a view eventually to transferring it to private hands.

According to Administrative Reforms Commission's Study Team Report, among all the three forms in which public undertakings have been organised, the departmental form is one that is generally regarded suitable only for undertakings that provide services affecting the totality of the community or the security of the country. The flexibility and autonomy that are needed for commercial and industrial enterprises cannot be provided by a departmental form. Such undertakings require a high degree of freedom, boldness and enterprise in management and must be free from the circumspection and cumbersome, time consuming and vexatious procedures of departmental administration. Both, the company form and the Public Corporation form, can provide for this flexibility and autonomy. It is not, therefore, possible to prescribe one of these forms as applicable for all types of undertakings and under all circumstances. The choice will have to depend on the nature of the undertakings, its importance, its magnitude and investment, and the role that it is expected to play in economic development capital formation and provision of goods and services. What is crucial, is the vigilance and responsibility with which autonomy is exercised and the meticulousness and spirit of co-operation with which autonomy is respected.

The Articles of Association of the Company or the Statutes of the Corporation can provide for Autonomy and operational flexibility. The Company form gives greater freedom to the Executive to determine the structure and autonomy by revising the Articles of Association. The Corporation is not set up an Act of Parliament. It is the embodiment of an expressed desire of Parliament to set up a new agency. It is, therefore, set up after a full and informed public debate on the needs, objectives, financial and economic obligations, and structure and autonomy of the new agency. Such a debate in Parliament and the decision that follows, invest the Corporation with the sanctity of national approval for its objectives, obligations and autonomy. This is essential for a public undertaking that is created by heavy investments from the scarce resources at the command of the exchequer. While the Company form may have all other advantages that Corporation may have, the sanctity and individuality that a Public Corporation alone can acquire are essential in democracy that nurses and depends on the efficiency of the public sector. There might have been reasons for learning heavily on the Company form at a certain stage of the development of public enterprises in the country. Nor can the Company form be discarded altogether as useless and unprofitable under all circumstances.

However, the weight of the considerations that we have detailed in the above paragraphs has led us to the conclusion that the form of Public Corporation is the one that is best fitted for the commercial and industrial undertakings in the public sector. We are convinced that the Public Corporation form has distinct advantages over those of the government company. We, therefore recommend that the Government should implement the declared intention of the Industrial Policy Resolution in this behalf and adopt the form of Public Corporation as the general rule for the industrial and commercial undertakings in the public sector in India.

Some Problems of Public Corporation

Public Corporation has succeeded in solving a number of problems. At the same time, however, it has created some others. Some of the more pressing problems confronting the Public Corporations are:

(a) How should we reconcile autonomy of the Public Corporations with public accountability, *i.e.*, accountability to Parliament?

(b) What should be the extent and nature of ministerial control?

(c) Should there be a standing Parliamentary Committee on Public Corporations?

The supreme considerations underlying the choice of Public Corporations in preference to other forms of state enterprises, are autonomy and freedom of business management. Admitting that the autonomy of the Corporations must be scrupulously honoured, the latter cannot be made wholly free from responsibility to parliament or from ministerial control. They are accountable to Parliament at least on those matters which lie under the control, direct or indirect, of the Minister. Parliament is certainly entitled to discuss the general policies of the Public Corporations, and the economy and efficiency of their administration. It should not, however, discuss day-to-day matters and details of administration. The need for reconciling autonomy of the Corporations with the accountability to Parliament is so crying that it has been repeatedly emphasised by the Speaker of the Lok Sabha. In 1993, for instance, he observed: "...my reaction is that the House is entitled to have all information that is reasonably necessary and just to judge whether the administration of a particular Corporation, which is autonomous, is being carried on properly or not. But it ought not to enter into details so as to interfere with the autonomy of the particular Coporation."

Accountability to Parliament

The Public Corporation is accountable to Parliament, because the latter is the custodian of the State's finances, and represents the shareholders (*i.e.*, the tax-payers). Potentially, the parliamentary control may be exercised in the following ways:

1. Parliamentary question.
2. Raising half an hour discussion on any enterprise.
3. Moving a motion for adjournment on a matter of urgent nature and public importance.
4. Raising of two hours' debate on a matter of urgent public importance.
5. Parliamentary debates about any enterprise or group of enterprises.
6. Budget debates.
7. Debates on Bills and Resolutions.
8. Discussion on annual and periodical reports.
9. Debate on Audit reports.
10. Parliamentary Committee-Public Accounts and Estimates Committees, and particularly, the Committee on Public Undertaking.
11. Debates on the report of the Enquiry Commission, if any.

Members of Parliament have, thus, numerous opportunities to express their views and obtain general information relative to the Public Corporations. Matters of detailed administration are—and should be—outside the sphere of their general control. As against thus, the Minister has been given extensive power to direct the Public Corporation in the public interest. In the words of William A. Robson, "It is to the Minister that the board submits their annual reports and accounts in the first instance, and it is he who can continue the members of the board. The minister has extensive power of control and influence over a Public Corporation which are much greater than those possessed by the shareholders of a commercial company in relation to the board of directors. Parliament has almost two positive powers. In theory, it can change the law; but in practice it can only pass, amend, or reject Bills introduced by the Government."

Extent and Nature of Ministerial Control

That the Public Corporations cannot be made immune from ministerial control and direction is universally conceded. Objectives of the Public Corporation cannot be separated from national objectives. In the final analysis, The success of this form (as any other form) will be judged by its contribution to the achievement of national objectives. The problem is, thus, one of establishing sound management standards and practices within the context of broader national policy. Hence, the necessity and desirability of ministerial control over the Public Corporations. Undue ministerial intervention, however, cripples the Corporation's freedom of action, and is consequently harmful in the national interest. It should mainly take the form of broad directives on such matters as development programmes, capital investment, personnel policies, and other issues possibly affecting national interest. At the same time, the Public Corporation must be protected from excessive government intervention, though it is true that 'flexibility' is sometimes wrongly interpreted by managers as meaning that they could work in exactly the same manner as private entrepreneurs. Well-drafted laws and rules may be helpful in establishing proper relationship, but the most important need is the development of appropriate conventions and of willing co-operation and mutual understanding between the personalities at all levels. Clearly enough, the proper balance between autonomy and ministerial control is a delicate one. Excessive government intervention may be attributed to the tendency of members of Parliament to concern themselves too much with the day-to-day working Corporation. This may also be attributed to a strong tendency for Government to get its own way in regard to the management of Public

Corporation while publicly disowning responsibility for the results. Indeed, there is ample British experience confirming this suspicion. Ernest Davies, for instance writes: "The consequence that whereas behind the scenes they have exercised a greater influence on the boards, they have not accepted public accountability for their actions. The have exercised their responsibility in private and not answered for it in public. This tendency was noticeable during the previous administration, but has been carried considerably further by present Ministers." Explaining such an unsatisfactory state of affairs, William A. Robson Writes:

"It may be due, in some instances, to a Minister not wishing to make himself liable to accept the blame of public odium for a particular policy which may turn out badly. In others it may be because the Corporations have not the courage to tell a Minister point blank that they refuse to adopt a policy he is urging on them unless he gives them a direction to that effect. A background factor is the widespread habit of English life of preferring an informal understanding or gentlemanly 'persuasion' to a formal instruction or a legal document.

"Whatever the reasons may be, this tendency to rely on influence or pressure rather than formal directions, is misplaced in the relations between Ministers and the nationalised industries…

"Minister must be prepared to face up to the responsibilities which they have assumed. They should not be permitted to remain in the twilight zone in which some of them love to dwell flitting happily from one private his meeting to another, talking things over with the chairman at lunch, in the club, in the House of Commons, in the department, without disclosing either to the public or to the Parliament the real extent of their intervention. This is not the way to strike the right balance between government power and managerial freedom."

If the Public Corporation, in Britain, can succumb to indirect and overt control by Ministers, one can easily imagine the extent of autonomy left with its counterpart in India where there is a strong tradition of subordination and surrender to those in power. Indeed, the enquiry commissions that have gone into the functioning of some of the Public Corporations, have revealed widespread ministerial influence, exercised in a manner not contemplated in the statute. The Damodar Valley Corporation Enquiry Committee, appointed in 1952, commented this: "It is curious that, on the one hand, the Central Government was reluctant to issue directions under Section 48, and, on the other, the Corporation regarded the issue of directions as a reflection on its own competence, and pleaded on occasion that directions should not be issued, while at the same time allowing to be influenced in a manner not contemplated by the Act." This situation contrasts radically the assurance given by the Minister while presenting the Report of the Select Committee on D.V.C. Bill to Parliament. The Minister had observed: "The general principles on which this Corporation will have to work, are that for all purposes it is going to be an autonomous body, that it will be free within the framework as contemplated in the provisions of this Bill—to manage the affairs of the Corporation. There is only one limit. . . . that in matters of policy the Central Government will have the final voice."

The ministerial control over Public Corporations broadly speaking takes the following forms:

(a) Appointment of members of the governing board and general manager, their removal, fixation of conditions of service etc.;

(b) Issue of general policy directions on matters like development programmes, capital investment, personnel policies and other questions affecting national interests;

(c) Issue of specific directions;

(d) Approval of certain categories of actions and policies; and

(e) Right to obtain information and periodic reports from the Corporation.

It would be fair to lay down that ministerial intervention in the affairs of Public Corporations should take the form of written directive. Further, the parliamentary control over Public Corporation should be co-extensive with the ministerial control. As Appleby succinctly points: "The Public Corporation must not be thrown into the arms of Ministerial father unless a fond Parliamentary mother in available to restrain excessive application of paternal discipline." This is an important issue, for whereas the ministerial intervention is increasing there in an averseness to answering a wide range of questions."

Parliamentary Committee on Public Undertakings

There had been a demand, since 1953, for the creation of a Parliamentary Committee on Public Undertakings to look into their functioning and to report its findings to Parliament from time to time. At the back of this demand was the general feeling that Parliament, despite the numerous opportunities it had of holding the public enterprise accountable to it, had not succeeded in exercising control over them in a meaningful and effective way. Rather, its control hitherto was chaotic, intermittent and inadequate, lacking thread of continuity

The need for such a Committee was first voiced in the Lok Sabha, in late 1953, in the course of the debate on the Industrial Finance Corporation Act (Amendment) Bill. Lanka Sundaran made a strong plea for the establishment of a Committee of Parliament under the direction of the Speaker specifically charged with the task of looking into the affairs of Public Corporations, Companies and institutions. His objective in making this demand was "to strengthen the hands of the Minister vis-a-vis the departments, and more than this... to put beyond shadow of doubt the competence of the House of the People to investigate into the working of the Public Corporations." The main points in his indictment of and Suggestions were:

(i) Public Corporations have become impervious to public control and public criticism.

(ii) The Auditor-General has no or limited power to report to Parliament on their financial transactions and accounts.

(iii) The seruring of their accounts and estimates by the Public Account and Estimates Committees is not effective. Moreover, these Committees are already overworked.

(iv) Each of the Corporation has become a monopoly without competition.

(v) Many of them have become something like an imperium in imperio-small kingdoms under the overlord ship of officials to whom they were entrusted.

(vi) The Committee of Parliament to look into the affairs of them is the way out. "This... will strengthen the hands of the Ministers, will affirm and enforce the authority of Parliament, and will give more than anything else... to the tax-payer an assurance that his moneys are properly husbanded."

The Finance Minister, however, could not be won over to this suggestion. He pointed out that, in reality. Parliament's control over the Corporation was and should be the Minister's control, and the power which the Minister had, were quite enough. He asked: "is it necessary for Parliament to be informed from day-to-day or session to session, as to how a particular Corporation is being run? Is it into better to enable the executive to manage these, and then to call the executive to account? This is a consideration which Parliament will have to bear in mind, before they take a decision on this matter." He cautioned against hurrying too much: "There is always the danger of our throwing out the baby with the bath water." He suggested, as an alternative, that a body, combining the Public Accounts Committee and the Estimates Committee, could be formed in place of the proposed committee. Or else, sub-committees of the Public Accounts Committee, which had already been used, be utilised for the purpose.

This issue again cropped up in1956, during debates on the Life Insurance Corporation Bill. This time Asoka Mehta argued in favour of constituting a standing committee which would have the necessary equipment and requisite quota of officers to make thorough enquires into the functioning of the nationalised enterprises. The members of the standing committee "will be in a position to come here and answer or challenge the Government on various important points with the requisite information and knowledge." He concluded: "My contention is that this Parliament will not be able to exercise its supervision unless it is aided and assisted independently of Government by as set of experts to find out what is happening to different Corporations." The Finance Minister, too, shared this feeling adding, "I am still trying to persuade them (*i.e.,* the members of the Cabinet) now to take steps to have a kind of committee established. This idea that there should be a committee of the House commends itself to me."

G.V. Mavalankar, the first Speaker of the Lok Sabha, had, in a letter addressed to the Prime Minister, advocated the appointment of a standing parliamentary committee to examine to working of autonomous Public Corporations. The Rules Committee to which the matter was referred by him, suggested that "there is no harm if a separate committee is appointed with limited functions, such as to examine reports and the working of such bodies after the reports are presented to or are otherwise circulated to members and on matters concerning their organisation, working and administration. The proposed committee will not go into the problem of day-to-day administration of such Corporations, but would only consider question of policy and their working broadly,"

The Krishna Menon Committee has also recommended the appointment of a standing committee of Parliament. "We look forward," it stated, "to the situation where this Committee, while by no means being an expert committee (such is not the intention), would be a well-informed committee, informed of all the circumstances in which the concerns functions. The purpose of our recommendation would be adversely affected if either the Committee of Parliament becomes imbued with the feeling that it is a fault-finding body or that it is super Board of Management. At the same time, there cannot be any fettering of its judgment and the expression of its views in good parliamentary tradition. The Committee would also, no doubt, bear in mind that any public expressions of views which are intended to correct errors or to provide greater incentives in respect of any concern or all of them, are not of such a character as would have the opposite result of lowering the concern in public estimation, or affect our credit or capacity to be well regarded abroad."

The plea for the Committee on Public Undertakings was, thus, gathering support from many quarters. The Planning Commission, too, had visualised the need for a Parliamentary Committee on Public Undertakings. It was being increasing realised that full parliamentary control over the ever-expanding public sector could be exercised only by such a special committee.

Arguments Against the Committee, As against these advantages discussed above, the critics of the proposed committee have apprehended a host of dangers involved in the setting up of the committee. Their main fears may be summarised in what follows. In the first place, the proposed committee would be, in effect, a negation of what Parliament had deliberately done in setting up a public corporation: It willingly restricted its control. The setting up of this committee would mean renouncing this self-denying ordinance. As Herbert Morrison bluntly put it, "Those who want detailed parliamentary accountability, must plump for state departmental management; those who favour publicly owned industry being vested in a Public Corporation must be prepared to face the consequence, namely some limitation on detailed accountability." Lord Keith characterised it as "Institutionalizing in a terrifying form the parliamentary question." Secondly, it is contended that the Committee on Public Undertakings is likely to concern itself with the day-to-day functioning of the enterprises. This would cripple the spirit of adventurousness and boldness in making decisions. Thus, the principal advantages claimed for Public Corporation "possessed of the initiative and flexibility of private enterprise" would be rendered ineffective. Herbert Morrison feared that the proposed committee would create "a rather red-tape, un-adventurous and conventionally Civil Service frame of mind." Sir Geoffrey Hayworth expressed a similar opinion. He said, "If people came to looking at everything I did in a year, after the event the shareholders would be horrified because they would see that some of these decisions were quite wrong in the light of after-events. The mere fact, therefore, that I felt that some one was looking over my shoulder all the time and was going to examine these things any time later, the less I would be inclined to take a decision and the less decisive I would become, and pretty well certainly, the less would be the results," Thirdly, the duplication of parliamentary committees is likely to lessen the responsibilities of the existing bodies, and may lead to disharmony and conflict between them. This argument may easily be countered, however, by public enterprise from a separate area and a separate pattern. The sphere of activity of the proposed committee can easily be separated from the area of activities of other committees. Fourthly, the constitution of the committee would lead to a terrific increase in official record-keeping. And lastly, the crux of the problem lies not in acquiring more information concerning the public enterprises, but in how best to make use of the information Parliament already has.

Notwithstanding these apprehensions and arguments, the British House of Commons constituted, in March 1957, the Select Committee of the Nationalised Industries. The terms of reference of the Select Committee are to examine the reports and accounts of the nationalised industries established by statute, whose controlling boards are appointed by ministers of the Crown and whose annual receipts are not wholly or mainly derived from money provide by parliament or advanced by the Exchequer.

Argument in Favour of the Committee. The protagonists of a Committee of Parliament of Public Undertakings put forward the following arguments in support of their demand. *First*, Parliament, being a busy body, is precluded from giving adequate time and attention to the problems of an over-increasing number of public enterprises. There is an apparent need for a smaller body drawing its personnel from amongst the members of Parliament and functioning under its subordination. Parliament is too unwieldy a body to discuss affairs relating to public enterprises in a systematic coherent way. It is further handicapped by lack of requisite expertise in so far as an overwhelming number of its members have little understanding of the complex problems confronting the enterprises, and consequently, not in a position even if they so desire, to exercise vigilance over them. A standing committee would keep itself as well as the Parliament informed about the aims, activities and problems of the Corporations. The members would acquire a certain degree of knowledge about these enterprises, and this would enable Parliament to perform its functions in relation to them more effectively and in a meaningful way. Discussions and debates would be informed and effective. *Secondly*, as the Krishna Menon committee indicated, the parliamentary procedures are inadequate and inappropriate for ensuring accountability to Parliament. There are many inhibitions and restrictions; and what is worse, even speeches are delivered for constituency consumption and from party angles. Commending the constitution of a select committee on the nationalised industries, Hugh Molson, a member of the House of Commons, observed: "In the past the House of Commons has always found it convenient, when confronted with a special problem to appoint a committee. I think the reasons for that are threefold. First, in order that a few members of Parliament may give intensive study to the problem; second, that there may be interrogation of witnesses and investigation of papers and maps; and third, in order that in seclusion of a committee room, there may be comparative freedom from political prejudice." *Thirdly,* the Public Account-Committee and the Estimates Committee are not fit instrument for exercising control over public enterprises. The former engages itself in a sort of post-mortem examination of the public accounts. This is largely a negative function. For exercising meaningful and effective control over public enterprises, the Parliament needs some kind of guidance on the basis of a review of past and present functioning and policies of the enterprises. This task could have been performed by the Estimates Committee. In practice, however, it could not do this, primarily because of a very wide area falling within the jurisdiction of the committee. Furthermore, both these committees are overworked. *Fourthly,* the public enterprises are comparatively late arrivals on the scene, requiring a new kind of parliamentary control and supervision. This can best be achieved by constituting a special committee. *Fifthly,* the officials of the public corporation have at present little opportunity of presenting their case or of explaining difficulties confronted by the corporation. The proposed committee would serve as a liaison between Parliament and the corporations, resulting in better understanding and mutual co-operation. Lord Hurcomb, the then Chairman of the British Transport Commission supported the demand for a Select Committee, observing: "One of the very greatest handicaps under which anyone in my position suffers, is that he gets no opportunity of stating his own case or explaining what are his difficulties direct to Members of Parliament." *Sixthly,* the proposed committee would act as the guardian of public interest. It will bring the statutory corporations in touch with public and parliamentary opinion. A Corporation may simply thrive at the expense of the general consumer. The committee would prevent the corporation from being, in any way, 'feather-bedded'. *Seventhly,* the British experience supports the demand for such a committee. The working of the British Select Committee on Nationalised Industries demonstrates the general usefulness of such a body in India as well.

Committee on Public Undertakings

In November 1963, the Lok Sabha formally resolved to form the Committee on Public Undertakings. The decision to constitute such a committee was a sequel to the report of the Krishna Menon Committee referred to earlier in this chapter. The Committee on Public Undertakings consists of fifteen members—ten from Lok Sabhaand five from Rajya Sabha. The members are elected according to the principle of proportional representation by means of a single transferable vote. The creation of this committee was long stalled as the Lok Sabha was not convinced of the propriety of allowing full fledged representation to the Rajya Sabha. The Lok Sabha originally agreed to retain the elders as the "associate member' and exclude them from participating in the work of this committee when it engaged in performance of functions currently discharged by the Estimates Committee. The Rajya Sabha objected to these limitations. The constitutional wrangle was finally resolved by the constitution of a joint committee.

Functions

The functions of the committee are:

(i) To examine the reports and accounts of the enumerated public undertakings;

(ii) to examine the reports, if any, of the Comptroller and Auditor-General on the public undertakings;

(iii) to examine, in the context of the autonomy and efficiency of the public undertakings, whether the affairs of the public undertakings are being managed in accordance with sound business principles and prudent commercial practices; and

(iv) such other functions vested in the Public Accounts Committee and the Estimates Committee in relations to the public undertakings as may be allotted to the Committee by the Speaker from time to time.

Tenure

The tenure of membership of this Committee is five years. One-fifth of the members, however, retire by rotation. The members to retire every year are those who have been longest in office since their last election.

Jurisdiction

At the time of its inception in 1963, the Committee had jurisdiction over the following:

(i) Damodar Valley Corporation.

(ii) Industrial Finance Corporation.

(iii) Indian Airlines corporation.

(iv) Air India.

(v) Central Warehousing Corporation.

(vi) Life Insurance Corporation.

(vii) Oil and Natural Gas Commission.

(viii) Hindustan Aironautics Ltd.

(ix) Bharat Electronics.

(x) Mazagon Docks, Bombay.

(xi) Garden Reach Workshop, Calcutta.

(xii) All government Companies.

At present the Committee on Public Undertakings enjoys an enlarged jurisdiction, and all public undertakings except the departmentally run ones and the nationalised banking institutions fall within its scope.

Limitations

The Committee is precluded from discussing matters of government policy as well as matters of day-to-day administration. Also, it has no jurisdiction over those companies in which the Government is the largest single shareholder. All these points came under parliamentary criticism when the Government motion to appoint this Committee was being discussed in the Lok Sabha. It was said that the Committee lacked adequate powers, and its membership was too small to permit an effective scrutiny of the growing public sector in the country. One member of the Lok Sabha even wondered why the Committee was not given all powers enjoyed by the Public Accounts Committee and Estimates Committee in respect of Public undertakings.

Sound administration demands that matters of day-to-day administrative details should not be discussed by the Committee. But it does not seem fair to exclude it from discussing matters of Government policy. Concretely put, the Committee, for instance, cannot discuss the pricing policy of an undertaking or its labour-management relations.

Evaluation

The Committee brought out its first report in April, 1965 and has since published over 150 reports about half of which have dealt with the action taken by Government on earlier recommendations.

Some of its more important reports are on subjects like:

1. Structure of Boards of Management of Public Undertakings.
2. Delays in Commencement of Productions, Business, Under-utilisation of Capacity and Related Matters in Public Undertakings.
3. Management and Control Systems of Public Undertakings.
4. Productivity in Public Undertakings.
5. Extravagant and In fructuous Expenditure on Entertainment by Public Undertakings

The Committee is doing a useful job, and had for ever put to rest the fears expressed by the critics. It is a fact-finding committee; its function essentially, is to help Parliament to have a more effective annual debate on the working of the public undertakings. As the Minister of Industry argued: "I submit that the House will be more adequately served by a special committee, which will confine its functions to public undertakings only. The committee, as I envisage, ill digest the annual report and accounts of each undertaking and its report will help both houses to have a more fruitful debate."

One should not, however, conclude that public undertakings in India are functioning very efficiently. Far from it, it is said that every fifth public undertaking was running at less than half of the installed capacity in 1977-78. This has happened because of several factors. Broadly speaking, public undertakings suffer from unduly long gestation periods, very low level of production or utilisation of assets and the consequential escalation of cost of projects, wasteful expenditure, over-staffing, groupism and unionism. What is more, many of them which are incurring heavy losses are recklessly spending on entertainments, consultancy and training.

11

Acceptance of Organisation Aims

Their power of control does not in any sense imply that the control group exercises an unlimited option to direct the organisation in any path it desires, for the power will continue to exist only so long as the controlling group is able to offer sufficient incentives to retain the contributions of the other participants…

United aims are not alone the product of goodness but of wisdom.

When employers, singly and in groups, are ready to propose this next step, what will they propose? They cannot successfully ask co-operation of employee representatives toward objectives which have been predetermined by employers. They cannot hope to convince employee representatives that the objectives chosen by the employer alone are necessarily good objectives for the employees. Difficult as it may seem, they must begin by seeking co-operation in the selection of the objectives, before they can successfully ask for co-operation in the achievement of the objectives.

It would be generally agreed that "common effort is the result of common intention." But we need to be reminded that common intention requires commonly accepted, and acceptable, aims. Commonly acceptable aims in turn are the outcome of shared needs, desires and satisfaction which have their source in comparable if not necessarily identical experiences. In other words, people in organised groups will work with enthusiasm for some end which they learn in action is yielding them some recognizable good. And in general as the nature of that "good" is found to bc somewhat durable or enduring, is productive of the growth and realisation of the person, or is intrinsically rewarding out of the pleasure of the action itself (as in the joy of fine of fine craftsmanship), the response to the ends or purposes of the organisation will be more sure and more lasting. The degree of individual commitment bears a reasonable constant relation to the degree of deep satisfaction experienced.

The previous chapter has shown that the likelihood of achieving truly shared aims is greater in *membership* organisations than in those where the typical relation is that of being an *employee*. For where employees are involved, the problem of knowing the aims, of agreeing with them, of experiencing good results from the effort to realize them becomes more and more complicated. It would be naïve to assume that acceptance of aims will come spontaneously or can be taken for granted. Indeed, the modern administrator has to appreciate that unless he is skilled in grasping the interrelations of corporate aims and individual motives, he has a defective idea of the nature of one of his major problems. He is failing to see his task in its most profound terms. For corporate aims which cannot be made validly appealing and attractive in a sustained why to all participants will obviously get only their nominal, grudging, or indifferent response.

Managers have to be experts in the clarifying, articulating and purifying of aims, in assuring the relative appeal of the several prevailing or possible ends, in bringing abot their persuasive communication, and in supplying the supporting conditions which make acceptance of them likely throughout the organisation. Nor is this a task that is ever finally completed. There has to be a perennial, dynamic effort on the administrator's part toward eager and widespread acceptance, for the outgoing of events can both deliberately and unconsciously bring shifts in the relative emphases among the plural aims in actual effect. Among other things, the motives and methods of either managerial or worker leaders can change in ways favourable or unfavourable to the enlistment of creative motives up and down the line.

The several typical kinds of corporate aims have already been identified. These include aims which are (1) legal, (2) functional, (3) technical, (4) profit-making, (5) personal, (6) public. And it now become necessary to ask:

1. Can employees be expected to become equally loyal to all of these; or in what respect do difference occur in their several appeals?

2. Is complete unity of aim, or "functional unity," possible and practicable?

And finally, because of the stress which this volume lays on the need for the conscious and affirmative agreement to aims,

3. Is employee acceptance of and agreement with the going corporate objectives a proof of their social validity?

The Appeal of Different Aims

I do not propose to expatiate further upon the appeal of the *legal aims* as affecting the rank and file of workers. The extent of their appeal to the generality of employees depends upon numerous factors. Any agency conducted with a reasonably defensible purpose can enlist some degree of interest on the part of the workers if that purpose is justified to them and if they are made to realize that genuine benefits do in fact accrue to them out of their labours. The real problem of positive employee motivation lies elsewhere. *How* are aims being justified? *Can* they be justified? Agree genuine benefits accruing, and are they as great as might be feasible in the situation? It is questions like these, beyond the legal phase, which press for answer.

It will therefore be more rewarding to extend the analysis of several of the other objectives. The aim of good *functional performance,* for example, is one which will be found to be susceptible of much greater common acceptancc by workers involved than is often true today. Indeed, there is an impressive body of supporting aims which it is as important and necessary for the employees to accept as for the management itself, if good functional performance is actually to be achieved. And the value of functional effectiveness can be shown to employees and to union leaders to be integral for them and their purposes. Once a clear grasp of the constituent elements can be extended into the experience and thinking of the rank and file, start will have been made toward a new awareness of possible and desirable common intentions. These elements of potential common purpose are:

1. The continuous operation of the organisation on a regularised and stable basis, brought about by the fact that it renders acknowledge benefits and values to whose whom it serves.
2. The smooth and efficient internal operation of the organisation in its managerial, supervising and technological phases; leading to;
3. The achieving of lowered costs which enable sales to be made at prices which attract a profitable volume of business.
4. The assuring of a product or service of such progressively good quality as to bring continued favourable consumer reception.
5. The employment of measures of safety, health, training, personal convenience and comfort, which will conduce to good work and to sustained worker fitness and development.
6. The adoption of terms of employment as to wages and hours which are deemed jointly to be reasonable and fair, together with the provision of measures which reduce worker anxiety about sickness, disability, old age and unemployment.
7. The utilisation of some acceptable form of collective negotiation and straightforward two-way communication which will provide shared decisions as to fair terms of employment and conditions of work and other contentious issues; and last, of course:
8. Sufficient profit from the operation to retain and attract such volume of capital as is required in order to assure the future stability of the business.

In short, when the conditions necessary to an organisation's survival are understood, there is a body of operating purposes which are essential to the survival and therefore to the self-interests of all who seek to be assured of continuing employment in that organisation. Obviously, there will be differences of outlook among the different groups in an organisation as to how in detail these several policies looking to functional competence shall be carried out. And careful analysis requires that the distinction be kept clear as between the acceptance of potentially common aims on the one hand and the reality of conflicts or divergences of group interests on the other hand, arising out of failures to agree upon the relative weight which should appropriately be placed from time to time on the several aims and also failures to agree as to the methods by which specific aims will best be implemented. The distinction here is important. There are, in short purposes to be served if the reason of any organisation for being is to be satisfied. And there are group interests within the organisation to be reckoned with as the effort to fulfill purposes goes forward. Provisions have, therefore, to be consciously made as an administrative concern both for achieving some unity of purpose and for confronting and attempting to reconcile differences among group interests. These are separate if kindred problems, each requiring its own kinds of explicit organised methods of communication and conference, which will be more fully considered later.

The point to be here stressed in relation to the desirably common purposes just enumerated is that they do have to be acknowledged and accepted by all groups if the ongoing of the corporate body is to be assured. This, however, does not mean that a complete unity of aims is easily achieved, for as we shall see, this would entail drastic changes in typical present policies.

Similarly, in the *technical* purposes to be served, there can often be far more sharing with the rank and file than is usually assumed. But the major conditions of sharing in this phase would be that the employees genuinely participate in the technical knowledge about process and product which would induce a sense of pride of workmanship, of being partners in a technical achievement which would truly tap the springs of workmanly creative capacity. Good workmanship at a high level of quality is, *other things being equal,* an effort that normal people would prefer to make. The failure to elicit this kind of productive application is typically due to a slighting or denying of all the other supporting provisions which would prompt a release of creativity.

THE APPEAL OF PROFIT MAKING

The aim of *profit making* presents us, from this point of view of employee involvement, with interesting and fundamental questions. There has come about in our economic history a considerable tempering of the single-minded pursuit of profit. Yet the nature of the underlying conditions of profit seeking which are still all to prevalent needs to be spelled out honestly, if we are to get to the bottom of this challenge of getting employee acceptance to as many as possible of the plural corporate aims.

In those employer-employee relations where the employees have no voice directly or indirectly in determining how and where the annual financial outcome of the operation is to be allocated, we confront a difficult situation *in terms of employee motivation. For the rank and file typically share in the creation of the profit, but they do not share in the profit.* Their connection with the corporate project is usually like that of an army of mercenaries. They are paid for serving a cause in which they have slight personal stake and with which they have only a precarious identification. They are compensated to help realize an aim they have no part in shaping and no direct gain from success in achieving. This has been called a "master and servant" relation; and obviously the characteristics of anything like a "partnership" or "one big happy family" are not present.

This statement admittedly puts the grimmest possible construction upon the relation of workers to the corporation. And it is undoubtedly true that, far short of the use of some form of profit sharing, a number of extenuating factors enter which help to enlist more employee energy and zeal than might theoretically be expected. We have seen that the profit purpose among managers is increasingly modified by other aims. Intelligent workers are coming to understand that some degree of profit (even if they do not share in it) is a normal condition of the survival of the business in which they are employed. To an extent, also, workers no less than others are clearly the beneficiaries of a profit system as they share in the higher standard of material consumption progressively enjoyed in this country.

All these among other factors obviously help to assure for the profit purpose in a particular company and for the profit system as such an acceptance in the minds of American workers which they seem only infrequently to call into question—except for those few who are well to the "left" in economic ideology. Indeed, if this acceptance were not tacitly as widespread as it is today, the productive capacity of our economy would not be anywhere near as ample and as expanding as its is.

Am I not, then, in raising any question about the failure of profit making to supply a powerful and positive motive for the productive of the rank and file in American industry, injecting a doctrinaire, theoretical, if not a false thesis?

The present analysis, I emphasize, is neither an indictment nor an apology. It is rather an effort to confront in psychological terms the same truth as that implied by an astute student who said that "in a profit motivated economy, profits have to be made popular." One cannot avoid being realistically concerned with announced objectives at work in our economic organisations, and with the relation of the large body of American workers to them. For the fact is that the receiving of profits and the labours of earning profits are largely dissociated. Any direct receipt of profits by the majority of workers is simply not the fact. For it is an overgenerous estimate that there are 14,000,000 stockholders of American companies in a population of 150,000,000 people and a working population of nearly 60,000,000. And if only the persons who own 100 or more shares are included, the estimates indicate that the number of stockholders would be reduced by half. Hence profit making as a direct aim being shared enthusiastically in common all down the line is not a reality. It plays little if any direct motivating role for the vast majority of workers. It is in most organisations negligible as an employee incentive, purpose, or source of direct satisfaction.

But it may with equal truth be urged that there is at present no strong articulate voicing of a desire for some explicit sharing in profits from the majority of workers. Efforts toward securing larger individual earnings look chiefly toward the gaining of more income in the pay envelope, either immediately or deferred into pension funds, and seem to get more or less satisfactory expression at this level.

Many executives, however, give evidence of expecting employees to *act as if* they are interested in the loyal to the profit aim; and of anticipating from workers the degree of effort which is requisite to the realizing of that aim. And this expectation—said or unsaid—does psychologically give rise to a potential, and sometimes actual, divisive influence between managers and men.

At bottom, loyalty to the central aims of an organisation is the basis for loyalty to the organisation. And loyalty to the organisation without loyalty to one of its central reasons for being is surely a truncated motivation—even when other aims are supervening to temper and improve the relationship and motives which exist.

Also, we have to remember that loyalty, in any true version, is a two-way relation. Individuals give, or should give, loyalty to an organisation only as it in turn gives evidence of being loyal to the individuals—loyal in terms of the presence of satisfying shared aims and supporting good conditions and outcomes, which are demonstrably experienced by the workers. The securing of unequivocal employee loyalty in the usual business corporation is thus a perennially complicated affair in its underlying psychological aspect. Appeals by managers for a "partnership" attitude, for "all-out cooperation," for "devotion to company welfare" must inevitably seem insincere to workers (and others) who fail to discover "what there is in it for them."

How sound and practical plans can be contrived for giving workers a valid sense of some explicit stake in the total outcome of a business presents a difficult problem. Perhaps a share of profits for employees may not be necessary in order to attain a real functional unity of aim throughout an organisation. I am not, however, prepared to admit this, despite the difficulty of bringing forward practical measures. For the present underlying psychological disparity of certain interests cannot be ignored.

That this is not just a theoretical view, moreover, is attested by the numerous and recurring efforts of thoughtful executive leaders for almost a century to utilize some form of profit sharing in their own companies. The best of these plans have been the outcome of a sincere desire to give employees a partnership stake in the enterprise and thus to share profits as a measure of equity and fairness and as a direct or indirect appeal to creative motives. And although the history of this movement is admittedly not one of unqualified success, the fact remains that where the will to work the plan has prevailed and where in a prosperous company the plan itself has been carefully contrived, the results have been on the whole satisfactory.

The sound conclusion is not that profit sharing is by itself an automatic means of bringing about complete unity of aim and harmonizing of conflicting interests. No such simple or naïve expectation can be realised. That the employee should ideally enjoy some stake in the final outcome of the business I believe to be a valid position, psychologically, economically, and ethically. But the ties which bind him effectively to the organisation for which he works include a variety of policies, practices and surrounding conditions all of which have to be satisfactory, before considerations of profit division arise, and whether or not a profit is earned.

Indeed, the importance of the profit factor in qualifying a possible unity of aim, might be refuted by some by pointing to nonprofit agencies and observing the unquestioned fact that in most of them deep-rooted employee loyalty is little if any more a reality than in the profit-making organisations. Nonprofit "mutual" savings banks, "mutual" insurance companies, many hospitals, educational agencies; philanthropic associations, and governmental departments and bureaus operate without benefit of the profit motive. Yet I am sure that no experienced executive would assert that in these instances employee morale is inevitably superior to that found in profit-making organisations. Is there, then, some other profound reason why unqualified corporate loyalty is so hard to attain?

I believe the second part of the total answer is to be found in the point that loyalty is the product of a two-way relation. Many agencies, irrespective of the profit factor, have no sound, consistent and through-going administrative policy of relations and dealings with their own personnel. The components of a personnel policy which will evoke favourable responses clearly include numerous factors besides the monetary return to the employees. Without a total "personnel approach" in administration it cannot be expected that workers will evince deep loyalty, because no genuine solicitude is being shown for their interests, aims and satisfactions. Nonprofit institutions can get a far greater loyalty if and when they put a sound and comprehensive personnel philosophy into practice. Indeed, without the complicating factor of profit motivation, they *should* be able to secure loyalty more readily and more profoundly, if fine leadership is present to really the group together for a soundly worth and well-interpreted purpose under well-administered personnel procedures.

The argument may also be advanced that the loyalty of employees to the corporation is not expected by management and is not needful. The company has its aims; the employees have *their* aims. If the workers can somehow be induced to do enough work to get the product out profitably, that is all that should be expected. It is a purely contractual relation of value given and value received; and what the underlying attitudes and deeper motives of the employees are need not greatly concern the employer.

This view ahs certainly wide acceptance in administrative circles over the years. But it is now longer satisfactory or universally accepted. It no longer works in terms of the worker attitudes which are needed and desired. The failure of this philosophy to persist as a valid attitude is due to multiple causes. These include the more enlightened attitudes of modern-minded administrators themselves, the outlooks of labour union heads and members, and the climate of public opinion as to what the organic and qualitative relation of people to their work has a right to be and can potentially be.

It certainly is true that industry "got away with" the policies implicit in this purely contractual approach to rewards in the years of America's rapid industrial expansion. Employers were in favourable, "cheap" labour market; and a more "hard-boiled" management attitude was normal. There are still companies operating tacitly on this premise of adherence to the literal terms of a joint contract. But under present conditions they do not enjoy competitively the productive and harmonious relations with their workers from which more wisely administered companies benefit.

I have no desire to exaggerate or distort the immediately practical consequences of this dilemma. I am as aware as anyone of the remarkable amount of loyal service which corporations today receive from employees on fixed weekly wages. And in numerous companies with a broadly conceived personnel programme (in which profit sharing as such is not included) the response in worker morale is good and seems on the surface to leave little to be desired. A *partnership attitude* and sentiment are undoubtedly more prevalent in a certain few American companies than ever before; and this ideal is proving contagious.

But this desirable attitude requires the substantiation of a *participation* which goes beyond the present body of personnel policies, essential through these are and will continue to be, a participation which *extends into the area of financial outcomes.* We already see in the policies and utterances of certain labour leaders and in their handling of wage disputes, a linkage of "wage, price, profit" facts which gives unmistakable evidence that the profit factor cannot remain outside the realm of joint consideration.

It has been necessary to elaborate the place of the profit motive because of its pervasive influence. But as respects the other two of the plural corporate aims—the personal and the public phases of purpose—the briefest comment will suffice. It is true that corporate conduct is sometimes controlled by strong-kind and self-willed top executives. And where this is the situation, the workers cannot collaborate in any advantageous way. Such personal aims may have some paternalistic expression, but more usually they are selfish. And in either case they are not working with the expressed needs or desires of the workers themselves. Rather the expression of employee interests would here take the form of acting as a check on an excessive exercise of executive personal power, even where it has a seemingly philanthropic intent. Here is a purpose which, normally, employees would have to oppose.

The corporate aim of taking account of *public* requirements is, on the other hand, one which has to be evaluated by employee groups on the merits of the public expressions. These expressions can take several forms. They can be local sentiment, they can take the form of legislation, they can be public policy as discerned in time of war or other public crises.

In general terms public pressures to be considered in the conduct of corporate groups will tend in directions which employees would find it in their interests to support. But in each specific instance employee groups and labour union groups and leaders will have to undertake a careful evaluation of the public pressures in order to determine what attitude they should take and what measures they should support.

This review of going aims and the part employees might take in sharing in their realisation supplies a needed background for what is to follow. Probably more aspects of aims are common to all employed in a given venture than is usually realised. The present extent of good work and good relations would certainly substantiate this statement.

There is a final common aim not as mentioned. It is the aim of doing everything possible to assure the presence of administrative leadership which will embody the kind of outlook here being described and advocated. Such leadership is surely destined to realize that the aims of corporate life cannot remain too separate from or inconsistent with the underlying human ends which life itself has to serve it is to enhance the well-being of the generality of individuals in a democratic society.

This discussion of the reality and necessity of knowing and stressing common aims has, however, to be viewed in a realistic context. The situation is not and will not soon be one of gentleness, sweetness and light. The issues of tension are real, basic and vital. On matters having a bearing on the ultimate financial outcome of operations, complete agreement and unity of interest are not readily achieved. There may perennially arise, moreover, such questions as the following: Shall a particular position fall into one pay classification or a higher one? Shall foremen's salaries be fifteen per cent or forty per cent above the level of wages in their departments? Shall a dividend of five, six or eight per cent be paid? To what amount should corporate surpluses be retained in the business? Does the price of the product militate against it acceptance by a wider public?

These are typical instances of the kind of issue as to which no absolute standards can be invoked, and as to which, therefore, differences of opinion and sharp conflicts of interest naturally arise.

We are now, therefore, at a point where the second question posed for examination in this chapter may be raised.

Is Complete Unity of Aims Possible?

A distinction between a working unity and a complete unity is valid in an attempt to analyze how *greater* unity may become a fact.

The signing of every collective agreement and every acceptance of going terms of employment in cases where such negotiation does not prevail actively give effect to a temporary accepted basis of accommodation under which work does go forward. If this were not so, the dissensions within organisations would threaten to disrupt and bankrupt them. Or to put it differently, an empirical working cooperation in fact exists wherever operations are going forward with reasonable productivity, solvency, and good feeling. But this kind of temporary empirical adjustment is not enough. Our society and our productive instrumentalities are entitled to more. And our managers and rank and file are entitled to more, as energetic and creative persons. Indeed, if the aims were influential which *might* validly be common if they were fully understood by all concerned, and it a serious effort were made by managers, by workers, and by union leaders *to agree as to what in terms of productive group effort they all wanted the workers to be loyal to,* a building of policies of collaboration which came close to unity of aim would become a real possibility.

But the attaining at present of any unity of aim and motive including all workers in a corporation is certainly not an easy task. Ultimate and complete functional unity has to be seen as a long-range possibility. For, ideally, its attainment would mean that every worker while on this job was always centered intensively on doing all he could to advance the agreed aims of the organisation. *Total mobilisation of total ability for total achievement of a unanimously accepted goal*—this would identify functional unity at its ideal level.

And as an appealing ideal—desired throughout his organisation by every wise manager—this is not to be dismissed as utopian. But it is essential to know the demanding conditions which would be the price to be paid for its realisation. It is essential also to appreciate that, *given the right attendant conditions,* this kind of all-out mobilisation has an appeal to normal human nature which is profound. It is interesting to see out of a wholly different kind of analysis the confirmation of this view of a basic human craving presented by another writer as follows:

> … the mind becomes possessed to a supreme degree of the desire to apply itself to its work with all its will to fine achievement, and to realize as effectually as possible the act of *one* against *all,* through *all*, and, ideally, for *all,* which is characteristic of its nature, and which the spectacle of human disorder demands of it.

In other words there is a human disposition to go *all out* for some socially justified project, if only the situation is demand propitious. But to shape the situation to be one that is deemed by all to *be* propitious is not simple.

We have, for example, to remind ourselves of the further complicating factor, in the striving for common aims, introduced by the claims of loyalty to the labour union with the collective agreement is negotiated. The reality of a dual loyalty here is not to be denied; nor is it likely to be diminished whatever changes in managerial policy may occur.

The interest and aims of the unions are not at all points identical with the interests and aims of the employing body. Indeed, by definition, they are to some extent not supposed to be identical, even though one may envisage important changes in emphasis in the future.

Also, most executives would readily acknowledge that employees will, and indeed should, have other loyalties than those to the employing organisation. And they would agree that all the employer currently has a right to expect is that degree of loyalty which assures good production in a friendly atmosphere. That there may be deeper reaches of collective collaboration which it is possible to attain in which the degree of harmonizing the aims can be intensified, is the happy outcome still to be explored.

Complete unity of aim is for the future. Yet it is not to be lost sight of. For such devotion as that of the football player to his team or of the musician to his orchestra has a quality which could valuably be extended to other groups with enormous benefit to all involved. It suggests an attitude of organisation-centered loyalty which managers would and should highly prize.

But short of such an ultimate, much remains to be done that could be done *now* and done with great benefit to industrial relations.

It is at once possible for wisely disposed managers to focus on employee understanding and acceptance of certain shared aims. It is at once possible for managers to supply a degree of heartening personal leadership toward present common aims. It is at once possible to provide methods to reconcile or minimize the more acute conflicts of interest about the implementing of common aims. It is at once possible for managers to strengthen the measures of two-way communication about policy and programme to common advantage.

There is, in short, plenty to be immediately undertaken in the direction of greater unifying of interests, and such efforts will benefit production and improve human relations.

Does Employee Acceptance of Agreed Aims Prove their Soundness?

In a world where organisations will increasingly seek employee concurrence in and active support of the purposes they want to realize, it is pertinent to ask; is acquiescence on the part of these associated in some venture, especially where it is affirmatively obtained, all that is needful as the basis for *social* sanction of the policies being given effect?

Certainly not. Agreement among the groups within an organisation as to desirable policies and practices is *not of itself* sufficient evidence that the right line is inevitably being followed.

This question is not raised to borrow trouble that in practice may rarely arise, or to strive for undue refinement of analysis about what some may regard as an academic issue. But I place so much emphasis upon the importance of searching for areas of agreement and for working out procedures designed to bring about unity of intention within organisations that almost inevitably one asks: Does mutual agreement prove social soundness?

One type of situation of which or history supplies bountiful illustrations is the programme of the paternalistic employer. In these instances the acquiescence is, of course, more *passive* in character. Yet as time goes on and more and more "generous" provisions are made, the acceptance of these by employees has often tended to be taken for granted. The managerial psychology which prompts such "handouts" is by no means defunct.

There are degrees of paternalism in action. The extreme cases is that of the company-owned town which may include all or some of the following: employee housing, schools, churches, stores public buildings, and athletic fields, all owned by the corporations. A less extreme example would be once where the company "welfare" programme is elaborate, including recreation features and community activities all financed and controlled by the company.

What difference does it in fact make how such benefits are supplied so long as the employees find that they enjoy them? Is not their use by employees the evidence that they are gaining some advantage?

There are two kinds of answer to such questions, The first is the practical one of past experience. The second derives from the philosophy which permeates this book. First, there have been enough cases of employees under paternalistic provisions who have *eventually* "revolted" and gone of strike, to raise doubts as to the wisdom and permanent acceptability of employer "generosity." Also, since such paternalism has usually existed in unorganised shops having no collective agreements with unions, the *eventual* demand in many instances for the initiation of collective dealings has demonstrated that all was not as serene and contented as managements had assumed.

It is revealing, moreover, that the reaction of managers of the eventual repudiation of their generosity, in favour of freer and more independent employee action, has been almost uniformly of the same character. Executives have been surprised, aggrieved, resentful, discouraged at the employee "ingratitude." Indeed, in some cases they have been led to abandon any basic efforts to get at the real sources of employee disaffection and of more permanently constructive employee attitudes. All too often there has been little or no realisation that generosity *down from above* comes to be suspect because it is "down" and is clearly identified by the giver and the receivers as "from above."

The second and more profound reason why paternalistic measures are not self-justifying is that they come sooner or later to be regarded as a substitute for autonomous and self-respecting participation by employees in affairs they eventually realize to be "their own." There is a point beyond which the long arm of the company is not desired or desirable in relation to the conduct of local community education, housing, recreation, worship and the like, since these are common *human* concerns and not directly production matters.

Put in another way, questions arise as to what welfare provisions may do to the character and attitudes of people, both donors and recipients. For example, do the welfare features give evidence of increasing people's powers of self-growth, self-initiative, self-responsibility for personal and community development? Do they enhance people's sense of self-respect, integrity, reasonable freedom to be themselves, awareness that they are needs in themselves and not the means only to the needs of others? Are a full belly, creature comforts and absolute security all the employees are looking for?

Is it, by way of illustration, better to have a company band resplendent with uniforms and instruments bought by the company and the occasions of its performances and the selection of its repertory determined by the company? Or is it better to have no band—*unless* the employees themselves largely take the initiative in having it *their affair* wholly or partially under their control and support?

Surely, if company-bestowed benefits are fostering employee docility, deference to management dictation on non-industrial aspects of living, dependence of employee political or religious opinions on managerial judgements, there is *in kind of society* little good to be said for them.

Rather the test of worth is whether they are helping workers as individuals and groups to have educational experiences which through their own voluntary and responsible participation in handling diverse affairs become occasions of learning and growth in individual self-respect and civic competence. The benefits fundamentally desires are those of *enriched and growing personalities.* And only provisions why supply educational and democratic self-assumed responsibilities can pass muster as justifiable. The measure of the soundness of whatever features the management may desire to provide *is the enhancement of the selfhood of all participants.* They have to be helped to grow toward a condition where a sharing of partnership attitudes and cooperative practices will progressively become the fact.

In short, the tacit or passive agreement found where paternalism is in practice is no indication whatsoever of its social acceptability.

Beyond the paternalistic situation, however, with its passive agreement to certain material advantages, there is the situation of collective agreement which can lend themselves to conspiratorial or monopolistic results. Instances are not unknown where, whatever the strictly legal interpretation, employers and unions together may agree upon a basis of joint operation which restrains trade, limits labor supply unwarrantedly, tacitly fixes prices, fosters monopoly, or embodies other restrictive features. Such agreement is clearly antisocial.

Again, cases could be cited where employees are tacit parties to the fabrication of a poor quality of product and misrepresentation about product; and parties also to undue price rises caused by agreement on an excessive scale of wage payments and company profits.

To cite another type of situation, an employer might in effect bribe with high pay a body of workers to continue employment under conditions which were unsafe or unhealthy comparatively with the best provisions possible in that industry. Workers' continuance at work under such unfavourable conditions constitutes an agreement of sorts. And if both parties are aware that safe or healthy provisions might readily be made by the application of up-to-date technical resources, tacit acceptance of bad working conditions is the more egregious. Hence, to say that the fact of such tacit agreement proves *ipso facto* the soundness of the working basis is obviously false.

The case might also be recalled of the company in a severe flu epidemic, which was urged by its medical staff to suspend operations when a substantial minority of its workers were out sick, but which at the insistence of the employees themselves did not close down. Joint agreement here did not, of course, prevent the exposure of more workers to infection and to expansive illness.

Finally, a *reduction ad absurdum* in uncritical acceptance might be illustrated by gang of counterfeiters of bootleggers. Their unity of aim and their agreement in action may well be above reproach. But that surely says nothing about the legitimacy or social validity of their behaviour. The notion of "honor among thieves" leaves much unsaid about the nature of the honour and the desirability of thievery.

On what matters is concurrence between managers and men being sought, for what purposes, and by what methods? These, in a word, are the questions which have to be faced before there can be a socially intelligent answer to the basic inquiry as to whether tacit acceptance or active agreement by employees constitutes assurance of a sound decision. In some form or other the ancient "bread and circuses" situation is always in danger of recurring in managerial attitudes and provisions. And where the weakness of the flesh leads employees to acquiesce in such situations, the outward serenity, security, or stability is profoundly misleading because it is based on precarious and temporary satisfactions.

There is, in short, little or no ground for believing that *fundamentally* employee or union agreement with company proposals (or company agreement to union to union proposals) is necessarily sufficient. Sooner or later from some responsible source, the question will be posed as to the larger social soundness of measures which promise dubious outcomes.

Managerial thinking and planning can, therefore, never rest content merely with the actuality that employee and union concurrence to specific measures is assured. This will be especially true in instances such as restrictions upon output, price increases, labour limitations, etc., as to which there is a growing body of opposed sentiment in the community at large.

Admittedly it is not possible to lay down a quick and easy test of social soundness. Agreements in violation of law and public regulation, offenses against accepted public standards of morals or taste—these are relatively easy to identify. But there is obviously a wide range of issues upon which the advance appraisal of public acceptance is not simply come by. Yet such long-run criteria as whether proposals are truly democratic and are contributing to a wide human friendliness, to educational experiences and to the personality growth of participants—these can be helpful.

There has to be mindfulness of the values of an effort by managers and workers together to identify and to evolved those policies they can wisely espouse. Nor can these be confined to or measured solely by *material* advantages, desirable though these may be. In numerous concrete ways commitment has to be to the value of a democratic way of life, to the applied use of scientific knowledge, technological and psychological, and to validity of a law of widening fraternal love in human relations. These are our central points of reference wherever efforts to agree are going forward between managers and men, no les than in other publicly reached decisions of practical policy.

Ultimately, it is the quality of personal and communal living which is at stake. For it is folly to forget that we are not laboring and producing in association merely for the sake of the work and its material rewards. Even while he is at work, every man is a whole man—producer, consumer, citizen free person with family ties and aspirations. And all of these aspects of personality have to be accounted for and ministered to. Only policies and practices which strengthen then the possibilities of this wholeness can defensibly get the concurrences of all parties at interest in productive activity.

CONCLUSION

Consideration has now be given to the difficulties of getting acceptance by the rank and file of the aims of organisations. It has been suggested that some aims are more appealing than others. It has been emphasised that a number of integral aims might well become more acceptable if they were better understood. It has been pointed out that common aims can be clarified and strengthened only to the extent that divergences of internal group outlooks and interests are reckoned with, and shared provisions are made or resolving whatever conflicts of interest may arise.

The requirements for virtual merging of interests among groups as to what organisations are to do and how they are to do it have been shown to involve conditions not easy to meet under typical present policies of operation. Yet the very suggestion of the value of such a unity of purpose indicates that it should not be ignored as we think ahead.

Finally, agreement entered into by employers and workers, whether tacit or overt, cannot ignore the truth that for social acceptability these agreements have to conform to—or at least look in the direction of strengthening—certain broader social standards.

The fact of agreement *of itself* proves nothing as to the social value of what has been agreed upon, even as affecting the agreeing parties.

The aims and policies of any organisation and the acceptance of these aims by those working in it have, in other words, to be scrutinised in their relation to a more inclusive foundation. Such an inclusive foundations is to be looked for to an important degree in a study of the claims and demands human nature itself makes upon life—its total up thrust for quality and nobility in search of human fulfillment. Clearly we are obligated to understand human nature in as abroad and deep a frame of its experience and its aspiration as we can discover and depict. Only with this knowledge will men's activities fall into a meaningful pattern—actual and potential.

Administrative leaders should be among the first to make use of the results of such discovery. The obtainable truths here should being to supply basis criteria for all they plan and create in their corporate relations with people. It is to such an inquiry, psychological in essence, that it becomes imperative next to turn. Only with the insights such a study should yield will management being to be equipped with a profound grasp of the human elements of its problem.

12

Boards and Commissions

The Commissions form of organisation has been extensively employed in the administration of public affairs, though, generally speaking unitary control of administrative services is now increasingly favoured. The history of this form of organisation dates back to Middle Ages when many European Governments created boards and commissions for conducting public affairs. The commission form of local government in the U.S.A., is largely modeled on this basis. In international administration, the boards and commissions have been in vogue since the nineteenth century with a view to giving representation to all independent States.

In Europe, the commission form has today fallen into disfavour. In the U.S.A., on the contrary, there has been a constant increase in the number and variety of boards. This increase is partly due to the looseness of the American administrative system, and partly to a desire to escape the pervasive influence of party politics in administration.

In India, too, boards and commissions have been extensively made use of. The Commissions in India may be classified into three broad categories from the point of view of their source of origin.

The Constitution of India mentions a few of such organisations; for example, the Election Commission, the Union Public Service Commission, etc. These organisations are, thus, backed by constitutional sanctity. Secondly, boards and commissions may be set up by Act of Parliament. The University Grants Commission, the Railway Board, the Central Board of Revenue, the Oil and Natural Gas Commission, the Atomic Energy

Commission, the Flood Control Board, etc., have been set up under statutes passed by Indian Parliament, Thirdly, the Commissions may be brought into being by an executive resolution of the Government. The Central Social Welfare Board, the Handicrafts Board, the Handloom Board, the Central Water and Power Commission etc., may be cited as examples of boards and commissions created by the resolutions of the Government.

Of these three categories, the commissions mentioned in the Constitution enjoy the greatest amount of autonomy: They are appointed directly by the President of India, and do not come under the general administrative control of any particular Ministry in their day-to-day functioning. The statutory boards are put under the general administrative control of the Ministry concerned, but are free from the regular departmental procedures. The third category of bodies like the Handloom Board, the Handicrafts Board, etc., are created for a specified period of time, and their existence depends upon the will of the Ministries concerned. They are attached to the Ministry and are knows as Attached Boards.

The Constitution of India enumerates the following bodies to be set up on the commission model: the Finance Commission, the Union Pubic Service Commission, the Election Commission, the Backward Classes Commission, and the Official Language Commission.

THE FINANCE COMMISSION

The Finance Commission is constituted at the expiration of every fifth year or at such earlier time as the President considers necessary. It consists of a chairman and four other members to be appointed by the President. The Finance Commission recommends on the following:

(i) The distribution between the Union and the States of the net proceeds of taxes which are to be or may be, divided between them, the allocation between the States of respective shares of such proceeds;

(ii) The principles which should govern the grants-in-aid of the revenues of the States out of the Consolidated Fund of India; and

(iii) Any other matter referred to the Commission by the President in the interest of sound finance.

The recommendations of the Commission are laid before each House of Parliament.

The Union Public Service Commission

The Union Public Service Commission conducts examinations for appointments to the services of the Union. It shall be consulted:

(i) On all matters relating to method of recruitment to civil services and for civil posts;

(ii) On the principles to be followed in making appointments, to civil services and posts, and in making promotions and transfers from one service to another, and on the suitability of candidates for such appointments, promotions, or transfers;

(iii) On all disciplinary matters affecting the Central Government employees;

(iv) On any claim by or in respect of Central Government employee in a civil capacity, that any costs incurred by him in defending legal proceedings against him in respect of acts done in the execution of his duty should be paid of the Consolidated Found of India; and

(v) On any claim for the award of a pension in respect of injuries sustained by a Central Government employee.

The members of the Union Public Service Commission are appointed by the President for a period of 6 years or till the age of sixty-five, whichever may be earlier. The authorised strength of the Commission is nine.

The Election Commission

The superintendence and control of all elections to Parliament and to the Legislatures of the States and of the President and the Vice-President of the Union, are vested in the Election

Commission consisting of a Chief Election Commissioner and such other Commissioners as may be appointed by the President. Originally, it was proposed to set up one Commission to deal with elections to parliament and separate Election Commissions for each State to be appointed by the Governors of the States. But now there is only one centralised Commission. "The centralised election machinery has, thus, stemmed from the national urge to curb and thwart any intention of the State Governments to project regionalism into the preparation of the electoral list."

The Backward Classes Commission

The Backward Classes Commission investigates the conditions of socially and educationally backward classes within the territory of India and the difficulties under which they labour and to make recommendations as to the steps that should be taken by the Union or any State Government to remove such difficulties, and to improve their condition and as to the grants that should be made for the purpose by the Union or any State Government. The report of the Commission is laid before each House of Parliament. This is not a standing commission.

The Official Language Commission

The Official Language Commission set up at the expiration of five years from the commencement of the Constitution and thereafter at the expiration of the ten years from such commencement, recommends to the President as to:

(i) the progressive use of the Hindi language for the official purposes of the Union;

(ii) restrictions on the use of the English language for all or any of the official purposes of the Union;

(iii) the language to be used for all or any of the purposes in the Supreme and the High Courts, etc.;

(iv) the form of numerals to be used for any one or more specified purposes of the Union; and

(v) any other matter referred to the Commission by the President as regards the official language of the Union

and language for communication between the Union and a State, or between the State and another and their use.

The Commission consists of a chairman and such other members representing the different languages as the President may appoint.

The Commissions envisaged in the Constitution itself manifest some common traits. The members are appointed by the President, and Commissions do not come under the general administrative control of any Ministry. Their reports are placed on the table of each House of Parliament. Further, the members cannot be removed from office except by a special procedure, ensuring thereby independence of members.

A study of all the three categories of boards/commissions reveals that their composition varies from one another. They may be composed of government officials who are full-time members, or the members may be non-officials including members of Parliament or State Legislatures, giving only a part of their time to the work of the Commission. Finally, the Commissions may consist of members holding offices under the Government may by virtue of such offices being *ex officio* members.

The relative merits of the Commission form of organisation have been debated in all countries. W.F. Willoughby argues that the Commission is better fitted than the Bureau:

(i) where duties involve the exercise of discretion on an important scale in the formulation of policies and rules affecting private rights and the adjudication of claims;

(ii) where the functions involve general control of character;

(iii) where it is desirable to have a number of different interests represented; and

(iv) where it is necessary to eliminate party politics and influence of pressure groups.

The Board or Commission type of headship is generally recommended if the public policy has not been fully finalised, and, therefore, joint discussion and deliberation should precede its formulation. Secondly, this form is appropriate in those areas where several interests are to be represented, adjudged, or reconciled, Labour disputes, involving the interests of capital and loabour, are usually entrusted to boards for settlement; for, a plural body, it is generally believed, commands greater confidence of concerned parties than a single individual. Thirdly, plural headship is appropriate where wide discretionary or controlling powers are exercised. The examples are the Public Service Commission, the Central Board of Revenue, etc. Fourthly, this form of organisation may be preferred in the interest of administrative integrity against external pressure. For, a single individual may more easily succumb to external pressures than a plural body.

The plural executive, however, suffers from a number of drawbacks which, in effect, severely restrict its large-scale adoption. It results in lack of unity of purpose, lack of energy in execution, absence of well-defined responsibility, and, not un-often, lapses of coordination. "While Commissions, at times, operate smoothly and energetically, they often develop friction and conflict among their members. Differences spread inevitably into the subordinative staff, forming factions, one of the worst type of administrative plagure." That The plural headship is a guarantee to sound decisions is also a doubtful proposition. The single executive, on the other hand, displays energy, vigour and courage in execution and is, therefore, to be preferred where the major policy has been settled, and work is of a routine character. Even where Commission type of organisation exists, the implementation of the decisions is very often entrusted to the charge of a single executive officer. "Substantially universal experience demonstrates the fatal weakness of the direction of day-to-day operations by a plural body. To 'administer' in this sense of the term is the job of one, not of many." The merits of the single executive are, thus outlined by Alexander Hamilton.

"A single man, in each department of the administration, would be greatly preferable. It would give us a chance of more knowledge, more activity, more responsibility, and, of course, more heal and attention. Boards partake of a part of the inconvenience of larger assemblies. Their decisions are slower, their energy less, their responsibility more diffused. The will not have the same ability and knowledge as in administration by a single man. Men of the first pretensions will not so readily engage in them; because they will be less conspicuous, of less importance, and have less opportunity of distinguishing themselves. The members of Boards will take less pains to inform themselves and arrive to eminence, because they have fewer motives to do it."

The above discussion does not establish a conclusive case for either of the two types of headship. Choice of one as against the other, should be determined by the administrative circumstance of each case. It may, nevertheless, be pointed out that plural executive lacks ingredients of effective management. Boards are expensive, cause delay, result in diffusion of responsibility, and precipitate occasional deadlocks. The board form renders difficult co-operation and co-ordination between different agencies. As L.D. White observes, "in general, the burden of proof is on the advocates of a board in preference to a single executive." John A. Fairlie observes, "For the conduct of administrative services, there should be a responsible single executive. There will remain, however, a place for boards in conducting inquiries and in planning new undertaking, as well as in the management of emergency or temporary tasks. Furthermore, they will find a function as advisory agencies and as regulators of general policy, even in cases where a responsible single executive will carry out the actual administrative work. This division of function has already developed to a considerable extent in the control and management of educational affairs; it promises the possibility of deriving from the use of boards the greatest possible benefit with the least possible disadvantages. There will of course, exist danger of conflict between the supervising boards and the administrative official."

It is appropriate tc point out her that the Indian Commissions are not like the Independent Regulatory Commissions of the United States. The former are not independent in the sense in which it is understood in the U.S.A. In that country, the Commissions are virtually free from the Presidential control. The Commissions in India do not enjoy such a degree of Independence. The U.S. Congress labours under perennial distrust of the Executive, *i.e.*, the President. Consequently, the Congress has preferred to create special bodies to regulate and control, when regulation and control become necessary with the economic advancement and industrialisation of the country. Of course, a feeling that quasi-judicial, quasi-legislative work should be entrusted to separate bodies independent of the executive has also been behind the creation of such bodies. Nevertheless, the paramount factor behind the emergence of the Independent Regulatory Commission has been the Congressional distrust of the President. It is, therefore, necessary to point out that India, with its parliamentary system of government, is not likely to have the Independent Regulatory Commissions of the U.S.A. model.

INDEPENDENT REGULATORY COMMISSIONS

The Independent Regulatory Commissions are characteristically American device to undertake public regulation of private economic activities. The need for such regulation and control became apparent with the growing industrialisation of the country during the nineteenth century. Appearing first at the state level, the first Independent Regulatory Commission, set up by the Federal Government, was the Inter-State Commerce Commission, established in 1887. At present there are the following nine regulatory Commissions in the Federal Government of the U.S.A.:

1. Inter-State Commerce Commission.
2. Civil Aeronautics Board.
3. Federal Power Commission.
4. Federal Communications Commission.
5. Federal Trade Commission.
6. National Labour Relations Board.
7. Securities and Exchange Commission.

8. Board of Governors of the Federal Reserve System of Banks, popularly called the Federal Reserve Board.

9. Tariff Commission.

Broadly speaking the Regulatory Commissions perform two sets of functions. First, they set up standards and rules to govern the behaviour of a particular industry in future. Secondly, they also enforce these standards and rules, and prosecute the defaulters. The Commissions are, engaged in administrative legislations (or, rule-making) and administrative adjudication. These bodies are marked by the following three features:

1. These Commissions are manned by experts and are relatively small.

2. They are collegial, consisting of a group of men discussing and arriving at decisions by majority vote.

3. They are relatively independent of the Chief Executive, *i.e.*, the President.

A Commission is set up under a statute passed by Congress laying down its constitution and functions. Though the members are appointed by the President with the approval of the Senate, they are not responsible to him. The overlapping of terms of the members also strengthens their independence of the President in the functioning of the Commission. The President cannot remove the personnel of the Commission except on grounds specified in the statute creating the Commission. The members of the Commission are not to be treated like the civil servants who can be removed by the President at his will. This position was established in the famous Humphrey case. It may, nevertheless, be stressed that the independence of the Regulatory Commissions is relative, not absolute. Their actions are subject to judicial review, which means judicial control in three principal aspect-(i) "in assuring the use of correct procedures in administrative action; (ii) in preventing action in excess of powers conferred by the legislature: and (iii) where administrative action depends on a factual record in making sure that the evidence in the record is sufficient." Further, the Commissions are subject to Congressional control. They receive annual appropriations from the Congress, which may order an investigation into the operations of the Commissions, amend its constitution, and, even abolish it; although this last step, in the words of the Hoover Commission Task Force, is a "blunt instrument and not likely to be resorted to except under the extreme circumstance." Moreover, in personnel administration, the Regulatory Commissions are controlled by the Civil Service Commission. Lastly, their budgets are subject to review by the Bureau of the Budget.

Regulation of private business activities is a difficult task. The organisation entrusted with this function must manifest impartiality to all concerned. At the same time, it must not be hampered by provisions which interfere with the discharge of the vital function of regulation of private business activities. "The industries affected by regulation are often powerful and politically influential, and regulation controls their profits, their services, and their finances. The combination of a wide administrative direction on the one hand, and great private influence on the other, plus high stakes in the relationships between them, involves serious risks of corruption and unfairness. In this situation, the independent Regulatory Commission seems most nearly to meet the need." Elucidating the merits of this type of administrative organisation, the Hoover Commission Task Force commented: "The number of members and their security of tenure are intended to assure freedom from partisan control or favouritism. The group is able to resist outside influence more effectively than an individual, and each member is free from a threat of removal as a source of pressure. Moreover, since the activities of the Commission may be more subject to public scrutiny than would be a single bureau in a large department, there is greater opportunity for exposure of pressures or improper actions. Finally, while provisions for hearings and similar safeguards against arbitrary actions are not peculiar to Commissions. They may be more effective when combined with group action."

Despite these advantages, independent Regulatory Commissions have been subjected to varied criticism. Indeed, there are fundamental difference of opinion regarding the suitable administrative organisation for the performance of regulatory functions in the economic field. The main indictments are summarised below:

In the first place, the system of independent Regulatory Commissions has created a 'headless fourth branch' in the U.S. Government, violating the accepted tripartite of powers. They are 'headless' as they are not subordinate to the President. They lie outside the administrative system. headed by the President, and may be called 'islands of autonomy' within the United States administrative organisation. Consequently, the later has become 'disintegrated', resulting in the diminution of the President's effectiveness as the Chief Executive. In the words of the Brownlow Committee (1937), "They (Independent Regulatory Commission) are in reality independent government set up to deal with the rail-road problem, the banking problem, or the radio problem. They constitute a headless fourth branch of the Government, a haphazard deposit of irresponsible agencies and un-coordinated powers. They do violation to the basic theory of the American Constitution that there should be three branches of the Government, and only three. The Congress has found no effective way of supervising them, they cannot be controlled by the President, and they are answerable to the courts only in respect to the legality of the activities." This Committee further declared that "though the Commissions enjoy power without responsibility, they also leave the President with responsibility without power."

Secondly, the combination of the functions of law-making, prosecution, and decision has been inherently unfair and is likely to lead to arbitrariness, endangering thereby the right of individuals. In this connection, Robert E.Cushman writes: "The Commissions are being asked to perform judicial task interwoven with determination of policy which at times are the subjects of acute partisan controversy or economic class antagonisms. This is not the atmosphere in which the right of individuals ought to be judged. It is a vital and inherent weakness of he Independent Commission system...."

Thirdly, it is argued that the Commission device has not been an effective one, either in protecting the public interests, or in assuring the long-run progress of the industry. This is because the Commissioner act through case-by-case procedure, and they are separated from one another. This defect impressed the Hoover Commission (1949), which pointed out: "The chief criticism that can be made of the Regulatory Commissions is that they become too engrossed in case-by-case activities and, thus, fail to plan their roles and to promote the enterprises entrusted to their care. Typical of this is the attitude by which the Civil Aeronautics Board and the Inter-State Commerce Commission have approached the problem of building a route structure for the nation."

Fourthly, the Regulatory Commissions are subject to the charge that they have been unduly lax. This slackness is engendered partly because the Commission, being relatively free from executive supervisions, are liable to drift into a condition of dependence upon the interests with which they deal, partly because "in practice, the Commissions are not responsible to the legislative body in any orderly way holding out the possibility of various forms of interference, and partly because of the Commissions' fear of being reversed by the courts." In the opinion of Arthur M. MacMahon, all these three factors may make the commissioners timid.

Fifthly, the Regulatory Commissions have been criticised on the score that the Commission type of organisation is inherently weak. This criticism can, however, be made pointless by developing the administrative role of the chairman. Indeed, the Hoover Commission has recommended the strengthening of the Chairman's role. As a result, the chairman's administrative role has been strengthened to some extent

Sixthly, the system of independent Regulatory Commissions has resulted in lack of co-ordination. This is because they adopt the case-by-case procedure, are outside the administrative system headed by the President, and are even separated from one another.

Attempts at Reforms

The independent Regulatory Commissions have been the subject of study and investigation by individuals as well as commissions. The President's Committee on Administrative

Management (popularly called the Brownlow committee) severely criticised them declaring that "thought the commissions enjoy power without responsibility, they also leave the President with responsibility without power." The Committee was of the opinion that the work of the Commissions should be assigned to appropriate department, the former to remain as autonomous adjudicatory boards within the departments for the handling of cases involving administrative adjudication. Such activities as planning, investigation, initiation of prosecution should be looked after by the bureau of the department. The Congress, however, rejected this recommendation. The Brownlow Committee's plea that the regulatory work should be sought under the departmental auspices, and the Regulatory Commissions should survive as the adjudicatory boards, was criticised by the Attorney General's Committee on Administrative Procedure, reporting in 1941. The Committee observed: "A separation of functions would seriously militate against what this Committee has already noted as being numerically and otherwise the life-blood of the administrative process-negotiations and informal settlements. Clearly, amicable disposition of cases is fare less likely where negotiations are with officials devoted solely to prosecution and where the prosecuting officials cannot turn to the deciding branch to discover the law and the applicable procedures." This Committee thus, defended the Commission system.

The second Hoover Commission called the Regulatory Commission 'an outstanding development' in the American federal government, though at the same time, it drew attention to the haphazard, un-coordinated nature of their growth in response to the immediate needs of the governments. The Commission said, "...it is found that a large part of the work of the Commission is not closely related to that of the rest of the Government and requires no active co-ordination to avoid conflicts." It pleaded for enhancing the powers of the chairman, and better salaries for the commissioners.

The independent Regulatory Commissions confront any scheme of federal administrative reorganisation with a challenging problem. In the words of Robert E. Cushman, they are 'areas of unaccountability' outside the sphere of Presidential direction and responsibility. How can they be made to fit into the broad pattern of the United States Government? There are the following four alternatives.

1. Integration of the Regulatory Commissions into the executive branch of the government making them subordinate to the President;
2. Strengthening of the Congressional control of the Commissions;
3. Strengthening of the judicial review of the Commissions' activities; or
4. Segregation of the legislative, administrative and judicial work of the Commission, each phase of work to be appropriately performed.

It appears that, despite their shortcomings, the independent Regulatory Commissions seem impregnable. James W. Fesler stresses the need for the recognition of certain fundamental factors in the functioning of the Commissions. He writes, "first the quality of men and women appointed to the Commissions is more important than the details of organisation. Second, judicial work should be carried on in an impartial manner, free from the bias characteristic of the prosecution function. Third, co-ordination of policy formulation and administrative management among government agencies is essential, especially during periods when government plays a positive role in the economy. The chief executive appears tc be the only responsible and effective focus for such co-ordination. And fourth, independent Commissions should be subject to the same control by the legislative and judicial branches that applies to all other regulatory and service agencies of Government."

13

Field Administration

New Delhi is the hub of administration—a centre, from where the whole country is governed and administered. In practice, however, there is a plurality of administative centres spread throughout the length and breadth of the country; and from the point of view of the citizens, these centres are decidedly more important.

There is no ministry/department of the Central or State Government which does not have numerous field offices all over the land. Take a central department like the Posts and Telegraphs which has about one lakh Post Offices scattered all over the country, all arranged in a hierarchy—circle, postal, district division, sub-post office area, ways, which has the following hierarchy of organisation.

"Headquarters"		— Railways Board
"Field"	Zone	— Zonal Manager
	Division	—Divisional Superintendent.

The picture is no different in the case of the administration at the State level. Take the Police and Revenue administration as an example. The hierarchy of organisation in these cases is as follows:

	Police	*Revenue*
State Headquarters	Inspector-General of Police	State Headquarters—Board of Revenue: Division—Divisional Commissioner

Range	Deputy Inspector-General of Police	District—Collector/ Deputy Commissioner
District	District Superintendentdent of Police	Subdivision—Sub-divisional Officer: Tahsil—Tahsildar
Circle	Circle Inspector	Revenue Circle—
Police Station	Sub-Inspector	Revenue Inspector
Village	Chowkidar or Patel, or the Headman	Village-Lekhpal or Patwari

DEFINITIONS

By the term 'headquarters', we mean the central or supervising office, usually in the capital, in contrast to regional or fieldoffice. Concretely put, the "headquarters organisation of the Government of India comprises a number of Ministries and Departments," to quote from the Report of the Second Pay Commission. In contrast to headquarters, the offices which usually should get the approval before taking administrative actions from the headquarters and are under the control and direction of the latter, are called ' field-offices'. In India administrative jargon, headquarters is synonymous with the secretariat, and the term 'field' refers to attached and subordinate offices.

IMPORTANCE OF FIELD

Just as proof of the pudding lies in its eating, the impact of legislation or any administrative action depends upon its 'administering'. Best intentions get thwarted by inefficient or soulless implementation. Since 'administering' is the responsibility of the field, the latter, in fact, makes the difference between good government and bad government. Importance of the field emerges from other factors as well, some of which are the following:

1. There are many times more public officials working in the field than at the national capital. Only one out of every 160 or so Central Government employees is in the headquarters at Delhi—the rest work in the field. This is true of other countries as well. In the U.S.A., for instance, "nine employees are stationed in the field for every employee stationed in

Washington," according to James W. Fesler. This is the trend all over the world.

2. Expansion of services now being provided by government committed to the ideals of the Welfare State.

3. Increase in the regulatory activities of government.

4. Technological advances—particularly in the field of transportation and communication—have played an important role in the expansion of field organisation.

5. Democracy, too, has necessitated the creation of field organisations. Citizens now want services at their door. Also, there is a demand for greater citizen participation in both, policy-formation and execution.

6. Some field organisations are inevitable under any situation. A country, for instance, must maintain its diplomatic missions abroad.

Field: A Neutral Concept

A word need be said about an erroneous belief that 'field' necessarily connotes decentralisation and 'grass-roots' administration. Historically, the field organisation has been a tool employed for both the centralisation and decentralisation of government. Centralist emphasis, for instance, dominated field organisation under Mughal and British administrations.

Criteria Governing Formation of Field Areas

An important organisational question is: Should each department have its own field area suited to its own convenience? Or, should all the departments agree to have one common area? We may pose the same question differently, *viz.,* should field areas be single-purpose (special) or multi-purpose?

Each method of organizing the field area has its merits as well as demerits. There is no virtue in either method. It may, however, be advised that the same area should be created for as many departments as possible. This results in—(i) citizen convenience, (ii) easy and direct communication between field officers of different departments operating in the same area in related problems, and (iii) pooling together of house-keeping activities with resultant economy and greater efficiency. District in India is the multi-purpose field area, common to most of the departments. Yet, single-purpose area may look necessary in view of the peculiar or different requirements of a department. Thus, railways and posts and telegraphs have their own field areas suited to their own requirements.

The criteria governing formation of field area may be listed as follows:

1. Administrative economy including availability of funds with a department, and manpower:
2. Political pressures and need for citizen convenience and participation;
3. Nature of work to be performed by the department;
4. Historical consideration; and
5. Topography.

Co-Ordination Between Field Level Agencies

The activities of field functionaries of different departments must need be effectively coordinated, as all these are engaged in the performance of activities which are interrelated, even interdependent, and which, when taken together, culminate in realisation or planned targets. All the departments are, thus, partners in the joint enterprise of a modern welfare state. Agricultural development, to give an illustration, requires supplies, in proper sequence, and, what is more, in a timely way, of fertilizer, seed, water and credit, and arrangement for storing and marketing. Involved in these various tasks are the departments of agriculture, irrigation, husbandry, co-operation, electricity, etc. Failure on the part of even one is liable to retard the achievement of targets, and, as a result, there could emerge a situation, which a block development officer describes in this manner:

"Although the state irrigation department provides overseers on almost all the blocks, there is, however, no coordination between the overseers and the block. He seldom comes to the block, and hardly consults the extension officers or listens to the problems or grievances of the villagers. As a result, the grievances of the villagers regarding channels etc., are not solved in time and effectively. These are dealt with through routine correspondence and area, thus, delayed."

Success in agricultural development programme depends upon how various departmental functionaries gear their efforts. Co-ordination of these various activities may be facilitated if all these departments adopt identical boundaries for their areas, and also locate their offices in the same town in close proximity to one another. In addition, institutionalised efforts are also called for, and in this respect, a brief reference may be made to the following three models: (i) in India the District Collector/Deputy Commissioner has been the traditional coordinator in the district committed to his charge, (ii) the Prefect performs this function in France, and (iii) some countries appoint a general area officer who provides common staff services to all others and also functions as the convener and coordinator for conferences of officials in that area.

Whatever be the method for effecting field-level coordination among various technical functionaries, one thing must be strongly emphasised. And, this is the paramount need for free, frank and frequent communication between field offices of various departments For, their tasks are interrelated to a much greater extent than is generally realised or visualised at the headquarters. This is the 'procedural' supplement to the institutional models described in the earlier paragraph.

Issues in Field-Headquarters Relationship

Major issues involved in the relationship between the headquarters and field are two: (1) territorial—functional dichotomy; (2) communications and control.

Territorial—Functional Dichotomy

The organisation of field establishments from the standpoint of overhead direction and control may take either of the two forms—territorial or functional. Willoughby calls them unitary or multiple. In the unitary or territorial form the central authority creates regional or area agencies which have overall charge of all the activities of the area. The officer in charge of the area is its head and the heads of all other specialised units at that level are his subordinates. All communications from the field station to the head office and back are routed through him, and he has responsibility for the acts of all other departmental heads. The position is very different in a multiple or functional form of organisation where the different divisions or branches of the headquarters office have their corresponding field establishments at different area levels and maintain direct contact with them. There is no co-ordinating or integrating authority at the area level; each service or agency is treated as an independent entity unrelated to other services or agencies and the line of authority runs direct from it to its headquarters office. A good example of the territorial unitary type of field organisation is the Prefect in France. He is not only the head of the department (the largest unit of local administration), but also acts as the agent of the Central Government. He exercises general control and supervision over a number of public services in his department, e.g., education, public health, poor-relief, hospitals, and the preservation of order. The powers and functions of the Prefect have been lucidly expressed by Barthelemy as follows:

"This political agent, appointed and dismissed for political reasons, dependent upon the ministerial department most vitally concerned with questions of policy, represents not only the Ministry of the Interior, but all other ministries as well. Within the limits of his department, he personifies administrative authority, and possesses the power of deciding matters and appointing executives. The Prefect does not confine himself to directing, surveying and managing penitentiary and charitable institutions, which are under the Ministry of the interior, ...he does not confine himself to acting the part of political watchdog upon officials of all kinds, magistrates, schoolmasters, officers, and drawing up a more or less secret and exact report on everyone of them, nor even to keeping an eye on the general police and the maintenance of public order. In addition, he takes decisions upon numerous technical matters and appoints a large number of technical agents."

The Indian counterpart of the Prefect is the Collector or the Deputy Commissioner in India, who, till 1947, was in a way the real executive chief and administrator of the tract of country committed to his charge, namely, the District. His relationship with other specialised agencies at the district level was described by the Montagu-Chelmsford Report of 1918, as: "Several other specialised services exist with staffs of their own... but in varying degrees the District Officer influences the policy in all these matters, and he is always there in the background to lend his support, or, if need be, to mediate between a specialised service and the people." The position of the Collector, however, has changed since, and today the District functions as a sub capital where the district offices of the various technical departments are located. The heads of these departments are technical persons who are directly responsible to their departmental chiefs at the state headquarters, and who are independent of the Collector's authority. There has come about a similar diminution in the authority of the French Prefect as there is apparent a growing tendency for the French Minister at Paris to handle economic and social problems in the various departments through their field officials.

The mechanism of the central control over field-offices has been graphically portrayed by Luther Gulick, who discerns three patterns of field organisation, namely—(i) "All Fingers"; "Short Arms, Long Fingers"; and (ii) "Long Arms, Short Fingers". In the "All Fingers" pattern, there are no geographical subdivisions and the field agencies are controlled by the headquarters office directly. In the "Short Arms, Long Fingers" pattern there are found centralised subdivisions, that is to say, these divisions are located in the central office itself, each with an extensive staff, and they communicate with and control field officers in their respective areas. Thus, the Ministry of External Affairs has a number of geographical sections, like Africa—I section, Africa—II Section, America Section, Burma-Ceylon Section, South-East Asia Section, Indo-China Section, Pakistan—I Section, Pakistan—II Section, etc. These sections are located within the Ministry itself and not in the areas with which they deal. Under the " Long Arms, Short Fingers" pattern geographical subdivisions are decentralised. In other words, regional sub-offices are established in the field, far removed from the headquarters. A good example of this pattern is the district office in our country.

The headquarters office of any organisation is subdivided into specialised units, each of which is concerned with a particular progrmme of a segment of the total operation. Thus, the railway management in India, has a number of functional departments, like, Civil Engineering, Mechanical Engineering, Electrical Engineering, Operating, Commercial, Signal and Tele-communication, Accounts, Personnel, Stores, Medical and Security. All these departments necessarily have an impact on the efficient working of the railways. Each one of these departments has a field office at the zonal and divisional levels. Side by side with these functional offices the railways have introduced area officers, namely, the General Manager, who is in overall charge of the Zone, and the Divisional Superintendent who is in overall charge of the Division. The relationships between the functional officials at different levels and the area administrators at these levels as well as their relationships *inter se* at the same level constitute the crux of the headquarters-field relationships. An examination of the railway administration at the ministerial, zonal and divisional levels will throw some light on this complex and difficult situation.

The Ministry of Railways at the secretariat level is organised as a Railway Board which is functional in character. The Railway Board consists of five members—the Chairman, who at present happens to be in charge of staff, the Financial Commissioner, in charge of Finance, and three other members, each in charge of Civil (including Electrical) Engineering, Mechanical Engineering and Transport respectively. The Chairman is responsible for intra-Board coordination and is the administrative head of the organisation. He has the status of a Principal Secretary to the Government and has authority to overrule the other members except the Financial Commissioner. The Board Members deal with all aspects of technical subjects of which they are in charge. These Members are assisted in their work by five Additional Members respectively in charge of Works, Mechanical, Transport, Staff and Finance. In order to give relief to the Members of the Board from the enormous amount of work involved in controlling Railways and to enable them to give some time for touring and studying the wider problems of Railway policy, the Board is assisted by a number of technical officers, designated as Directors, each placed in charge of a Directorate. There are 16 such Directorates, namely—Civil Engineering, Establishment, Efficiency Bureau, Finance, Health, Mechanical Engineering, Railway Planning, Railway Stores, Railway Co-ordination. Security, Signals and Telecommunications, Traffic, Transport, Statistics and Economics, Wagon Production and Vigilance.

The level next below the Board in the field is the Zone, like the Centrla Zone, Northern Zone, Western Zone, etc., at the head of which is the General Manager. He is a top level official in the railway hierarchy and is in overall charge of the zonal railway system, and is the Chief Executive at that level. He is assisted by a number of official heads of various departments or branches, *viz.*, Chief Engineer, Chief Operating Superintendent, Chief Commercial Superintendent, Chief Personnel Officer, Chief Signals and Telecommunications Engineer, Chief Electrical Engineer, Chief Mechanical Engineer, Chief Medical officer, Chief Security Officer, and Chief Accounts Officer. All these technical officers are subordinate to the General Manager, and are directly responsible to him for their work. The General Manager writes their 'confidential report'. He is responsible for bringing about coordination at the zonal level between all departments. All communications from to New Delhi to any departmental officer are routed through the General Manager except in purely technical and routine matters where the departmental officers are free to correspond directly with the technical officers, that is, Directors at the New Delhi headquarters.

Zones are divided into Divisions which are in overall charge of the Divisional Superintendent. He is a prototype of the General Manager in the Division, and is assisted by as many technical officers who are "Deputies" to the "Chief" at the zonal level.

The above organisation may be presented in the form of a chart given ahead.

Communication and Control

One of the real areas of difficulty in headquarters-field relationship is the establishment of a system of good communications between various levels. In our opinion, the chief reason for non-implementation or partial implementation of policies and programmes in our county is the absence on the part of field officials of a proper understanding of the purposes and objectives of programmes. These officials are seldom taken into confidence in determining policies and preparation of programmes; nor do they have any appreciation of the overall plan or objective. They are not even sure of the methods and techniques they use for executing these programmes. The only channels of communication open to them are 'noting on files' and Manuals. Communication is usually one way, *i.e.,* from the top to the bottom in the form of orders, directives, notifications, circulars and memoranda. Above all, there are the 'sacred' Manuals laying down in categorical terms the role of officials at various levels. Feedback from below to upwards is not encouraged, if not frowned upon. As regards Manuals, the complaint of the field officials is that the procedures and rules prescribed therein do not always fit the situation and often do not take into account operating realities. Dimock and Dimock call this phenomenon "Manualties" which is defined as "an occupational disease, generally found in Government....that causes people to assume that everything in administration can be reduced to rule and embalmed in a procedure manual for the guidance of all employees in the organisation."

Another aspect of this relationship is the exercise of control by the headquarters over field agencies. There are a number of commonly accepted techniques and devices by which administration at one particular level of an organisation may control the performance of subordinate field agencies. Such techniques may be in the nature of control before action is taken, for example, prior approval of individual projects before initiation by an operating unit; the promulgation of service standards; budgetary limitation upon the magnitude of operations; approval of key subordinate personnel. Field agencies in the States find themselves particularly handicapped by the imposition of detailed financial control by the

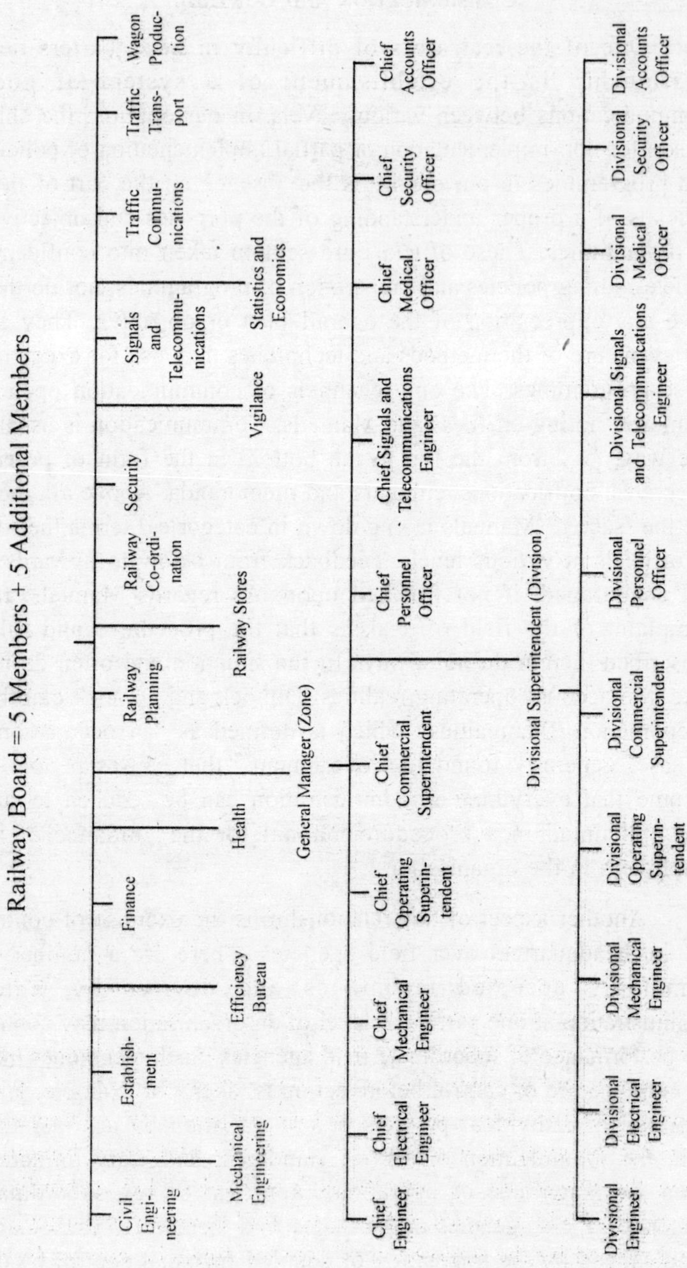
Railway Board = 5 Members + 5 Additional Members
Civil Engineering
Establishment
Finance
Railway Planning
Railway Co-ordination
Security
Signals and Telecommunications
Traffic Communications
Traffic Transport
Wagon Production
Mechanical Engineering
Efficiency Bureau
Health
Railway Stores
Vigilance
Statistics and Economics
General Manager (Zone)
Chief Engineer
Chief Electrical Engineer
Chief Mechanical Engineer
Chief Operating Superintendent
Chief Commercial Superintendent
Chief Personnel Officer
Chief Signals and Telecommunications Engineer
Chief Medical Officer
Chief Security Officer
Chief Accounts Officer
Divisional Superintendent (Division)
Divisional Engineer
Divisional Electrical Engineer
Divisional Mechanical Engineer
Divisional Operating Superintendent
Divisional Commercial Superintendent
Divisional Personnel Officer
Divisional Signals and Telecommunications Engineer
Divisional Medical Officer
Divisional Security Officer
Divisional Accounts Officer

Finance Department as also by the insistence on prior approval of the departmental headquarters office before any programme can be executed.

Control after action takes the form of reporting, audit, inspection and investigation. One of the traditional methods of exercising control over subordinate offices is for the headquarters to insist on receiving information from the field agencies in the form of returns, reports and statistics relating to the progress of field operations. The trouble with this method is that the returns and reports tend to multiply, thus entailing untold burden on the offices concerned. Audit may be defined as an independent examination of every financial transaction. The main purpose of audit is to prevent embezzlement, fraud, carelessness, errors, unauthorised expenditure, expenditure of excess allotment, and non-compliance with rules and laws. Two things to be noted about audit are: first, audit is a *post facto* function and is in the nature of a post-mortem scrutiny; and second, it has the limited function of examining compliance with rules and regulations in financial transactions. Inspection, literally speaking, means looking carefully at or over; viewing closely and critically. Inspection is designed primarily to ensure that the existing rules, regulations, procedures and practices are observed. It ensures compliance with instructions. In this respect, it resembles the audit function. What audit is to financial transaction, inspection is to administrative transactions. Such a limited view of inspection, however, is out of date in the present context of administration. Inspection to be useful and effective, must develop a positive and affirmative character, and its scope should be widened to include some sort of audit of performance. It is not enough in a planned economy like ours, which calls for action mindedness, that rules laid down in the Manuals are complied with the inspection authority must also evaluate the performance of the inspected agency as to whether it has fulfilled the purposes for which it had been set. Again, inspections have to develop an O and M angle, that is to say, they should not stop at criticizing the lapses but go further and suggest improvement organisation systems, methods and procedures with a view to increasing efficiency. Lastly, inspection is not a mere fault-finding process, and one of its essential elements should be instructing and guiding the person working in the inspected agency, and actually demonstrating on the spot as to how defects have to be rectified and discrepancies reconciled. In an ideal system of inspection, the inspectors have to regard themselves as a part of the administrative process and assume responsibility for the successful working of the office or project in the same sense as other officials engaged in the work. The effectiveness of an inspection system should be judged in the light of the above ingredients. Investigation is an inquiry into some alleged or suspected malpractice or abuse of authority. Its main purpose is to discover the guilty person and to prosecute him. Investigation is often personal and particular in character, and is usually on an *ad hoc* basis.

Successful Administration of Field Offices

"It has been said that there is both a headquarters and a field way of life, the groups often viewing each other with smugness and suspicion. Field-workers insist that headquarters does not understand their problems.....Headquarters is characterised by an intellectual or research approach to problems in contrast to the field's practical approach." This statement has universal application. A general feeling is that a posting at the headquarters means a comfortable life, more amenities, special pay allowance, higher status, better 'contacts' and more powers. This feeling is obviously detrimental to the efficient administration of field offices.

Among the essential prerequisites to successful administration of field offices, the following may be enumerated:

1. Effort should be made to create at the headquarters as well as in the field a full appreciation of the particular field situation so that they get induced to arrive at a decision appropriate to the situation. Orders should be, in the words of Mary Parker Follett, 'the composite decision of those who give and those who receive them' and this will maximise the chance of their acceptance Follett calls this process as the 'law of the situation'

2. Field offices must be staffed by trained and competent personnel in adequate number, who can take sound decisions on matters falling within the sphere of their responsibility.

3. The responsibility of the fieldofficer must be clearly defined, and their limitations, too, should be made clear to them.

4. There should be free, frank and frequent communication between field-officers of different departments in the same area on related problems.

5. The powers given to field-officers must relieve the headquarters of unnecessary work. Because powers have been handed down, it does not follow that they will be used.

6. Special facilities including financial incentives should be provided in 'hardship' areas to attract competent staff.

7. Periodic transfers from field to headquarters and *vice versa* and between fields are useful in inculcating a balanced outlook on local requirements and national policies. The existing 'tenure system' needs to be strengthened.

8. Formal inspections, submissions of periodic returns and reports should be supplemented by informal visit by headquarters officers. These help build up rapport between the headquarters and field.

9. Training courses and conferences between field-officers and headquarters officers make them more competent, and keep them aware of each other's problems. This also results in the building-up of community of interests.

10. Field and headquarters officers must possess adequate knowledge of local needs and opinions, and, within the framework of the governmental policy and procedures, strive to meet these.

11. Before a person is posted in the field he should be given briefing by the headquarters on his own assignment and the problems and issues involved in it. This helps him in understanding his new job quickly and more completely. Likewise, there should be de-briefing when he completes his

field-assignment. De-briefing may take the form of a few terminal interviews with the headquarters personnel wherein he communicates the operational problem and difficulties he encountered in his work. This would provide the much needed feed-back to the headquarters.

14

Planning and Administration

In talking about Planning and Administration. I shall confine attention to the situation in India. In fact therefore the talk will be a Planning and Administration in India today. Also, I shall be concerned here not with plan formulation or evaluation but with the aspect which has closest connection with administration namely plan implementation.

For understanding the existing administrative situation in India it is necessary to look back at the British period. The existing administrative structure has changed very little from that developed in British times, and procedures, methods, attitudes have to a considerable extent continued in the present from the colonial past. The main characteristics of the older situation were as follows. The total scope of Government activity was then extremely limited. Keeping law and order, administering justice, collecting revenues were the main activities. Economic policy was predominantly *laissez faire* and the scope of development and welfare activities, including Education and Health, directly undertaken by the State was highly restricted. Lord Morley vetoed even the establishment of a department of Industry by a provincial Government. There were no set goals to achieve as those of economic development or of social welfare. This was underlined by the inaction and the complete lack of policy in the face of the severe depression of the thirties. Discriminating protection was the only exception introduced in inter-war years; but no aspect of this was integrated into the administrative system.

The second notable feature of the situation was the exercise of power fairly directly by the top civil service itself. Before the Mont-ford Reforms this exercise was direct. During inter-war years, for a limited number of subjects, a form of authority was vested in elected politician Ministers. But in effect the exercise of this authority was highly limited and in very few important cases were the political ministers in a position to ignore the wishes of powerful civil servants. The main difference made by the Mont-Ford Reforms was to add the responsibility of managing legislators and ministers to the other work done by the top civil servants.

The top civil servants were in effect the representatives of the British in India. Till the first world war they were overwhelmingly British. During inter-war years an Indian element was progressively introduced in the composition of the highest services but this made no real change to the structure, attitudes or operations of the civil service. There was high concentration of total authority in this body of civil servants. As within this body there was considerable delegation of authority to the member of the service at the lowest tier. "Trusting the man on the spot" had a specific limited meaning in British times. It meant trusting the district Collector or an official at even lower level of local authority if he was member of the civil, service. No such delegation was intended for or effected in favour of any officials outside the civil service. This had the other side of insisting upon working strictly to orders, according to a scheme or a blue-print, for all lower official cadres below the British civil servants. There was neither delegation nor exercise of independent judgment allowed at those levels.

As the official was the symbol of externally imposed authority, it was held to be of the utmost importance to maintain high his prestige in the eyes of the Indian public. This was meticulously insisted upon. To a certain extent even the Indian officials at lower ranks were vested, by a process of transfer, with this position or sense of prestige and the British system protected this aspect as against members of the Indian public.

The total operations of the bureaucracy and, in particular, of the nuclear British civil service were as those of an outsider. It was an outside element involved neither in the affairs nor the passions, emotions of the ruled that was running administration.

The basic ultimate purpose of the administration were objectives and purposes of British interest and policy. To the extent, however, that proper maintenance of law and order and of British prestige, involved maintenance of certain standards of justice, etc., as between Indian and Indian, and the observance of the rule of law, considerable importance was attached to these. When Indian became members of this civil service, it was insisted that they should keep themselves aloof from involvement in Indian society in order to preserve the role of functioning as outsiders.

During inter-war years the political situation was undergoing continuous change. However, this meant no change either in the structure of the civil service or the rest of the administrative apparatus or in the relations of the nuclear civil service with the rest of the administration. It meant also no change of attitude either of the part of the official or of the public towards each other. The major change was that members of the civil service found it necessary and expedient in certain contexts to conceal the basic sanction of force at the back of exercise of power by the British and to be occupied to a large extent with managing and manipulating politicians and other leading elements in Indian public life.

This environment and situation changed suddenly with the coming of independence. The most important new factor was the emergence of the Indian politician as the effective ruler. The civil servants at the top of the administrative apparatus no longer acted as representatives in Indian of the English crown, but had to act as servants of Indian Ministers. This could have meant a very large change in the situation of civil servants and in the functioning of the administrative system. However in effect, no large change took place immediately. This was largely because the Indian politician did not appear anxious in any way to affect the prestige and operation of the administrative system and particularly of the top operators. He did not evidently want to change the position of members of the Indian Civil Service in any way and they were guaranteed, like princes, a number of privileges. Even so, the exercise of political power by Ministers and later by legislators ordered gradually the privileged position of the top civil servants, and they had to learn more and more the art of management of their political masters. The change in relations between the highest civil service cadres and other elements of administration was more gradual.

The other extremely important aspect of the changed situation was that the civil servant could no longer look upon himself as an outsider or representative of an outside authority. He began by slow degree to function more and more as part of Indian society. The distinction of ruler-ruled did not become completely blurred but the involvement of the civil servant in public affairs, in particular groups, or interests, his affiliation with regions and castes came more obviously to the surface. However, even 20 years afterwards the transition has not been completed and in a large part vestiges of the older situation remain. The vestiges that are most important from our point of view appear to be as follows:

The "generalist" i.e., the Indian civil servant and his successor, the I.A.S., still completely dominate the scene. There is an enormous concentration of power on top in this strata and elements of specialists or managers of business still rank low in prestige and authority. The I.C.S. and the I.A.S. function as an exclusive club and it is openly alleged that you cannot function effectively in top positions in administration unless you belong to this group. The attitudes of the public towards officials and of the officials towards the public tare still coloured largely by the older situation and this has special meaning in the context of the plan of development.

The British concept of the single British District Officer or Collector, coordinating all authority in all departments over an entire area in his hands still continues to be and important feature of the local administrative structure and colours the whole of its operation.

The civil service enjoys very great effective power even to day. However, an extremely important aspect is that the older combination of power and responsibility are no longer to be found. In the older regime when power vested largely in their hands, the senior groups of members of the civil service also accepted accompanying responsibility. They were responsible ultimately to the crown for proper management of Indian affairs and always behaved with a full sense of this responsibility. Today the civil servant no longer feels responsibility in this manner because power is supposed to reside in and directly wielded by the political Minster. The curious situation that exists at present is, therefore, that while the actual day-to-day exercise of the power rests in the hands of the civil servant, the civil servant no longer feels any overall responsibility. This he feels rests with the Ministers who exercise it fitfully largely on the advice of the civil servants themselves. However, as this exercise especially in relation to personal or party matters may be on considerations other than those accepted by the civil servant or put forward by him, the advice is likely to be disregarded in some contexts and occasions. This change seems to have relieved the civil servant from any feeling of carrying the overall burden of administration. The informal operation of a group of top civil servants as generally looking after the total situation has, therefore, vanished and the Cabinet or an inner group of Ministers have not taken over this function in any effective manner; it has thus ceased to be discharged.

As against this background one has to consider the relevance and appropriateness of the present state of administrative arrangements in India to the specific requirements of the effort at planned economic development. Apart from the results of transition to self-rule after independence, it is planned economic development that has added enormously to the dimensions of Government effort. The activities of Government have increased tremendously both in width of coverage and in depth and intensity. The direct responsibilities that government now undertakes cover large of social and economic life. Government takes upon itself the responsibility of erecting the structure of public services and utilities required for development of a modern industrial society and of continuously maintaining that structure. It undertakes in addition a large variety of welfare activities and conducts a large number of industrial production businesses which are basic to the industrial structure. Government occupies large sections of trading and it tries to regulate for many other aspects of social and economic life. The number of administrations at various levels required in Government service has increased enormously and the qualifications needed by them have become extremely varied. The contrast with the situation in, say, 1939 is extremely glaring.

Not only has the sphere of direct Government activity and of official regulation of socio-economic activity immensely widened but also the conduct of operations has become extremely detailed. The task undertaken by government, of the transformation and activisation of rural economic society is in itself immense. This in effect means operating on the millions of small dispersed units of farming and other rural activities. Development of agriculture and its improvement are essentially specialised task which must be performed in relation to every locality. In British time, in some States the collection of revenue was related to maintenance of detailed village records and village officials. However, in the landlord provinces the rural administrative structure was very rudimentary. Looking at the area of the landlord provinces and of the Indian States, it may be said that for the larger part of the country an administrative structure for regulating or directing activities of individual local communities was not available at independence. This had to be constructed, widened and strengthened.

Apart from undertaking multi-fold activities and activizing or regulating economic life all over the country, planning requires continuous maintenance of a long-term and coordinated direction to socio-economic development. This is both a highly important and difficult function which is made all the more important and difficult because of the large size, the diversity and the federal political structure of the country. Administration had to be geared to all these ends. It will be thus seen that very large ground had to be covered as between the highly limited Government activity of British times for which the particular structure was fashioned and the requirements of the administrative system of the planned development era.

It must, in the first instance, be recognised that the Indian administrative system had grown rapidly, adapted itself partially to the changed situation and tried to meet the large and manifold new requirements. Inefficiency and corruption may have increased, but there has been no real breakdown of the system and this itself is creditworthy. However, huge problems remain unsolved and it is necessary to pay urgent attention to these. I shall deal with some indicated by the analysis above. Two major difficulties are related to the dominance and the changed attitude of the generalist I.C.S. and I.A.S. service personnel at the top. This first is the lack of a co-ordinated view and of a frame of considered policy. In fact this indicates a failure on the part of the Council of Ministers but it is also related to the short-term, departmental view that Secretaries and others take. This flows partly from their lack of specialisation and partly from the absence of conjoint operations. *Ad hocism* in policy decisions is the result. The second and even more important difficulty is sheer incompetence resulting not only from the lack of expert knowledge of the generalist but also equally from the degradation and frustration of the experts and specialists in government service. The first difficulty will be dealt with later. Relating to the second, action had to be divided in two parts. Firstly, even for ordinary departmental administration, much more diversified and wider based methods of recruitment have to be adopted. This will enable direct recruitment of a certain number of specialists and technically qualified personnel for administrative posts at appropriate levels. Even more important is making it possible for them to operate side by side on similar positions of authority with members of the generalist civil service. The recent appointment of Dr. I.G. Patel as Special Secretary in Finance is a case in point. Some leaven of such "outsider" on parallel positions could alone modify the older narrow and highly hierarchical tradition of generalist administration.

Secondly all operations other than the strictly administrative should be put outside the purview of the generalist service. The large number of public enterprises, autonomous corporations for performing a variety of specialised functions either of research or of administration or of quasi-business activity should be put outside the sphere of the generalist administrator. In these activities which are essentially spheres of the managers and the experts it should be insisted that the running would be by people who are professionally competent and are committed to a career in that particular line of activity. In business management, it is the experience even of Communist countries that the manager has to have considerable power and autonomy. This is necessary in order to allow him to manage his business flexibly. It is equally necessary to enable giving him due credit or fixing blame on him for good or bad management. The present arrangements by which the generalist looks upon all these areas as his privileged preserves into which he moves in and out at will and regarding mismanagement of which no responsibility is ever fixed on him must cease at the earliest. As a corollary it follows that the power of generalist secretaries over such branches of activity must also be abolished.

The next desirable change is essentially a change in attitudes, the attitudes of top civil servants to lower ranks and *vice-versa.* It is admitted on all hands that there is considerable administrative talent and considerable enthusiasm to be found among all lower ranks specially of local administrative personnel among departmental staff all over India. However, the whole of the tradition of colonial rule has imposed a pattern of behaviour which prevents any free expression of opinion or exercise of initiative by these large elements. This is a heavy handicap especially in a society which talks of democratic decentralisation. Means must, therefore, be found to vitalize the lower level of the administrative structure and by suitable encouragement and incentives to give scope for independent expression of views and some types of independent action by staff at the lower levels.

Reference to the untapped potential among the subordinate official staff naturally leads to consideration of problems of local administration and local planned development. Increased requirements in these regards were met in recent years largely through the expanding community development administration. It may be noted that this was in essence adoption of an older approach that was embodied, for example, in the Gurgaon experiment of Brayne which was much publicised at one time.

However, it became clear at an early stage that the Community development approach was inadequate. For effective local development a non-official community structure had to be built up and emphasis, therefore, shifted to the Panchayati Raj institutions. Establishment of local primary cooperatives had been recognised as being necessary, even earlier, as agencies of local economic activity and development. The recognition of the importance of building up Panchayati Raj and Cooperative institutions was the result of experience of successful development planning. They are not fads or ideologies but are essential systems without which planned development cannot proceed far. The difference made to rural development in various regions with different degrees of development of these agencies clearly proves this. Planning except at a highly generalised level has to be related to local situational variations, responses, references and feasibilities. Such relation can be established only locally. Moreover, planning also requires an agency which can communicate to vast numbers of dispersed farmers, artisans, etc., the scheme and intentions of planners and which can, in turn, interpret their wishes and difficulties to planners. Such agency cannot be wholly official; that would be both highly costly and ineffective.

Planning at the State and District level is thus intimately connected with administrative problems of Panchayati Raj institutions and Cooperatives. Once special problem that arises out of the working of the Panchayati Raj institutions is that of coordination at the district level. Fortunately, Panchayati Raj constitutions mostly provide for coordination at the highest level through a series of area and subject committees and a superior executive committee. However, the problems of coordination with the sphere of Collector and in some cases of the proper integration of the Community Development officials are still unsolved. Others are in part problems of the superior civil service and of lower ranks discussed above. They are also in part similar to problems of relations between civil servants and ministers. This is an area in which conventions need to be evolved based on recognition of mutual responsibilities and limitations. Some problems also arise out of reluctance to devolve and finance to local authorities and officials on the part of ministers, secretariat officials and departmental heads, and out of the propensity of ministers and superior officials to interfere in the working of Cooperatives. It is only when it is widely recognised that the successful establishment and healthy operation of the local institutional structure is a *sine qua non* of further progress that these problems will begin to be solved.

Finally, successful plan implementation also requires maintenance by Government of a consistent long-terms economic and social policy. For purposes of planning this requirement is so essential that it cannot be satisfied by the ordinary coordinating arrangements within a Cabinet. As indicated above, for a variety of reasons, *ad hocism* appears to be the rule today.

It is at the same time obvious that the ordinary day to day administration of various Ministries, departments and offices should not be hampered by the functioning of any outside body with a general over-viewing function. The way out is specifically to ensure that all important decisions which have relevance or significance for other activities or for future arrangements or operations should be subject to tests of consistency with policy laid down in this behalf or if there is no policy already laid down should be viewed in the possible frame of such policy. An organisation which looks at policy decisions from this point of view would not only be highly useful but for any long-term detailed planning, highly necessary. It does not appear essential to vest such organisation with any direct power. All that would be necessary is to ensure that in each such case informed and detailed comment in the light of accepted, coordinated, long-term policy decisions or perspectives should be fully expressed and should be carefully considered before action or decision is finally taken by the supreme organ of Government.

At the national level the Planning Commission could property perform this function and does so already to some extent. If organisation for plan formulation such as Planning Boards are created at the State level they could be similarly used. Apart from these it would be useful to have planning cells in all ministries and departments and planning officers at the District level. This could ensure that the planning aspect of all decisions and activities would be continuously brought to the notice of authorities and the functioning of important organs of Government would acquire a much needed orientation towards planned development.

D.R. Gadgil

15

Decentralised Planning and Development—A Non-Conventional Agenda

Our Experience of planning and development has indicated not only the need for careful planning but also for effective administration and management. Evaluations of successive Five Year Plans have highlighted fact that while planning had been carefully done, bottlenecks in administration at various levels could not result in implementation of desired goals.

Apart from land, labour and capital organisation and management are also importan. factors of production. Unfortunately the latter two factors have not attached the attention they deserved and hence the pitfalls that we have faced in successfully carrying out of our planned programmes.

Perhaps the most important development in economic sphere in recent years has been the emergence of a liberalised economy. Obviously the role of the Planning Commission in the altered situation cannot be the same as before. However, one has not witnessed any significant changes in its methods of operations even during the post-liberalised era.

In a parliamentary debate the then Prime Minister Shri I.K. Gujral had rightly stated that statutory status should not be given to the Planning Commission. While we agree with this, it is to be seen as to whether in the altered economic climate, the country's demands for development cannot be met by the full utilisation of the statutory responsibility of a constitutional authority, viz. the Finance Commission. As originally envisaged, the Finance

Commission was to provide necessary programme, funds and mechanism for balanced regional development. It was also expected that all financial transfers from the Union to the States, 'whether revenue or capital', were to be made on the recommendations of Finance Commission. Unfortunately the Finance Commission had not been allowed to flower in full in view of the emergence of a powerful Planning Commission. In its 'general observations', the Third Finance Commission had made certain suggestions to deal with the existence of these two bodies. One of these suggestions later on found favour with the authorities and a member of the Planning Commission was put also as a member in successive Finance Commissions. Unfortunately, that member invariably did not remain in the Planning Commission to fully coordinate the task.

In a liberalised economy with a more federalistic polity and a multiplicity of political parities holding power in our States, it is increasingly necessary to provide an institutional set-up which is more in tune with the constitutional provisions. We would, therefore, reiterate our suggestion that the Finance Commission should become a 'Standing' Commission, if not a permanent one. Further, the existing Planning Commission should be reorganised as a similar body in the shape of a Economic Policy Advisory Council.

Transformation of Planning Commission into an Economic Policy Formulation Advisory Council

In an era of liberalised economy while the need for tight control exercised by the Planning Commission diminishes, the need for well-thought out and coordinated economic polices in the spheres of industry, commerce, agriculture and foreign investment increases. The new EPAC should be under the Chairmanship of the P.M., with a full-time policy 'technocrat' as Deputy Chairman. The P.M., and not more than five experts should be its part-time Members. Ministers in-change of industry, Commerce, Agriculture, and Foreign Economic Affairs should be invited when their sectoral policies are under discussion.

Apart from advice regarding well-coordinated central policies, this council could also offer suggestions regarding their effective implementation at State and cutting-edge levels.

Finance Commission

As per the spirit of the constitution it would be more desirable to provide all ascertainable flows of funds from the Centre to the States through the mechanism of the Finance Commission. For performing this task the Finance Commission has to be made a standing commission if not a permanent one. Fortunately our constitution is flexible enough to accommodate this within the existing framework of Article 280. The obligatory requirement under this Article is that the Finance Commission should be appointed by the President atleast once in five years. There can, therefore, be no objection if this body is brought into existence every five years during which period it could remain as a standing Commission and meet as often as necessary. This may of course require some changes in the composition and terms of appointment of members of the Finance Commission. Unless the work of the Commission so develops that it requires full time attention of most of the members, it would be better to have only one or two persons as full members. Others could remain as part-time members and attend the meetings of the Commissions when these are convened.

For ensuring proper linkage and continuity tenure of all the members of the Finance Commission need not be co-terminus. Initially, some of the members maybe appointed for a period of two or three years and the rest for a full term of five years. Afterwards all appointments could be for a full five-years term. Thus, some new members will be joining the Commission every two or three years. This will provide the necessary fresh outlook from time to time while still preserving continuity in membership to a certain extent.

It should be possible for the Finance Commission to interact with political and professional technocrats for programmes of more balanced regional development. The members of State-level Development Commission should be of Special help. Discussion papers could be prepared for less developed areas or comparatively neglected sectors to bring up their development. More grants could be provided for States which for historical and other reasons had lagged behind in development their resources. The 'advanced'

States could depend on market mechanism for further enhancing their development activity.

The Finance Commission, under its Constitutional authority, could check with State authorities about utilisation of funds as agreed to earlier and also ensure that non-plan development programmes do not dry up until they reach their final goals.

Panchayati Raj Institutions

One of the more significant achievement toward decentralised planning and development has been the recent constitutional amendment to provide for setting up of Panchayati Raj institutions in our States in the shape of village panchayats, block level samitis and district level zila parishads, and the provision of a Panchayati Raj Finance Commission to devolve funds from the States to PR institutions. Almost all the States have provided for necessary legislation to implement the provisions made for Panchayati Raj institutions in the central legislation. In several States Panchayati Raj Finance Commissions have also made their recommendations. However, in many states the necessary administrative authority for appropriate planning and development activity at the three-tier levels has yet to emerge. It is said that the members of State Legislatures, while adhering to the desire of the Centre, do not wish to lose their hold and authority in favour of the elected representatives in the three-tier Panchayati Raj. How should we resolve this dilemma? In my view, we should add another tier of decentralised planning and development at the level of existing revenue divisions (or at similar levels if the revenue divisions have formally ceased to exist). We can call this new Panchayati Raj tier, which will be below the State Assembly but above the zila parished, by the name of Kshertriya Parished or Regional Panchayat.

All MLAs representing this region in State Assembly should be ex-officio members of this Kshetriya Parishad (KP). All Chairmen of Zila Parishads and may be one other representative of each zila parishad in the region should be members of this body. All the Members of Parliament from the region should be permanent invitees to KP meetings so that their advice may be available for drawing up desirable development plans keeping in view past aberrations in plan implementation. The Divisional Commissioner who is very often a very senior IAS officer and who is perhaps not over-worked at present, should function as the Chief Executive Officer of this body. The members of KP should elect one of the MLAs as their Chairman unless the legislation provides for the senior most MLA to occupy this position. Hopefully, the MLAs in the State Assembly and wherever necessary the MPs in the Parliament will carefully watch the interest of development of this region and try to avoid all the bottlenecks in implementation. They should be able to provide better informed guidance to Zila Parishads and act as their spokesmen in the Assembly and with the State Government. The Kshetriya Parishad will be a useful Coordinating agency and a significant brain-storming forum. Except for a limited number of inter-Zila Parished development programmes, the rest of the programmes will be carried out under the auspices of Zila Parishads.

A very important corollary for effective implementation of Panchayati Raj plans will be to decentralize State level administrative and allied services.

The members of the State services should be recruited by the State Public Service Commission on a competitive basis and, on the basis of their preference and performance, allotted to one of the regions of the State so that by and large major part of their career is spent in the region, apart from some postings at the State Headquarters (this should be somewhat on the pattern of recruitment of members of IAS who are centrally recruited and then assigned to States). The regional authorities should have major control over the functioning of the services in their respective areas. Thus, it should be possible for the Panchayati Raj institutions to have the much needed coordination between elected representatives in the existing three-tiers and the elected representatives in the State Assembly and the Central Parliament together with appropriate control over senior civil service to ensure proper implementation of development programmes. Appropriate authority and control over subordinate services and staff should be formally devolved at the other tiers of Panchayati Raj.

State Level Development and Finance Commission

At present some States have provided for State level Planning Commissions or Planning Boards and some others have Planning Advisory Bodies. States like Kerala, Tamil Nadu and West Bengal have provided for a full time Deputy Chairman or Vice-Chairman and some full time member of these Commissions, the Chief Minister of the State being invariably the Chairman of these bodies. We would like to suggest that all States should provide for a State level Development and Finance Commission with several full time members assigned with responsibilities for key sectors of development in the State. This body should be responsible for development planning, non-plan development activity and flow of funds from the State level to the various tiers of Panchayati Raj institutions. If necessary, to implement statutory provisions of Panchayati Raj legislation, some members of the Commission could be constituted as Panchayati Raj Finance Commission when the occasion arises. This combination of triple functions is necessary to avoid the existing purely accounting distinction between 'plan' and 'non-plan' development activities and their much needed coordination between the State level and the various tiers of Panchayati Raj institutions. This will also provide professional coordination between the Central and State authorities and continuing overseeing of development activities not only for a plan period of five years but as long as proper carrying out of even 'non-plan' development demands.

The members of DFCs will be in a much better position to put forward their claims, well-supported by technical papers, before the Finance Commission. As Finance Commission will be available all long, it should be possible to plug holes in effective implementation as soon as these are discovered.

State DFCs should also ensure that appropriate machinery for planning and implementation is in place in the Z.P., P.S., and Panchayats.

Linkages With Educational Institutions

We suggest that for improved planning and development, Universities, Professional and 'General' Colleges, Polytechnics, and senior secondary institutions should be optimally linked with various tiers of Panchayati raj bodies, specially for purposes of basic surveys, orientation and training of PR staff and NGO personnel, and evaluation of plan-programmes. In many cases the teaching staff of these institutions happen to be the best available 'brain-power' under on institutional roof in the area or PR tier concerned but we have not fully utilised and moulded this human resource. They can help in natural and human resource surveys in villages and townships, putting forward specific programmes of development in selected sectors, and writing out 'development' manuals at micro levels. They could also perform a useful role in carrying out 'evaluations' of completed or ongoing programmes at village and Samiti levels. In the process these College teachers will enrich their own knowledge and become more 'relevant and proficient teachers'.

CONCLUSION

We have offered a somewhat non-traditional agenda, within the framework of existing Constitution, to devolve more authority, responsibility and opportunity for innovative thing for decentralised development to succeed. It is our belief that when action is taken nearer the people the possibility of dealing more effectively with problems of poverty, illiteracy and disease increases. Action on the lines proposed in this short article can be one of the best 'gifts in the Celebration of fifty years of India's Independence.

M.V. Mathur